Ethnopolitics and Transition to Democracy

D1557518

Ethnopolitics and Transition to Democracy

The Collapse of the USSR and Latvia

———⟫◆⟪———

Rasma Karklins

The Woodrow Wilson Center Press
Washington, D.C.

The Johns Hopkins University Press
Baltimore and London

Editorial offices:
The Woodrow Wilson Center Press
370 L'Enfant Promenade, S.W., Suite 704
Washington, D.C. 20024-2518
Telephone 202-287-3000, ext. 218

Order from:
The Johns Hopkins University Press
Hampden Station
Baltimore, Maryland 21211
Telephone 1-800-537-5487

9 8 7 6 5 4 3 2 1

Library of Congress Cataloging-in-Publication Data

Karklins, Rasma.
  Ethnopolitics and transition to democracy : the collapse of the
USSR and Latvia / Rasma Karklins.
    p.   cm.
  Includes bibliographical references and index.
  ISBN 0-943875-60-9 (alk. paper). — ISBN 0-943875-61-7 (pbk.)
  1. Soviet Union—Politics and government—1985–1991.   2. Soviet
Union—Ethnic relations.   3. Latvia—politics and government—1991–
4. Latvia—Ethnic relations.   I. Title.
DK288.K363   1994
323.1'47—dc20   93-42362
                                                          CIP

Woodrow Wilson
International Center for Scholars

T HE CENTER is the "living memorial" of the United States of America to the nation's twenty-eighth president, Woodrow Wilson. The U.S. Congress established the Woodrow Wilson Center in 1968 as an international institute for advanced study, "symbolizing and strengthening the fruitful relationship between the world of learning and the world of public affairs." The Center opened in 1970 under its own board of trustees, which includes citizens appointed by the president of the United States, federal government officials who serve ex officio, and an additional representative named by the president from within the federal government.

In all its activities the Woodrow Wilson Center is a nonprofit, nonpartisan organization, supported financially by annual appropriations from the U.S. Congress, and by the contributions of foundations, corporations, and individuals.

W OODROW WILSON CENTER PRESS publishes the best work emanating from the Center's programs and from fellows and guest scholars, and assists in publication, in-house or outside, of research works produced at the Center and judged worthy of dissemination. Conclusions or opinions expressed in Center publications and programs are those of the authors and speakers and do not necessarily reflect the views of the Center staff, fellows, trustees, advisory groups, or any individuals or organizations that provide financial support to the Center.

Contents

Contents

Contents

Tables

Figures

Acknowledgments

This study was supported by several institutions and individuals. I am especially grateful to the John D. and Catherine T. MacArthur Foundation for providing me with one research and writing grant during 1991–92. The Woodrow Wilson International Center for Scholars was kind enough to make me a member of its International Workshop on Comparative Ethnicity, which met in Washington, D.C., during the summer of 1992. The collegial discussions of this group greatly encouraged and inspired me. My work has also been supported by a travel grant from the International Research and Exchanges Board and by a sabbatical leave from the University of Illinois at Chicago.

Colleagues in Latvia were most helpful during my seven research trips to Latvia between March 1990 and December 1993. I extend special thanks to the scholars at the Philosophy and Sociology Institute of the Academy of Sciences of Latvia, in particular Elmārs Vēbers. He and others were especially helpful in discussion and leading me to data sources. The generosity of members of the Social Research Center of Latvia, headed by Brigita Zepa, in allowing me to use their survey data is also greatly appreciated.

This study would have been much delayed without the excellent assistance of Vida Kuprys, Juris Osis, and David Franklin.

Introduction

⟫⟶◆⟵⟪

This study seeks to clarify three issues: the political consequences of ethnicity, the process of transition from a nondemocratic to a democratic regime, and how the two are linked. As for the first issue, it is clear that in the 1990s ethnicity and nationalism—not only in Eastern Europe and the former Soviet Union but all over the world—constitute one of the major subject areas in comparative politics.[1] The same is true for the transition to democracy. Since 1975 dozens of authoritarian regimes have been replaced by democracies, and many more may soon follow.[2] In this volume I analyze the links between such transitions and changing ethnopolitics.

The experience of the former Soviet region shows that empirically such analysis is needed, but we do not yet have the theoretical foundation to fulfill that need. There are few references to multiethnicity in the growing social science literature on the transition to democracy. Similarly, most writings on ethnopolitics are inattentive to political regimes and regime change. I examine the impact on ethnic relations when a multiethnic state is ruled democratically or by a Soviet-style autocracy. I also explore how ethnicity is relevant in the transition to democracy, how it can be a constructive rather than a destructive force.

To the extent that social scientists have discussed the relationship between democracy and multiethnicity, they have advanced contrasting theories. Whereas some analysts argue that the acceptance of ethnopluralism has developed hand in hand with the promotion of democracy, others have argued the exact opposite. In a typical exposition of the latter view, Russell Bova argues that ethnic heterogeneity hinders efforts at democratization because "political energies released by the process of regime liberalization are diverted from the quest of democracy by travelling down the road of national separatism instead."[3] He also points to the tendency of reactionary forces to exploit ethnic strife to stay in power.

The perception of ethnic political behavior as dysfunctional in a modern democracy is widely held. In a recent article William Safrann outlines the assumptions underlying this thesis, and then challenges it with specific counterarguments.[4] Most important for this study, he argues that different types of pluralism tend to fortify each other. Rather than being incompatible with individual rights, the acceptance of ethnopluralism has often accompanied their advancement.[5] He challenges the view of Robert Dahl that although "subsystem autonomy" in institutional or economic terms helps maintain polyarchy, this is not true for ethnocultural differences because they are inherently more divisive.[6] On this point Safran concurs with Arend Lijphart, who links the revival of ethnic demands in Western Europe to the new wave of democratization. The new activists were more concerned about minority rights—in line with the priorities of ethnic groups—than about majority rule. This was true also for their prescriptions for reducing the new Leviathan "to a more human scale" through regionalism, autonomy, and grass-roots democracy.[7] I argue here that a similar process occurred in the Soviet Union, most notably in its northwestern regions.

This study demonstrates that the empowerment of ethnic and civil communities in the former Soviet Union evolved in a complementary way, with one reinforcing the other. This was especially true in the Baltic states, as I show in the case of Latvia, where ethnic pluralism served as a means for promoting civil and political pluralism. This is not to say that such is always the case, but in a world so often driven by ethnic conflict it is worthwhile to study the conditions under which ethnicity has taken on a constructive democratizing role.

As a first step toward clarifying the links between ethnic and political pluralism, I discuss the consequences of a Soviet-style political system for both, and then contrast these to the institutional and attitudinal principles underlying pluralist democracy, especially consociationalism. Whereas the latter builds consensus, the Soviet regime's ethnic policy was built on control. As the Soviet political system began to change in the late 1980s, its ethnic control system changed as well. Democratization was linked to the reemergence of nations, including a redefinition of the identity of Russia and the interests of Russians. Although the regime-led reforms of Mikhail Gorbachev did not foresee the devolution of power from the center to the republics, the emancipation of union republics was a crucial step in democratization developing from below. The cases of Russia and Latvia are highlighted to illustrate this process. I also emphasize the shift in political culture among a segment of the Russian population that came to believe it was in its own best interests for Russia to renounce its imperial legacy.

The changing self-definition of Russians was crucial for the collapse of the USSR. During the late 1980s more and more Russians rejected a Soviet identity and opted for the self-rule of people and peoples. Russian and non-Russian democrats rejected the Soviet Union both as a political system and as an empire. This was an epochal event for Russian democracy. The unwillingness of Russian liberal democrats to accept national self-determination for non-Russians after the February Revolution of 1917 was a crucial reason for their failure to stay in power.[8] Moreover, the clash between nondemocratic imperial Russian interests and the quest for equity and self-rule by non-Russian nations served as a catalyst for ethnic conflict throughout the Soviet era.[9] Although individual Russian democrats, such as Andrei Sakharov, always argued that the fate of democracy in Russia was linked to the acceptance of self-rule for non-Russian nations, the proliferation of this belief in the late 1980s changed the course of history. It allowed the formation of new political alliances, such as the alliance between Boris Yeltsin and democrats in the Baltic states. Russia was among the first states to recognize the independence of Lithuania, Latvia, and Estonia, in July and August 1991; when the Union of Soviet Socialist Republics followed suit on 6 September 1991, this was but a symbolic confirmation of its own political demise.

A large part of this study emphasizes the emergence of multiethnic democratic movements and coalitions in the late 1980s, especially as they evolved in Latvia and between Latvia and Russia. This emphasis seems warranted due to the historically innovative nature of these movements and because their emergence exemplifies an instance of successful ethnic conflict resolution. Yet analysis also suggests that this was possible only due to a favorable political context. Until the demise of the USSR, democrats in Latvia and Russia had a common interest in weakening the Soviet regime. Once the context changed with the dramatic events of August 1991 and Latvia and Russia became self-ruling states, new political divisions began to emerge between them. Most of these issues, such as the presence of ex-Soviet troops on Baltic territory, originate from Soviet policies that Russia has repudiated in principle, but not always in practice. In late 1992 Russian leaders became ambivalent about rejecting the Soviet past in Latvia and by the end of the year relations had become less cordial. As Russia debated policies toward its neighboring states on issues such as military presence and the status of Russian settlers, imperial impulses began to resurface.[10] In 1993 the search for an unequivocal identity for post-Soviet Russia remains undecided. The resolution of this question is linked to Russia's success in making the transition to democracy. As noted by Paul Goble, "Those who prefer a resurrected empire tend to be more authoritarian in disposition than those who prefer independent countries."[11]

This study combines a theoretically informed analysis of the issues of regime change and ethnopolitics in the former Soviet Union with an in-depth analysis of the case of Latvia. Latvia was in the vanguard of democratic change "from below" and in many ways presents a model case for processes in the former Soviet Union. In addition, it appears imperative to conduct geographically focused research of change in the former USSR if one wishes to add to existing knowledge. I concur with Max Weber in seeing social science as a science of historical reality.[12] In its last years Soviet politics

changed so swiftly, took so many turns, and affected so many dimensions of
social and political life—with regional variation—that only in-depth case
study promises new insight. Moreover, innovative politics requires that its
analyst examine original documents and data sets, interview participants
about events, and, if possible, observe events on the spot as they unfold.
This in turn requires knowledge of local conditions and languages, facilities
that I gratefully acknowledge in the case of Latvia.

In my investigation of ethnopolitics and the democratic transition in
Latvia I have used numerous primary sources including statistics on demography, voting patterns, and education. In order to analyze changing public
attitudes I have made extensive use of survey research undertaken by colleagues in the former Soviet Union, Russia, and Latvia. While rooted in
empirical data, my approach is that of interpretive analysis with reference to
comparative theory and experience.

I hope that this study contributes to knowledge of regime change, transition from communism, and ethnic change. Clearly we need to take stock of
ethnopolitics in Eastern Europe and the former Soviet Union, and we need
to do so in a theoretically informed way. Yet this calls for the analyst to be a
pioneer in more ways than one, particularly since theories of ethnopolitics
are not as developed as they should be in light of the high saliency of the
topic. As noted by Donald L. Horowitz, "Western scholarship long regarded
ethnic and racial relations as backwaters of intellectual endeavor and was
slow to adjust conceptions to the rush of events."[13] Western studies of Soviet
nationality politics faced the related problem of being viewed with skepti-
cism by comparativists and having to fight the Russocentric bias of the
Soviet studies field.[14] As for Soviet work on the topic, ethnicity was one of
the most censored areas of research. The director of the Moscow Institute for
Ethnography had this to say about Soviet scholarly writing on nationality
problems: "Thousands of books and brochures were written, thousands of
dissertations defended. In the most part this constituted a giant campaign of
lies, comparable to the Lysenko affair in biology."[15] The notable exceptions
consisted of empirical studies conducted by ethnosociologists in the 1970s
and 1980s.[16]

This book is divided into seven chapters. Chapter 1 outlines topics that
need to be rethought to bring comparative ethnopolitical theory in line with
the Soviet experience. I contrast the concept of ethnopolitics to the concept
of nationalism and outline competing assumptions about the basis of ethnicity in politics. I argue that regime structures and political culture influence all ethnopolitics and that close links exist between political and ethnic
pluralism. I compare the policies of the old-style Soviet regime with consociationalism and movement toward democratic ethnopolitics during the systemic crisis of the USSR. A plural democracy accepts minority nations as

corporate political entities, grants them territorial autonomy, and forms a multinational coalition for the purpose of consensual policy making.

Chapter 2 uses the theoretical arguments of chapter 1 to outline actual regime change and ethnopolitics in the USSR during its final years. Policies of democrats during the collapse of the Soviet Union approximate the ethnoplural paradigm. The years 1986–91 also mark a related shift of political culture among a segment of Russians and non-Russians.

Chapter 3 focuses on the distinctions among ethnic, state, and regime identities and argues that the ascription of ethnopolitical identity to whole groups is misleading. People have multiple identities and the way they align in various contexts determines the specifics of ethnopolitics. Ethnic accommodation works best if a program is supported by people on the basis of several of their identities. The three identities focused on stem from an individual's relation to the ethnic community, the territorial state, and the political regime. After differentiating between ethnic communal identity and identification with particular states, I analyze how they and regime identity interacted during the perestroika period. I show how coalitions based on overlapping interests were significant until the question of regime type was resolved in August 1991; a realignment emphasizing territorial state differences occurred after that.

Chapter 4 analyzes links between political and ethnic pluralism by focusing on the emergence of grass-roots movements in Latvia. Civil society is a precondition—and a dimension—of democracy, but how can civil society be constructed in a nondemocratic system that deliberately limits social autonomy? I propose that communal ties provide an informal network that can form the nucleus of an emergent civil society. In the Baltic ethnicity and memories of the independent states of the interwar period played a constructive role in democratic self-organization "from below."

Chapter 5 discusses the role of ethnicity in political mobilization during the transition to democracy and the formation of new polities, nations, and states. Popular mobilization is a crucial component in the liberalization of authoritarian regimes. In Latvia, mass activism was expressed from 1987 onward in a wave of demonstrations, petition drives, picketing, and other events. Elections were additional catalysts for democratic mobilization. I describe how repressive hurdles were overcome and show links between grass-roots activism and civil disobedience, especially in reaction to the armed crackdown of January 1991.

Chapter 6 focuses on the international dimension of ethnopolitics in Latvia and explores whether it is best seen as a client state of Russia, a settler state, or a self-determining nation. Politics in Latvia cannot be understood without reference to its forced incorporation into the USSR during World War II and the continuing legacy of problems related to that event. As of

1993 ex-Soviet military forces remain in Latvia, as does a huge settler community with strong ties to Russia. I outline the demographic, social, and political dilemmas resulting from this.

Chapter 7 weighs the capacity of current and future models of ethnic policy to deal with the Soviet legacy in Latvia. I emphasize the need to recover the nationhood of Latvia and its people as a basis for harmonious internal and external relations. In particular I focus on policies regarding citizenship and language use in public life and education.

The regaining of Baltic independence has been remarkably peaceful. Except for the violent acts of the hard-line Communist putschists in January and August 1991, there have been no incidents comparable to what has been experienced in Northern Ireland, Catalonia, Los Angeles, or, for that matter, in the Caucasus or the former Yugoslavia. Whereas ethnicity in the Balkans is becoming synonymous with irrational strife, the opposite model has emerged in the Baltics. For this reason, if for no other, the present study should prove worthwhile.

NOTES

1. Howard J. Wiarda, *Introduction to Comparative Politics: Concepts and Processes* (Belmont, Calif.: Eadsworth, 1993), 113.
2. Samuel P. Huntington, *The Third Wave: Democratization in the Late Twentieth Century* (Norman: University of Oklahoma Press, 1991).
3. Russell Bova, "Political Dynamics of the Post-Communist Transition," *World Politics* 44, no. 3 (1991): 135.
4. William Safran, "Ethnicity and Pluralism: Comparative and Theoretical Perspectives," *Canadian Review of Studies in Nationalism* 18, no. 1–2 (1991): 1–12.
5. Safran, "Ethnicity and Pluralism," 5–6.
6. Safran, "Ethnicity and Pluralism," 8, in reference to Robert Dahl, *Polyarchy: Participation and Opposition* (New Haven: Yale University Press, 1971).
7. Arend Lijphart, "Political Theories and the Explanation of Ethnic Conflict in the Western World: Falsified Predictions and Plausible Postdictions," in Milton J. Esman, ed., *Ethnic Conflict in the Western World* (Ithaca: Cornell University Press, 1977), 61–62.
8. William Rosenberg, *Liberals in the Russian Revolution* (Princeton: Princeton University Press, 1974); Roman Szporluk has emphasized that the "Russian question" is crucial to the solution of the entire nationalities question in the USSR: "The most remarkable process now taking place in the Soviet Union is the resumption by the Russian leaders—the elite, the intelligentsia—of the process that was interrupted in 1917 and during the Civil War—i.e., the process of the formation of a modern Russian nation." Roman Solchanyk, "Roman Szporluk and Valerii Tishkov Talk about the National Question," *Report on the USSR*, 1 June 1990, p. 20; also Roman Szporluk, "The Imperial Legacy and the Soviet Nationalities Problem," in Lubomyr Hajda and Mark Beissinger, eds., *The Nationalities Factor in Soviet Politics and Society* (Boulder, Colo.: Westview Press, 1990), 1–23.
9. For example, Teresa Rakowska-Harmstone, "The Nationalities Question," in Robert Wesson, ed., *The Soviet Union: Looking to the 1980s* (Stanford: Hoover Institution, 1980), 137.
10. Compare Igor Torbakov, "The 'Statists' and the Ideology of Russian Imperial Nationalism," *RFE/RL Research Report*, 11 December 1992, 10–16; on the historical legacy compare S. Frederick Starr, "Tsarist Government: The Imperial Dimension," in Jeremy R. Azrael, ed., *Soviet Nationality Policies and Practices* (New York: Praeger, 1978), 3–38.

11. Paul Goble, "Russia and Its Neighbors," *Foreign Policy* (Spring 1993): 81.
12. For this interpretation of Weber compare Charles Ragin and David Zaret, "Theory and Method in Comparative Research: Two Strategies," *Social Forces* 61 (March 1983): 731–54.
13. Donald L. Horowitz, "How to Begin Thinking Comparatively about Soviet Ethnic Problems," in Alexander J. Motyl, ed., *Thinking Theoretically about Soviet Nationalities* (New York: Columbia University Press, 1992), 13.
14. Alexander J. Motyl, " 'Sovietology in One Country' or Comparative Nationality Studies?" *Slavic Review* 48 (Spring 1989): 83–88.
15. V. N. Tishkov, "O novykh podkhodakh v teorii i praktike mezhnatsional'nikh otnoshenii," *Sovetskaia etnografiia* 1989, no. 5, 5; for a similar assessment compare Ovsey I. Shkaratan, "*Perestroika* and the Rise of Mass Nationalism in the USSR," paper presented at the Conference on Nationalism in the Age of *Perestroika*, Columbia University, New York, 16 October 1990, p. 2.
16. For extensive references see Rasma Karklins, *Ethnic Relations in the USSR: The Perspective from Below* (London and Boston: Allen and Unwin, 1986), and G. V. Starovoitova, *Etnicheskaia gruppa v sovremennom sovetskom gorode* (Leningrad: Nauka, 1987).

Ethnopolitics and
Transition to Democracy

1

—————≫◦◦◦≪—————

Rethinking
Ethnopolitical Theory

The recent breakup of the Soviet Union provides rich material for rethinking the assumptions and propositions of comparative ethnic theory. Although neglected in the past, "ethnicity as a distinctive field of multidisciplinary, comparative inquiry is clearly coming of age."[1] This development is due to the maturation of theories of ethnopolitics as well as empirical trends the world over. Observed reality in the 1960s triggered works outlining problems of nation building in the developing world,[2] and the new volatility of politicized ethnicity in Belgium, Canada, and other Western democracies led to new theoretical work on these polities.[3] A similar reassessment is due after the demise of the USSR and other multiethnic Communist states. They too confirm that social scientists cannot stick to "the comfortable integrationist presumptions of the 1950s."[4] New theoretical and empirical work is essential.

Most analysts of the ethnopolitics of the former USSR have found it difficult to apply comparative theoretical perspectives, and have been faulted for this by comparativists.[5] Yet the major theorists themselves have had little to say about the Soviet Union, despite its being one of the most intensely multiethnic polities around.[6] Implicitly, and sometimes explicitly, both comparativists and Soviet area specialists have asserted that the USSR is a unique case. Uniqueness implies incomparability. I prefer to think of the Soviet system as a highly unusual case that can be assessed within a comparative framework if its distinctiveness is explicitly addressed. This requires

1

that a broad framework be used and that the salience of regime types for ethnicity be clarified. The latter also allows us to pinpoint links between the transformation of political regimes and changing ethnopolitics.

Comparative analysis is the art of making sense of both what is similar and what is different. The more traditional vein of comparative politics focuses on dissimilarities, for example by providing typologies of polities. More modern comparative political science aims at general theories useful for analyzing all polities, yet it faces the dilemma that many phenomena are particular and that generalizing about them is unscientific.[7] The response to this quandry has been either to abstain from comparing what is blatantly dissimilar—which explains why Communist systems are rarely included in comparative works—or to proceed as if the dissimilarity were inconsequential.[8] Some analysts have searched for functional equivalents of phenomena, a difficult task that rarely meets with success.

My approach is to follow the more traditional path: to confront dissimilarity head on and try to conceptualize consequences, mainly by clarifying links between regime types and ethnic policies. This approach is in line with the renewed emphasis on "bringing the state back in" to political science. Since the 1950s political scientists underemphasized governmental organization in favor of society-centered ways of explaining politics.[9] Recent theory argues for renewed attention to regime institutions, and such attention is compelling because regime change and the transition to democracy have been *the* issue in Soviet politics, as well as elsewhere. This empirical trend urges us to ask how exactly democracy differs from other types of regimes, and in the case of multiethnic democracies, how their ethnopolitics differs from that of nondemocratic systems. Answering these questions can help interpret what happened in the ethnopolitics of the former Soviet Union as it struggled to become a democracy.

My approach is to start analysis at the level of the polity and to ask how it deals both with pluralism in general and with ethnic pluralism in particular. The Soviet case shows that once regime transition has begun, the effect of the structural makeup of a polity and its political culture on minority nations comes into play as well. The basic contrast is between a polity oriented toward central control and a polity based on principles and values of power sharing. Another key in linking comparative theory to the analysis of the disintegration of the Soviet Union is the concept of ethnopolitics as it emerged in the 1980s and as further developed in this study. It is analytically more useful than the concept of nationalism, because it is generic and subsumes all political arrangements of ethnicity.

In sum, it is possible to use a comparative theoretical framework in analyzing the breakup of the USSR, but only if one differentiates between types of regimes and types of ethnopolitics. I turn to this distinction after first analyzing problems with the concept of nationalism and various propositions about the nature of ethnic identity and interests.

The Complexity of Nationalism

I prefer not to use the concept of nationalism in this study, because it is complex and does not reach to the core of some of the issues under discussion. Specifically, it does not allow us to discuss "nonnationalist" forms of ethnopolitics, one of which is the treatment of ethnic distinctions as irrelevant; another form, and more important for this study, is democratic ethnic pluralism. As shall be elaborated on, nationalism is a subtype of ethnic politics. I use ethnic politics, or ethnopolitics, as a concept that refers to all types of politics involving ethnic entities. And, just as social politics is not the same as socialism, ethnic politics is not the same as nationalism.

As a concept, nationalism is complex and ambiguous. At the core of its many meanings is "the self-assertion of ethnic groups,"[10] or nations. Yet while this self-assertion can focus on strengthening the group's identity, it can also assert superiority and be aggressive. "Nationalism is a state of mind, in which supreme loyalty of the individual is felt to be due the nation-state,"[11] and this loyalty too can be a positive or negative motivator. As a political doctrine nationalism strives "to make culture and polity congruent."[12] As such, it has been at the root of the democratic doctrine of national self-determination, but also has led to conflicts about the inclusion of cultural minorities in particular states.[13]

Nationalism has varying historical and value connotations in different societies. Some people see it as a modern form of patriotism that stimulates people to work for the good of their nation, whereas others demonize it as backward, irrational, and intolerant. As a political doctrine, nationalism has been connected to manifold historical movements. It has been linked to the emergence of democracy in England[14] and other countries; it has been linked to anti-imperial struggles the world over, including in Eastern Europe; and it also has been linked to xenophobic dictatorships encroaching on ethnic minorities or on other nations.

A historical typology of nationalism is that provided by Carlton J. H. Hayes, who differentiates between the humanitarian nationalism of the Enlightenment, the Jacobin nationalism of the French Revolution (including the traditional nationalism evoked in response to it—the liberal nationalism of Jeremy Bentham), and integral nationalism. This last form focuses on the exclusive pursuit of national interests and sees the nation as an end in itself, illiberal and tyrannical.[15] Yet there also exists enlightened nationalism that views its own nation's good as interrelated with the good of other nations.

3

Nationalism can be a great unifier within nations. It transcends class and other divisions and binds individuals into a larger community. In the words of Liah Greenfeld, "Nationalism locates the source of individual identity within a 'people,' which is seen as the bearer of sovereignty, the central object of loyalty, and the basis of collective solidarity."[16] The idea of "the people" is also tied to the emergence of democracy,[17] and the struggles for national and political emancipation often go hand in hand. I argue that this was the case in the former USSR, especially in the Baltic region.

At the core of nationalism lies the idea of the "nation," another elusive concept that will be discussed throughout this study but especially in chapters 3 and 7. The nation denotes both a territorially rooted ethnocultural entity and a political community. Both ethnic and political nationhood are powerful legitimating visions for governance. What principles to use for democratic nation building in regions marked by ethnic diversity is the question pursued throughout this study. I propose that it is possible to reconcile a nonassimilationist conception of ethnic nationhood with nonexclusivist political nationhood.

The Concept of Ethnopolitics

Lately, many scholars use the term "ethnopolitics" as a neutral concept referring to any politics among ethnic entities, be they big or small, historical nations or various types of minorities. Ethnic politics or "ethnopolitics" has been defined as any politics that impinges on the relative power or position of ethnic groups.[18] This focus on power emphasizes the perspective of political science rather than related disciplines such as sociology, psychology, and economics.

The study of ethnopolitics focuses on the causes, content, and consequences of politicized ethnicity. As an inclusive term, ethnopolitics includes both autocratic policies aimed at dominance and democratic policies aimed at consensus, coalition building, and power sharing. The concept is an analytical tool; it is up to the analyst to determine under what conditions one or the other form of ethnopolitics comes into play. Whereas the concept of nationalism implies that members of the same nation share the same views, ethnopolitics also allows for the possibility that people decide on the merits of ethnic issues as they see them. Often, individuals with the same ethnic background support the same side on an ethnic issue, but not always. There are instances when ethnic nominalism does not apply, such as when members of one nationality support the rights of another because they accept them as valid or because they share overarching interests.

Another advantage of the concept of ethnopolitics is that it avoids thinking of ethnicity in politics primarily as ethnic conflict. Rather, ethnic politics is seen as having a manifold nature: though it can be conflictual, it can also

4

be competitive, or cooperative.[19] The latter aspect is significant in light of the prevalence of casual references to "ethnic conflict" whenever ethnic issues emerge. As noted by Martin Heisler, the frequent use of the term "ethnic conflict" has led to a loss of analytical insight about ethnic relations.[20] Ethnicity does not have to be associated with conflict, and where it is, it bears remembering that some thinkers view conflict as natural and even creative. As noted by Georg Simmel, conflict can be an integrative force because "conflict resolves the tension between contrasts."[21]

One premise of the concept of ethnopolitics is that politics in any multi-ethnic state inevitably takes on an ethnic dimension. If ethnicity does not appear to be salient, it may be because ethnic issues are harmoniously arranged, but more typically problems are hidden behind the integrative rhetoric of a dominant group. Dominant nations or ethnic groups rarely define themselves as ethnic, and implicitly assume that they represent the norm to which minority members should want to assimilate. Dominant groups also like to imply that they stand above ethnic concerns and are the benefactors of minorities.

In sum, ethnopolitics is a generic concept referring to all types of politics between and among ethnic entities. It is value-neutral and as such encourages empirical analysis of the distribution of power and the processes surrounding it. Focusing on ethnic politics as politics is a crucial step beyond the many anthropologically, psychologically, and economically oriented theories of ethnicity on which political scientists have tended to rely. The concept of ethnopolitics includes a broad spectrum of political arrangements and programs, and though some focus on an individual nation and its interests, others involve multiethnic coalitions. The latter is a notion that nationalism cannot conceptualize, except as a negation of itself. Yet it is possible to recognize and reconcile multiple ethnic interests through pluralist structures and policies, a situation we will discuss more in the section on political regimes.

The Nature of Ethnic Identity

Our interest is in the political consequences of ethnicity, but this requires a definition of its nature. Contemporary scholars tend to take either an essential or a situational view of ethnicity. The essentialists see ethnicity as a fundamental empirical fact of social reality and emphasize the naturalness and stability of cultural, religious, historical, and emotional links within communities. Due to their primordial nature these ties are seen to have intrinsic consequences for the individual, although early socialization into a community is significant as well.[22] In contrast, the proponents of the situational view see ethnicity as an artifact "imagined" by cultural and political leaders for instrumental reasons.[23] They emphasize the fluidity of ethnic boundaries in history and note that the salience of group ethnicity depends on particular contexts. Individual ethnicity too is seen as situationally defined, since ethnicity is just one of many personal identities that acquire significance depending on social roles, interests, contingencies, and subjective choices.

Adopting one or the other definition means adopting an implicit view of the political consequences of ethnicity. People who view ethnicity in essentialist, primordial terms explain ethnic conflict by ancient hatreds and irreconcilable clashes of values. Because this view sees differences between communities as objective and immutable, it implies a permanency of political consequences, and thus cannot explain (or expect) political change. If ethnicity is a sociocultural given, group goals are so deeply ingrained as to be stable and unaffected by political regimes or other contexts. This approach tends toward ethnic nominalism, for example the ascription of ethnic labels without specific evidence regarding the nature or intensity of identity.[24] Ethnic nominalism is defined here as the tendency to impute ethnopolitical goals to an individual or group without empirical assessment.

I argue instead that the pertinency and consequences of politicized ethnicity have to be assessed in each context separately, not equally, everywhere, without evidence. The situational and instrumental view of ethnicity accepts the latter proposition because it sees ethnicity as susceptible to being redefined by situations and the subjective interpretations of participants.[25] The main problem with this second approach is that it implies that ethnicity has no content of its own and is used instrumentally wherever it appears advantageous to politicians. In addition, it pays no attention to the structures and values of political regimes and focuses instead on the usefulness of ethnicity in the pursuit of socioeconomic or general political goals. Political entrepreneurs recognize that ethnic solidarity has "instrumental utility in the struggle for power"[26] due to its psychological appeal. Ethnicity, in this view, is nothing but a tool for pursuing nonethnic goals.

In contrast Donald Horowitz has argued that the widespread conception of political power as a means to some other end leads to a misunderstanding of ethnic politics, in which power itself is often the core aim.[27] To this one can add that the distribution of power is a central concern of the subunits forming a multinational polity. And if it is true that different political regimes distribute power differently, the type of regime is of concern to ethnic groupings. Thus the instrumental approach is too narrow in that it disregards political issues of legitimacy, values, and conflicts over decision making, and basically implies that ethnicity is manipulated by elites rather than being able to develop mass support and agendas. The problem with the essentialist view is that it implies that ethnic mass support and agendas remain the same, no matter what.

A synthesis of essentialist-primordial and situational-instrumental arguments about ethnicity appears to be the most useful approach. In sum, nations and ethnic groups are objectively distinguished by language, religion, and other marks, and they are also subjectively distinct in that they interpret their history and future according to distinct values and psychological precepts. No single ethnic characteristic is necessary for a group to exist, since in essence ethnicity is marked by a sense of community, whether "imagined" or not. As noted by Nathan Glazer and Daniel P. Moynihan, ethnicity is "a tendency by people to insist on the significance of their distinctiveness and identity and on the rights that derive from this group character."[28] Although usually based on objective distinctions, such as language, at heart "identity is perception."[29] In other words, the perception of the salience of identity—and how it should be expressed—changes according to context. A sense of community is shaped by political institutions, leaders, events, and processes. Therefore the political consequences of ethnicity can be of minimal, medium, or strong significance, and they can involve different goals and either democratic or autocratic means of expression.

Ethnic and National Interests

Different types of ethnic groupings exist, and in the unusually complex multiethnic reality of the former USSR, the main difference is between historical nations and recent migrants.[30] For the latter—such as Ukrainians in Latvia—the core ethnopolitical concern is the role of individual ethnic identity in life situations, whereas for territorial nations—such as Latvians in Latvia—the main concern is their power and rights as corporate units. In essence, the difference is between the ethnic interests of individuals and those of groups.

Ethnopolitics differs depending on whether it accepts multiethnicity as an individual or group phenomenon.[31] If the focus is on the individual, the central issue is individual nondiscrimination of ethnic identity, as is the case in the United States. If, however, ethnic identity is group-based and the survival of a culture or the self-rule of a territorially rooted community is seen as the goal, then the focus of ethnopolitics shifts to how the regime addresses communal rights. Nations are more than aggregates of individuals with certain ethnic traits—they have group identities and interests. For nations, the core issue is the competition for relative power and position. Although this statement sounds like a platitude to analysts of international politics, it is less than clear to many analysts concerned with political interaction within a multinational state.

When distinct ethnocultural nations are discussed, it is important not to refer to them as minorities. As noted by Vernon Van Dyke, use of the term "minorities" suggests weakness in the face of the strength of a majority.

7

Terms such as "multiple nations" help us "get away from intimations of subordination and domination, and instead suggest groups of whatever size that live side by side, all of them with legitimate claims to equal treatment in terms of status and rights."[32] Chapter 3 addresses in detail what a nation is or is not. For the discussion here we define a nation as a culturally and historically distinct people concentrated in a region seen as its homeland.

Territorially based nations have specific interests that they want to see safeguarded in politics. The common denominator of these interests is the quest for self-rule and for the preservation of a distinct identity. This quest has both concrete and symbolic sides. Although nations defend concrete language rights, for example, they are also concerned about symbolism and the acceptance of their rights as legitimate and worthwhile. When Quebec voters supporting "sovereignty association" in 1980 were asked about their motives, the largest group (56 percent) cited "respect for the French language."[33] Acceptance matters a great deal in ethnic relations, as will be elaborated in the discussion of political culture in chapter 2.

The concrete interests of nations involve political power, cultural rights, and economic distribution. Politically, the central concern is the extent of self-government and participation in the decision making of central authorities. Self-rule of territories inhabited by minority nations is also expressed in extragovernmental forms of civic life such as political parties, trade unions, and so forth. The staffing of regional civil service institutions is an additional political issue, which also has a socioeconomic dimension.

Each nation has an interest in the broadest possible acceptance of the worth and survival of its culture. Take the language issue as an example: if several language communities live side by side, what is the emotional and social value of each language? Are all languages truly seen as equally worthwhile, or is one propagated as having superior qualities, such as providing links to world culture? In addition, what is the day-to-day situation regarding language use, especially for the minority languages?

Nations and ethnic groups have economic interests as well, and the core concepts are again those of control and equality. Issues surrounding distribution tend to loom large in conflicts over interests, especially in a state-controlled economy such as existed in the USSR. What matters are not just actual economic arrangements, but perceptions as to whether they are equitable. As I have written in an earlier work, "The quality of ethnic relations is affected by the perception of nationalities as to how well their basic interests are safeguarded. This, as well as the question of who decides the distribution of values, constitutes the political core of ethnic relations."[34]

The quest of territorial nations for political and national self-rule was a primary catalyst of the collapse of the Soviet Union, and it is important to use the concept of nation to clarify exactly what happened.

Do Regimes Matter?

As noted, the problem with applying ethnopolitical theories to the breakup of the Soviet Union is that most of them fail to address the significance of political regimes and therefore cannot explain national movements focusing on regime change. Although many theorists ask what economic, social, or other factors promote or assuage ethnic assertiveness,[35] few examine the links between types of political regimes and types of ethnic politics. The Soviet experience suggests that regime type is crucial to whether nations want to identify with an established multinational state or seek to form new states.

When a multinational polity consists of nations and historical minorities with distinct identities and interests, how this polity deals with its multiple nations is at the core of regime definition. Regimes can be distinguished according to whether or not they recognize national subunits as corporate entities with political rights, and whether the established political culture is based on negotiated consensus or on control. A structural as well as procedural recognition of ethnic pluralism is necessary for minority nations to identify with the state.

Ethnopolitical theory has to make politics the primary focus of its discourse. The statement that "the stability of culturally plural societies is threatened not by communalism per se, but by the failure of national institutions explicitly to recognize and accommodate existing communal divisions and interests,"[36] is an apt analysis when applied to the breakup of the Soviet Union. Ethnic politics cannot be separated from general politics in a situation where the nature of the polity itself is in question. Above all, the political struggle in the Soviet Union was over regime change, and this struggle drew attention to the question of how political regimes make a difference to ethnic politics. Does it matter whether a multinational state—be it the former USSR or another state—is ruled autocratically or democratically, and if so how? Moreover, once a transition to democracy starts, does multiethnicity play a constructive or destructive role, and under what conditions?

Few theorists of ethnopolitics have addressed these questions. Some analysts imply that regimes are important by focusing their work only on Western democracies or the developing world,[37] but many others implicitly or explicitly argue that theories of ethnic politics developed elsewhere can be adapted to nondemocratic systems. Lee Dutter, for example, states that "the Soviet Union represents yet another variation on the general theme of politics in plural societies."[38] Consociationalism is one of the few ethnopolitical theories that explicitly focuses on regime type, but it discusses forms of democracy rather than comparing democratic and nondemocratic systems. Nevertheless, this analysis is helpful. Arend Lijphart and others have enumerated the traits of democracy that have succeeded in keeping

9

plural societies within the same polity.[39] They have outlined a power-sharing form of democracy that provides a comparative paradigm helpful in identifying the nondemocratic features of the Soviet policy and explaining why Gorbachev's reforms fell short of saving the union. The use of this paradigm does not mean that it has to fit in every detail. In his more recent work, Lijphart has emphasized that the power-sharing model can be creatively applied to various situations since it "consists of a set of general principles, not specific rules and institutions."[40]

Empirically, too, consociational thinking can be applied to the Soviet case by focusing on territorially based nations. Even though the Soviet Union contained significant dispersed nationalities, at heart it was a geographically segmented multinational state. The dominant issue of ethnic politics in the Union of Soviet Socialist Republics was the extent of self-rule for the fifteen nations that provided their names to the constituent union-republics.

Students of ethnopolitics assess under what conditions ethnicity becomes salient. I argue that the political system of a state has a distinct impact, in terms of both institutional arrangements and specific policy processes. If this is true, then the change from one regime to another will also affect ethnopolitics. During the attempted transition to a new system, differing political agendas of competing political movements are at the heart of the ethnic struggle. Aside from the different programs for dealing with multiethnicity, new conflict groups as well as multiethnic coalitions are formed. If a movement aims at a power-sharing system, multiple identities have to be accommodated in the formation of a coalition based on strong common goals. In the next chapter I argue in detail that the democratic movement in the USSR did precisely that.

Regime Structures

Comparison shows that the most promising instances of conflict resolution in multiethnic states have taken place in democracies. What exactly is it that makes certain democracies so effective in dealing with national distinctions and conflicts? The recognition of multiple power centers and group rights appears to be most crucial. Democratic regimes such as those in Switzerland, Belgium, or Canada are based on the recognition of group pluralism, including the rights of minority nations.

Definitions of democracy that focus on groups are legion. To cite Giovanni Sartori, democracy is sustained by safeguarding a "network of primary democracies—small communities and voluntary organizations."[41] There are several clusters of theories of democracy; next to the radical participatory and the classic liberal-democratic theories, the pluralist-competitive theories emphasize the role of groups. Plural democracies base their policies on accepting the distinct rights of minority nations as corporate entities, but crucial group rights are also granted to political parties, interest groups, and voluntary associations. None of these have been recognized under Communist regimes. On the contrary, a Communist system is based on the rejection of autonomous group pursuits as detrimental to the good of the people as a whole. The single institution allowed to have an identity separate from the state is the Communist party, because "the Communist Party of the Soviet Union is the leading and guiding force of Soviet society, the nucleus of its political system and of [all] state and public organizations."[42] All this is well known, but its significance for ethnic identity and self-rule has been insufficiently explored.

The link between pluralist group politics and democratic ethnopolitical arrangements is twofold. There is a direct link in that many democracies incorporate ethnic autonomy into their structures and political culture. In addition, self-rule is granted indirectly by other pluralist structures of the polity. Thus pluralism in the vertical distribution of power means that considerable authority rests with lower levels of government such as provinces, cities, or local authorities. If such units have an ethnic identity, they attain de facto a degree of autonomy without ethnic pluralism coming into play. The same principle applies to the horizontal structuring of political power: the higher a political system's level of group and individual autonomy, the greater the scope of ethnic pluralism.

An illustration of this point would be that a democracy does not regulate book publishing and therefore it is up to ethnic groups whether books reflecting their concerns are published. The Communist state is in charge of all publishing, however, and thus there is an actual or potential political constraint on ethnic cultural autonomy. A similar example concerns the religious aspect of ethnicity: most democracies proclaim a separation of state and church whereby churches organize religious life, and relations with the state are unaffected by what they do. In contrast, the position of organized religion becomes an ethnopolitical issue in a Communist system, where the state actively regulates religious affairs. Thus there are indirect effects of regime structures on ethnic autonomy. This is especially evident if one studies American democracy with its extensive limits of the role of the state in religious, cultural, and communal matters. Whereas the experience of Switzerland and other consociational democracies illustrates how ethnopluralism can be accommodated directly, the American experience suggests ways of doing so indirectly.

In contrast, a Soviet-type system imposes both indirect and direct limits on ethnic political autonomy. The Communist Party of the Soviet Union (CPSU) saw it as its duty to prevent the emergence of alternative political or social groupings, whether they were ethnic or nonethnic, and the same applied to internal factions. According to Leninist principles, the pursuit of subgroup or ethnic interests was outlawed. When individual Communists tried to pursue the interests of their nationality, typically they were purged.[43] The nominal republican subunits of the CPSU were controlled by central party authorities who, for example, chose the party secretaries in the non-Russian republics. As noted by Horowitz, "Lack of group autonomy in leadership selection is a sure sign of ethnic subordination,"[44] but at least pre-Gorbachev leaders were sensitive to symbolic meaning and usually chose members of the titular nationality of a republic for visible positions. Gorbachev's insensitivity in this regard accelerated the rise of demands by non-Russians; when he replaced the first party secretary of Kazakhstan with a Russian in December 1986, ethnic rioting ensued. An open rift between central party authority and subgroup autonomy arose when the Communist Party of Lithuania seceded from the CPSU in December 1989.[45] This was a revolutionary act leading to regime change, because subunit autonomy soon became a fact.

Another direct limit on subgroup autonomy in the USSR involved its version of state federalism. Weak to begin with, formal federalism was systematically undermined by the unitary and hierarchical Communist party. A federal system consists not only of a sharp division of powers between the federal and regional governments, but of other political arrangements as well: "Among them are the party system, the role of pressure groups and political movements, and the effect of political attitudes on the system."[46] None of these was present in the old Soviet regime.

On paper, the Union of Soviet Socialist Republics had been a federal state since 1922. Theoretically this concession to national autonomy held considerable promise, because extensive federalism serves to accommodate nations living in distinct territories. Federalism has been a core principle of structural power sharing, with Switzerland being the classic example.[47] The basis for such accommodation is the recognition of minority nations who want to govern themselves extensively, and who have a group right to participate in common institutions. Power-sharing democracies expressly vest political power in such entities as the language communities in Belgium, which are specifically mentioned in its constitution.

As Lijphart and others argue, the emphasis on group rights distinguishes plural democracies from liberal democracies.[48] Even though liberals recognize the rights of states on the international level, they generally put priority on the rights of individuals over groups. Pluralists see extensive self-rule of nations in a multinational polity as the only way to accommodate their distinct identities. Also, some individual rights are seen as being inherently tied to group rights, especially cultural identity. Language and other expressions of culture gain meaning only through a communal interaction that requires certain structural givens. If people from a small language group live in close interaction with a larger group using another language, this tends to lead to the eventual extinction of the language of the smaller group. Unless such a minority is protected, interaction with the majority will undermine actual language use, and thus, language rights. This is the main argument in support of group cultural rights, for example the dominance of a language in a designated territory, such as particular Swiss cantons or the province of Quebec. Equal individual rights may be insufficient to guarantee real equality if more than one culture is to be preserved, or if there has been systematic discrimination against one group. A collective right may take precedence in such a context.[49]

The power-sharing approach to linguistic equality as practiced in Switzerland, Belgium, Canada, and elsewhere is twofold: for one, all languages are treated equally on the federal level (for example all languages are used in the federal legislature and civil service), and secondly and more important, a single culture has precedence within the homeland of each smaller nation. Complete linguistic and cultural autonomy on their own territory is seen as the only way to guarantee the rights of smaller nations. The French-Canadians have expressed this rationale best when emphasizing that every culture needs full development opportunities, that is, it has to be a "société globale." They have defined this as a social environment in which they can function completely as French-Canadians, without a need to switch to English for certain tasks.[50]

Language policy in the Soviet Union did not come close to this model. Not only did native languages not have this exclusive role in union republics, but even true bilingualism was lacking, as most Russians settling in these republics never bothered to learn local languages. The result was that indigenous people had to learn Russian, or else risk not being understood when trying to communicate with public officials, many of whom were Russians. Symbolically, this was difficult to accept, but there were practical problems for people with little knowledge of Russian. At a congress of the Writers' Union in Uzbekistan, a poet reminded members of his audience that if they became ill in Tashkent, or if one of their homes were to catch fire, they would be unable to get help by telephoning in Uzbek.[51]

The democratic approach to ethnicity includes full linguistic rights for distinct nations within their home territory. The significance of such rights extends beyond intrinsic value since the position of cultures also affects social stratification. If there is a dominant language for political and social success—such as Russian was throughout the Soviet Union—people with a native command of this language have a built-in career advantage.[52]

In contrast to the pluralists, liberals argue that ethnic identity should be reserved for the private sphere and that the state cannot recognize communalism in any way. As Jeff Spinner has written, "The individual is the primary political actor in the liberal state, not the group. . . . Liberals do not argue that groups should not exist; they merely say that these groups should have no political standing."[53] In contrast, pluralists define the exemplary state as one where public authority devolves on a plurality of groups. To guarantee the rights of individuals, it is essential to fortify the rights of private associations. Individuals are helpless against the monolithic power of the state and therefore power has to be pluralized.[54] In many ways the transition to democracy in the former Soviet Union substantiates this thesis.

A democratic regime requires vertical and horizontal pluralism vis-à-vis centers of political power. Democracy means extensive self-government of lower-level state units, even more so when ethnic diversities are grouped territorially. Self-rule is a democratic good in itself, but in addition, a multi-layered state structure helps to resolve conflicts overall: "In a federal system, with its multiple political arenas, any given group may be simultaneously in subordinate, equal, and superordinate positions in different cantons or provinces and at the federal levels."[55] Such multiple forums with differing balances of power help keep relations in harmony.

In the USSR the secondary level of government involved the fifteen union republics, each named after an indigenous nation. Beginning with the late 1980s a quest for self-determination was led by these republics. Formally, the Soviet Union was a federal state that looked similar to other federal states, but formal comparisons can be highly misleading. It is a stricture of comparative analysis that one cannot assume that what looks alike is alike; analysts should establish what is truly equivalent.[56] Most of all, the formal federalism of the Soviet state was undermined by the monopolistic and centralizing role of the Communist party, a role without an equivalent in other federations. In addition, the scope of central bureaucratic authority was unprecedented and applied to the economy and spheres that are typically under the purview of lower-level governments, such as education. Thus every course plan at Vilnius University had to be approved by the Moscow Ministry of Higher Education.[57] The multiple inadequacies of Soviet federalism were revealed as the regime crisis progressed after 1988. For instance, the debate about economic decentralization showed that only between 4 to 10 percent of each republic's industrial enterprises were under its authority.[58] By late 1990 Gorbachev himself called Soviet federalism nothing but concealed unitarism.[59]

Another crucial structural pillar of democratic multinationalism is a group-based right to participate extensively in the decision making of the federal government. Thus the members of the Swiss Federal Council represent not only their political parties and themselves as political leaders, but also one of the Swiss subnations.[60] Politicians in a consociational state have a mandate to represent the interests of their group; such pluralism is encouraged as an expression of democracy where the good of the people as a whole is seen as emerging from the balance of group interests. One crucial means of achieving this is "government by a grand coalition of the political leaders of all significant segments of the plural society."[61]

Again the contrast to the old Soviet system is striking. The central government saw the pursuit of ethnic group rights as divisive and an expression of bourgeois nationalism. Every politician was supposed to represent only the interests of the unitary Communist party, whether he or she was a Russian, Ukrainian, Georgian, or Kazakh. Although some attention was paid to the symbolic uses of nominal ethnic identity—such as having ethnic quotas in the rubber-stamp parliaments—actual ethnopolitical identification was a breach of party discipline. Furthermore, the loyal ethnic cadres were supposed to deter primordial strategies and undermine the rise of counter-elites.[62] As with all aspects of the old-style Soviet regime, this strategy became increasingly ineffective as autonomous centers of power began to emerge and were supported by a segment of the old elites. Once even the Russian republic under Yeltsin demanded self-rule, the central authorities were fighting a losing battle.

Although the power-sharing approach is important in the case of a political union between established nations, it should be noted that East Central Europe has provided another model of pluralist ethnopolitics. Early in this century the Austrians Karl Renner and Otto Bauer recognized that it was impossible always to draw territorial federal boundaries between ethnocultural groupings. They therefore advocated a corporate form of federalism. The key principle is that nonterritorial cultural communities are given collective rights. This model found practical application in interwar Latvia and Estonia, especially in the form of publicly funded minority school systems.[63] Other precedents focusing on legally and structurally guaranteed cultural rights were provided by the Minority Treaties sponsored by the League of Nations; specific cases involved all of Eastern Europe as well as Austria, Upper Silesia, the Aaland Islands, Turkey, and Iraq.[64] In the postwar period the same idea has found application in the 1960 Constitution of Cyprus[65] and partly in Belgium with regard to Brussels.[66]

Values and Process

Institutional arrangements are insufficient for power sharing to be effective; a strong commitment to pluralist values is also necessary. Values are important both as beliefs underlying the sharing of power at all times and as the result of the quality of specific interactions. The quality of interactions is cumulative; though one or two divisive incidents are unlikely to undermine basic confidence in power sharing, a number of incidents can change the whole atmosphere.

The expressed goals of the major political players, be they elites or mass movements, are extremely important. The main distinction is between a democratic power-sharing culture and a culture of autocratic control. Ethnic claims focus on notions of group entitlement in terms of both legitimacy and group worth,[67] and a power-sharing culture accepts this as a positive aspect. Its core value is that granting power to all constituent nations benefits everyone. Although "it is always much harder for majorities than for minorities to seek or accept power-sharing solutions,"[68] the majorities develop an enlightened view of self-interest as tied to the common interest. For power sharing to work, there must be a political culture that sees diversity as enrichment and the granting of rights to minorities as a strengthening of the rights of everybody in the state.

It helps if contention is seen as normal and accommodation as achievable. Ethnic accommodation involves commitment to dialogue and negotiation, as well as legally binding agreements on the basis of free will and reciprocity. In a truly federal system power relationships are characterized by "bargains, compromises, and balances" within formal and informal structures.[69] In contrast, the control model's intent is to make ethnic diversity and its political consequences disappear by defining it away and by exercising structural control.[70]

The quality of interactions over time is another crucial determinant of ethnopolitical evaluations. It matters whether the concerned groups feel that the initial entry into a common state was forced or voluntary. In addition, the cumulative effect of consensual or divisive interaction is significant. For the cumulative effect to enhance pluralist values, participants need to perceive that genuine attempts are being made to accommodate everyone's interests. If control or dominance by one group emerges as the pattern, prospects for power sharing are undermined. Focal events involving a cataclysmic experience can have a major impact, and can have either positive or negative results, or both. As argued in the next chapter, the hard-line crackdown in the Baltic states in January 1991 included elements of both: it was a negative focal event that discredited the old-style USSR, but due to Yeltsin's decisive rejection of the violence it also was a positive focal event strengthening future ties between a democratic Russia and Baltic leaders.

The central question about the political process is how to reach accord in a diverse society. Consociationalism is based on the assumption that this result is possible only through deliberate accommodation of distinct identities. The majority needs to be sensitive to minority concerns and accept real and symbolic claims as legitimate. Ignoring or trying to undermine minority interests will create the opposite effect. As noted by Lijphart, "Because of the tenacity of primordial loyalties, any effort to eradicate them not only is quite unlikely to succeed, especially in the short run, but may well be counter-

productive and may stimulate segmental cohesion and intersegmental violence rather than national cohesion."[71] Recognition of group identity and
rights is more likely to lead to integration into a political community.
Whereas in the short run institutions and values that accommodate pluralism strengthen distinctiveness, this quality decreases in salience in the long
run as mutual acceptance increases.[72]

It is critical to be clear about the assumptions analysts make about group
pluralism. Some analysts assume—implicitly or explicitly—that distinct
groupings necessarily cause fragmentation that has harmful effects on a
polity. Other analysts call this thesis simplistic and argue that one needs to
distinguish between subcultural awareness and political enmity.[73] Culturally
diverse groups can coexist amicably, and the deliberate accommodation of
diversity can make it a source of political pride and consensus. Switzerland is
the classic example. Rather than trying to "melt" ethnocultural groups into
a new cultural whole, it has used the affirmation of distinctiveness as the
cement that binds them into a political whole.

If one assumes that ethnocultural diversity necessarily undermines the
political community of a state, this leaves secession or assimilation as the
only options. The multitude of new states in the contemporary world attests
to the attractiveness of separate statehood, yet most of the new states themselves contain ethnic minorities. Thus we come to the question of cultural
assimilation of groups. I emphasize groups, because the assimilation of individuals, especially those who have migrated to new environments, is a different issue.

The dilemma is that in a multiethnic or multilingual environment there is
no such thing as ethnically or linguistically "neutral" policy. If, for example,
a specific language is used in public life and education (and unless this
language is Esperanto), it is the language of one group. Intriguingly, members
of the dominant language group typically deny that this is a form of cultural
dominance. Thus in the Soviet Union the proponents of the dominant role
of Russian called themselves "internationalists." Although such claims
seemed Orwellian to minority members, they reflected a sincere belief that
for Russians to insist on the use of Russian language was not nationalism,
but for Latvians to insist on the use of Latvian language was nationalism.
This assumption reflects the worldwide phenomenon of dominant groups
ignoring their own specificity. As noted by Marion Young, the assimilationist ideal presumes that there is a general group-neutral human identity,
unmarked by particularity: "The ideal of a universal humanity without
social group differences allows privileged groups to ignore their own specificity. Blindness to difference perpetuates cultural imperialism by allowing
norms expressing the point of view and experience of privileged groups to
appear neutral and universal."[74] In our context, "others" are marked by a

particular language, such as Latvian, whereas the use of Russian is not seen as the use of a particular language, but rather as the use of a "universal" and "international" language.[75]

Under these circumstances, a politics that asserts the value of group difference is liberating and empowering. Moreover, as also argued by Young, "asserting the value and specificity of the culture and attributes of oppressed groups . . . results in a relativizing of the dominant culture"[76] and its self-discovery as specific (for example, the Russian language). While this discovery proved to be liberating and empowering for many Russians in Russia and Latvia, others found it to be unsettling. As outlined in later chapters, "Russian-speaking Soviets" have become uncertain about their identity. As a result, some would like to return to the good old times, some others try to assimilate to what they see as the new dominant norm, and still others search for new ways to have a "neutral" identity. This could mean social anomie or moving to an immigrant country with a clearly assimilationist ideology.

In sum, an analysis must ask how a polity deals with pluralism overall and with ethnic pluralism specifically. Are autonomous social groups seen as disruptive, as was the case in the Soviet Union, or are they seen as legitimate political actors, as is typically the case in democracies? It is significant whether or not minority nations are seen as distinct entities with legitimate interests and as the bearers of crucial rights. In the case of territorially based nations, it is important whether they have extensive self-rule and participate in central decision-making institutions. The assumption of consociational and cultural autonomy arrangements is that safeguarding plural ethnic identities and interests leads to attitudinal political integration into a larger polity; the same idea underlies the European Community.

Conclusion

The recent collapse of the Soviet Union presents an interesting case for the study of comparative ethnopolitics, but it also adds to our theoretical knowledge. One problem in applying existing theories to the Soviet case is that most of them assume some stable givens, but in the ex-Soviet region everything has been in revolutionary flux. In most multiethnic states the state itself, its nations, and the political regime are clearly established and one can determine who the main players are and what are the basic rules of interaction. The Soviet Union and its successor states have been states in profound crisis and redefinition, including state boundaries, national identities, and the nature of political regimes. Yet this draws our attention to the nature of such core givens. The Soviet case raises questions about comparability and the appropriateness of specific concepts. I argue for the use of a neutral concept of ethnopolitics and for paying attention to the nature of regimes. Regimes matter in themselves, but even more so during periods of regime change. The next chapter will explore this point in more empirical detail, but here I have tried to make the theoretical case for a statist approach to ethnicity. Theda Skocpol has called this a "Tocquevillean" approach, because Alexis de Tocqueville urged us to pay attention to the organization of polities:

> In this perspective, states matter not simply because of the goal-oriented activities of state officials. They matter because their organizational configurations, along with their overall patterns of activity, affect political culture, encourage some kinds of group formation and collective political actions (but not others), and make possible the raising of certain political issues (but not others).[77]

In sum, political regimes matter, and for consensual and stable ethnopolitics to emerge in the region the old Soviet regime had to change fundamentally in regard to its structures and underlying processes.

Contemporary arguments about ethnic politics emphasize its contextual nature. Ethnopolitics in the USSR during its final years can be understood only if one links it to the revolutionary transformation of the Soviet polity from an ossified Communist autocracy into a participatory democracy. This transformation proceeded gradually and with interruptions, but crucial changes did occur. The link to changing ethnic politics is extremely strong, to the point that much of what was commonly interpreted as "ethnic conflict" was part and parcel of the struggle over democratization. Democratization meant new conflict and competition, but it also meant new forms of cooperation and the formation of a new political culture among a segment of the population. As will be explicated in the next chapter, in the former USSR the entire democratic movement, including the Russian one, supported national independence for republics. The democrats increasingly came to believe that the only chance of forging a mutually acceptable union was to base it on purely voluntary integration. The first step toward that goal was to accept each other's sovereignty unequivocally. This could be done by accepting the demands of non-Russian nations as inextricable from the new ideology of participatory democracy.

New values and perceptions are crucial for the strengthening of democratic ethnopolitics. The downfall of the old system was marked by the increasingly prevalent perception on the part of all actors that they were losing, and by the search for a new order in which everyone would be winning. This nonzero-sum approach was the basis for new thinking.

NOTES

1. Crawford Young, "The Temple of Ethnicity," *World Politics* 35 (July 1983): 652.
2. Walker Connor, "Self-Determination: The New Phase," *World Politics* 20 (October 1967): 30–53; Cynthia H. Enloe, *Ethnic Conflict and Political Development* (Boston: Little, Brown, 1973).

3. For excellent surveys see Joseph V. Montville, ed., *Conflict and Peacemaking in Multiethnic Societies* (Lexington, Mass.: Lexington Books, 1990).
4. Young, "Temple of Ethnicity," 656.
5. David D. Laitin, "The National Uprisings in the Soviet Union," *World Politics* 44 (October 1991): 139–77.
6. Alexander J. Motyl, ed., *Thinking Theoretically about Soviet Nationalities* (New York: Columbia University Press, 1992), expressly challenges theorists in the field to address the Soviet case, with mixed success.
7. Adam Przeworski and Henry Teune, *The Logic of Comparative Social Inquiry* (New York: Wiley, 1970).
8. The use of concepts developed on the basis of Western democracies such as "interest group" and "political participation" has been controversial. See H. Gordon Skilling, "Interest Groups and Communist Politics Revisited," *World Politics* 36 (October 1983): 1–27, and Mary McAuley, "Political Participation under Review," *Studies in Comparative Communism* 17 (Fall-Winter 1984–85): 241–51.
9. See Theda Skocpol, "Bringing the State Back In: Strategies of Analysis in Current Research," in Peter B. Evans, Dietrich Rueschemeyer, and Theda Skocpol, eds., *Bringing the State Back In* (Cambridge: Cambridge University Press, 1985), especially 4.
10. Uri Ra'anan, "The Nation-State Fallacy," in Montville, *Conflict and Peacemaking*, 9.
11. Hans Kohn, *Nationalism: Its Meaning and History* (New York: D. Van Nostrand, 1965), 9.
12. Ernest Gellner, *Nations and Nationalism* (Ithaca: Cornell University Press, 1983), 43.
13. Anthony Smith, *Theories of Nationalism* (New York: Harper and Row, 1971), 171.
14. Liah Greenfeld, *Nationalism: Five Roads to Modernity* (Cambridge, Mass.: Harvard University Press, 1992), 14 and passim.
15. Carlton J. H. Hayes, *The Historical Evolution of Modern Nationalism* (New York: Macmillan, 1931), especially 16–17, 45–57, 87–88, 165–66; for an outstanding historical analysis of nationalism see also Greenfeld, *Nationalism*.
16. Greenfeld, *Nationalism*, 3.
17. Ibid., *Nationalism*, 10.
18. Joseph Rothschild, *Ethnopolitics: A Conceptual Framework* (New York: Columbia University Press, 1981).
19. Ibid., 84.
20. Martin O. Heisler, "Ethnicity and Ethnic Relations in the Modern West," in Montville, *Conflict and Peacemaking*, 27.
21. Georg Simmel, *Conflict*, trans. Kurt H. Wolff, and *The Web of Group-Affiliations*, trans. Reinhard Bendix, in one volume (Glencoe, Ill.: Free Press, 1955), 14, see also 17.
22. See Anthony H. Richmond, "Ethnic Nationalism: Social Science Paradigms," *International Social Science Journal* 39 (February 1987): 3–18.
23. See especially Benedict Anderson, *Imagined Communities: Reflections on the Origin and Spread of Nationalism* (London: Verso, 1983), 12 and passim.
24. Heisler, "Ethnicity," 26.
25. A strong argument for the situational character of ethnicity and ethnic politics is presented by Nelson Kasfir, "Explaining Ethnic Political Participation," *World Politics* 31 (April 1979): 365–88. The many theories linking modernization to increased or decreased ethnic pertinency constitute a subtype of the contextual approach.
26. Rothschild, *Ethnopolitics*, 5. For a succinct summary of the contrast between instrumentalists and primordialists, see Young, "Temple of Ethnicity," 652–62.
27. Donald L. Horowitz, *Ethnic Groups in Conflict* (Berkeley: University of California Press, 1985), 185–86; for an application of the interest approach see Rasma Karklins, *Ethnic Relations in the USSR: The Perspective from Below* (London and Boston: Allen and Unwin, 1986), especially chap. 2.
28. Nathan Glazer and Daniel P. Moynihan, "Introduction," in Nathan Glazer and Daniel P. Moynihan, eds., *Ethnicity: Theory and Experience* (Cambridge, Mass.: Harvard University Press, 1975), 3.
29. Greenfeld, *Nationalism*, 13.

30. The complex differences between ethnic groupings in the USSR were clearly shown by John Armstrong with his typology of Soviet nationalities. John Armstrong, "The Ethnic Scene in the Soviet Union: The View of the Dictatorship," in Erich Goldhagen, ed., *Ethnic Minorities in the Soviet Union* (New York: Praeger, 1968), 3–49.

31. Vernon Van Dyke, "The Individual, the State, and Ethnic Communities in Political Theory," *World Politics* 29 (April 1977): 343–69. I see ethnicity and ethnic politics as being situationally defined; for excellent expositions of this general approach see Kasfir, "Explaining Ethnic Political Participation," 365–88, and Richmond, "Ethnic Nationalism," 3–18.

32. Vernon Van Dyke, *Human Rights, Ethnicity, and Discrimination* (Westport, Conn.: Greenwood Press, 1985), 247.

33. Maurice Pinard and Richard Hamilton, "Motivational Dimensions in the Quebec Independence Movement: A Test of a New Model," in Kurt Lang and Gladys Engel Lang, eds., *Research in Social Movements, Conflicts and Change*, vol. 9 (Greenwich, Conn.: JAI Press, 1986), 248.

34. Karklins, *Ethnic Relations*, 11.

35. Links between ethnic assertiveness and modernization are discussed in Saul Newman, "Does Modernization Breed Ethnic Political Conflict?" *World Politics* 4 (April 1991): 451–78, and Enloe, *Ethnic Conflict*.

36. Robert Melson and Howard Wolpe, "Modernization and the Politics of Communalism: A Theoretical Perspective," *American Political Science Review* 64 (December 1970): 1130, as cited in Arend Lijphart, *Democracy in Plural Society* (New Haven: Yale University Press, 1977), 142. For a similar point see Kenneth D. MacRae, "Theories of Power-Sharing and Conflict Management," in Montville, *Conflict and Peacemaking*, 93–94.

37. For example, Horowitz, *Ethnic Groups*, entire, and Heisler, "Ethnicity," 24.

38. Lee Dutter, "Theoretical Perspectives on Ethnic Political Behavior in the Soviet Union," *Journal of Conflict Resolution* 34 (June 1990): 312. He does mention regime type as one of many influential factors, but he does not see it as a crucial variable.

39. Lijphart, *Democracy in Plural Society*; see also MacRae, "Theories of Power-Sharing," 93–106.

40. Arend Lijphart, "The Power-Sharing Approach," in Montville, *Conflict and Peacemaking*, 496.

41. Giovanni Sartori, *The Theory of Democracy Revisited* (Chatham, N.J.: Chatham House Publishers, 1987), 9.

42. Article 6 of the 1977 Constitution of the USSR, cited in Robert Sharlet, *The New Soviet Constitution of 1977* (Brunswick, Ohio: King's Court Communications, 1978), 78.

43. Walker Connor, *The National Question in Marxist-Leninist Theory and Strategy* (Princeton: Princeton University Press, 1984), 533–80.

44. Horowitz, *Ethnic Groups*, 222.

45. See, for example, V. Stanley Vardys, "Sajudis: National Revolution in Lithuania," in Jan Arveds Trapans, ed., *Toward Independence: The Baltic Popular Movements* (Boulder, Colo.: Westview Press, 1991), 11–24; Martha Brill Olcott, "The Soviet (Dis)union," *Foreign Policy* 82 (Spring 1991): 118–37.

46. Michael B. Stein, "Federal Political Systems and Federal Societies," *World Politics* 20 (July 1968): 723.

47. Jürg Steiner, "Power-Sharing: Another Swiss 'Export Product'?" in Montville, *Conflict and Peacemaking*, 107–14.

48. Arend Lijphart, *Democracies: Patterns of Majoritarian and Consensus Government in Twenty-One Countries* (New Haven: Yale University Press, 1984); Van Dyke, *Human Rights*, entire.

49. Raymond N. Morris and C. Michael Lanphier, *Three Scales of Inequality: Perspectives on French-English Relations* (Don Mills, Ont.: Longman Canada, 1977), 10; also Van Dyke, "The Individual, the State," 365.

50. Erwin C. Hargrove, "Nationality, Values, and Change: Young Elites in French Canada," *Comparative Politics* 2 (April 1970): 475, 479. See also Milton J. Esman, "The State and Language Policy," *International Political Science Review* 13, no. 4 (1992): 381–96.

51. *Report on the USSR*, 22 September 1989, p. 17. See also the discussion in chapter 7.
52. See also Karklins, *Ethnic Relations in the USSR*; especially chap. 2.
53. Jeff Spinner, "Liberal Citizenship and Ethnic Identity," paper presented at the Midwest Political Science Association, Chicago, April 1992.
54. Henry S. Kariel, "Pluralism," *International Encyclopedia of the Social Sciences*, Daniel L. Sills, ed., vol. 12 (New York: Macmillan Company and Free Press, 1968), 164–69.
55. MacRae, *Theories of Power-Sharing*, 102.
56. Przeworski and Teune, *Comparative Social Inquiry*, 103–16.
57. Author's interviews with officials of Vilnius University, December 1990.
58. Uwe Halbach, "Nationalitätenfrage und Föderation," *Osteuropa* 11 (November 1990): 1020.
59. Speech by Gorbachev to the plenary session of the CPSU Central Committee, 10 December 1990, *Pravda*, 11 December 1990, p. 2. See also Stephan Kux, "Soviet Federalism," *Problems of Communism* (March–April 1990): 1–28.
60. Steiner, "Power-Sharing," 111.
61. Lijphart, *Democracy in Plural Society*, 25.
62. See Philip G. Roeder, "Soviet Federalism and Ethnic Mobilization," *World Politics* 43 (January 1991): 196–232, especially 206–7; Connor, *National Question*; Gerhard Simon, *Nationalism and Policy toward the Nationalities in the Soviet Union: From Totalitarian Dictatorship to Post-Stalinist Society*, trans. Karen Forster and Oswald Forster (Boulder, Colo.: Westview Press, 1991).
63. Georg Von Rauch, *The Baltic States: The Years of Independence, 1917–1940*, trans. Gerald Onn (Berkeley: University of California Press, 1974).
64. For a survey of the protection of minorities by the League of Nations, see Oscar I. Janowsky, *Nationalities and National Minorities (With Special Reference to East-Central Europe)* (New York: Macmillan, 1945), 110–92 as well as C. A. Macartney, *National States and National Minorities* (Oxford: n.p., 1934).
65. Carl J. Friedrich, *Trends of Federalism in Theory and Practice* (New York: Praeger, 1968), 124.
66. A similar form of self-government—this time based on religious identity—existed in the Ottoman Empire. Members of a specific religious community (*millet*) dispensed law in areas of personal status according to religious precepts. Ra'anan, "Nation-State Fallacy," 17.
67. Horowitz, *Ethnic Groups*, 185–228.
68. Lijphart, "Power-Sharing Approach," 496.
69. Stein, "Federal Political Systems," 733; see also Lijphart, "Power-Sharing Approach," 492.
70. Ian Lustick, "Stability in Deeply Divided Societies: Consociationalism versus Control," *World Politics* 31 (April 1979): 325–44.
71. Lijphart, *Democracy in Plural Society*, 24.
72. Ibid., 228.
73. G. Bingham Powell, Jr., *Social Fragmentation and Political Hostility: An Austrian Case Study* (Stanford: Stanford University Press, 1970), 3–5.
74. Iris Marion Young, *Justice and the Politics of Difference* (Princeton: Princeton University Press, 1990), 165.
75. The reference here is to language use within a specific country. "Universal" languages have played a considerable role in international relations, and continue to do so in specific subfields. Thus Latin until recently was the universal language of medicine and the Catholic church, French is the universal language of international postal services, and English has become the language of international commerce and air traffic.
76. Young, *Justice and the Politics of Difference*, 166.
77. Skocpol, "Bringing the State Back In," 21.

2

⋙◦⋘

Regime Change and New Ethnopolitics

S ince the late 1980s a systemic crisis and the struggle over regime change determined Soviet ethnopolitics. Simply put, the struggle was between forces in favor of a basically unchanged USSR—with subgroups favoring partial reform or no reform—and those favoring a radically new system with extensive vertical and horizontal pluralism. As highlighted in the theoretical discussion in the previous chapter, for the Soviet polity to make the transition to democracy, a fundamental change regarding group rights was crucial. Pluralism had to emerge in every sphere, including the rights of nations as corporate entities. Structural shifts had to be accompanied by shifts in political values and interactions showing acceptance of general as well as ethnic pluralism.

There are two choices in the approach to ethnic policy: power-sharing or control. As outlined in the previous chapter, the power-sharing approach to dealing with multiple nations within a single state involves a host of basic principles. It includes the principle of group rights and decentralization in all spheres, both as a value in itself and as an indirect boon to ethnic pluralism. Territorial nations are recognized as corporate entities with distinct rights. The main consequences for state structure are strong federalism and group participation in common decision making. The consequence for political culture is that policy making is characterized by dialogue, accommodation, and legal safeguards for basic minority rights, and that certain values are respected.

In a power-sharing arrangement the essential value is that granting power to all constituent nations benefits everyone. Majorities, in particular, develop an enlightened view of self-interest as tied to the common interest. For power sharing to work, there must be a political culture that sees diversity as enrichment and the granting of rights to minorities as strengthening the rights of everybody in the state. Thus the underlying psychological outlook is nonzero-sum: if one member of the community wins it is not at the expense of other members; instead everyone gains by creating harmony and conciliation.

Official Soviet political culture had little in common with power-sharing, except in its ambivalent rhetoric. The principal ideological strictures denied the significance of ethnicity and established the goal of a new international community, the Soviet people. Yet, since Lenin's time, there also was some acknowledgment of the rights of nations, as expressed, for example, in the nominal federalism of the USSR and constitutional articles about sovereignty and the right of union republics to secede. As shall be analyzed below, this rhetoric backfired once pressures for real power sharing arose in the late 1980s.

The classic formulation of the control model is by Ian Lustick,[1] although one can also derive its definition by imagining opposites to the consensus model.[2] As argued by Lustick, a multiethnic state can achieve stability—or apparent stability—through control over minorities. In the Soviet case, control meant rule by central bureaucracies and a partocracy hidden behind nominal federalism and the rhetoric of internationalism. "The mark of the efficient control system is its relative invisibility or low salience,"[3] including limits on open and outright repression. The Soviet Union under Leonid Brezhnev's rule fits this model rather well, but in the Gorbachev era underlying power arrangements became visible and were challenged. Lustick sees such a change toward the overt use of coercion as a sign of the breakdown of domination.[4] Clearly this prediction fits events in 1991 that began with the brutal crackdown in the Baltics and led to the coup attempt in August.

In the late 1980s it became increasingly clear that the central authorities under Gorbachev were unable to move from control to real power-sharing. Yet their partial reforms allowed the emergence of alternative political forces, raised expectations, and finally led to a radicalization of demands due to the repeated frustration of these expectations. In ethnopolitics, the group Democratic Russia and other movements developed a basically consociational agenda as an alternative to both hard-liners and wavering reformers. The democratic alternative was able to institute the decisive break with the old regime during the hard-line coup in August 1991. This cataclysmic event followed similar focal events in a number of republics and, together with the deepening trauma created by the revelations of glasnost, created an epochal change in political culture.

After briefly outlining the emergence of general group pluralism in the Soviet Union, I shall focus on the emancipation of union republics. Here I discuss mostly the debate over the Union Treaty and changes in political culture. For our purposes the most significant phenomenon was the emergence of a multiethnic coalition between democratic Russians and non-Russians based on the acceptance of the sovereignty of each participant.

The Emergence of Group Pluralism

Group pluralism is a crucial characteristic that sets democracies apart from a Soviet-style system. The literature on democratization emphasizes that even limited social pluralism is essential for a successful transition to democracy, because it creates alternative institutions and leaders. Groups independent of state control have to emerge, as Daniel Levine writes: "Such groups develop and ultimately press claims of collective identity and autonomous action against states and social elites long accustomed to dominate through corporatist and patrimonial manipulations."[5] Philippe Schmitter also sees organized modes of interest intermediation as significant aspects of the transition to democracy,[6] and Ted Gurr makes a similar point in his systematic study of regime change, in which he assesses the change of political regimes by measuring the extent of political competition, the scope of pluralism in top governmental organs, and the intensity of decentralization.[7]

In the Soviet Union groups increasingly called for "self-determination by the community of citizens."[8] Growing pluralism became a symptom of as well as a motor for political change after 1987. Unofficial organizations mushroomed and became increasingly independent. When popular fronts first emerged in the Baltic states, Communist reformers in Moscow encouraged them as new mass organizations that could enhance perestroika.[9] The union republic branches of the CPSU tried to control the fronts by indirect means, but they soon developed strong autonomous tendencies (see chapter 4). By late 1989 similar popular movements proliferated in other parts of the USSR and openly challenged the CPSU's legal preeminence of political organization as expressed in Article 6 of the Constitution. When this constitutional article was revoked in March 1990, group pluralism was officially legitimized. Next, various mass movements, and even parties, were institutionalized by strong showings in local and republic elections throughout 1990 and 1991.[10] By mid-1991 political group pluralism posed a serious challenge to the Communist party. Now the Soviet system was dualistic, with remnants of the party's institutional control coexisting with alternative groupings. This dualism between a party claiming monistic power and nascent pluralism ended when the CPSU was suspended after the aborted coup attempt in August 1991. Thereafter a truly pluralistic regime began to emerge in which all political groupings—including new pro-Communist organizations—coexisted on equal terms.

As noted in the previous chapter, this structural regime change indirectly increased ethnic pluralism by, for example, allowing cultural and religious groups to act without interference from the CPSU and state authorities. In addition, autonomous ethnic social and political groupings emerged in all regions of the USSR. The ethnic agendas of these groups differed, but many, especially the Popular Front of Latvia, *Rukh* in Ukraine, and the Democratic Russia movement in the RSFSR, emphasized the need to form multiethnic coalitions within and between republics. These groups saw each other as allies in a common struggle. They expressed support for each other at the mass as well as elite levels by exchanging delegations, sending messages of support, and organizing common activities.[11] This cooperation among regional elites fits the principles of consociationalism.

Parallel to the emergence of autonomous sociopolitical groupings, a similar process developed within the CPSU. The founder of the party, Lenin, had insisted that no internal factions be tolerated, and centralized hierarchical control was indeed preserved against all factionalism throughout the Soviet period. The breakdown of this control during the last few years of the USSR was another sign of the party's decline. In the course of the last few years a twofold political rift emerged in the party: an ever-deepening split between orthodox Communists and liberals, and a second split between central and regional party organizations. In some areas the latter rift included an ethnic dimension, most prominently so in the Baltic republics. The Lithuanian Communist party under Algirdas Brazauskas was the first to demand organizational independence from Moscow. This was something the center could not accept, and in the end the autonomists split off to form their own reformist Communist party in December 1989.[12] For the first time in the history of the CPSU even the central party's insistence on retaining the old control pattern could not keep group pluralism from developing.

When the Communist Party of Lithuania split in two, the larger part became an independent Communist party, and the smaller part, composed mostly of non-Lithuanians, remained loyal to the CPSU. The confrontation led to a decline in party membership: though the old Communist Party of Lithuania had more than two hundred thousand members in December 1989, one year later the renamed and autonomous Democratic Labor Party of Lithuania had about sixty thousand members and the Lithuanian Communist Party (CPSU) had about forty thousand members.[13] Similar tendencies of membership decline and factionalization were notable in other republic parties.[14] These splits underlined the increasing polarization between pro-Moscow and proindependence forces. The Latvian case is remarkable in that due to its unusual ethnic composition the larger part of the old Communist Party of Latvia (CPL) remained loyal to Moscow. The party formally split on 7 April 1990, when 242 of 700 delegates left the party congress to form the separate Independent Communist Party of Latvia. The basic disagreement was over independence and the status of the CPL, but in addition the reformist program tended toward West European socialism whereas the conservatives wanted to retain the ideological and political status quo.[15] The political split coincided with a split along ethnic lines. Most of the reformist party members were Latvian, whereas the old-style Communist Party of Latvia consisted mostly of Russians, except for a small group of high-level Latvian *apparatchiki* led by First Secretary Alfrēds Rubiks. Even *Izvestiia* noted the untenability of the situation by saying, "A Latvian Communist party without Latvians is, pardon the expression, nonsense."[16]

Splits such as those of the Baltic Communist parties led to some increase in political and ethnic polarization in 1990, but they were also accompanied by the parallel formation of new multiethnic coalitions among the forces struggling for autonomy. Thus the independent Baltic Communist parties established close ties in the summer of 1990. At a meeting in Riga in late June 1990, they outlined the future role of their parties as one of democratic and human socialism, providing alternatives during the coming period of social upheavals and suffering.[17] A new regional compact was also formed by top government and party officials of the five Central Asian republics at a meeting in June 1990. In addition to an agreement on economic, scientific-technical, and cultural cooperation, the meeting also issued "An Appeal to the Peoples of the Republics of Central Asia and Kazakhstan." This appeal, and other statements, called for unity on the basis of common Central Asian traditions and blamed ethnic strife and other problems on the central authorities.[18]

The Emancipation of the Union Republics

Parallel to the ascent of new social and political groups in the late 1980s, union republics increasingly pressed for autonomy. While the vertical pluralization of power involved breaking the Communist party's power monopoly, horizontal change involved a drastic devolution of central authority to lower levels of government. The two processes were interrelated. In a large quasi-federal state, democratization necessarily includes the quest for self-rule by ethnically or nonethnically based territories, and even more so if the existing powers of republic governments are minimal. The republics had no independent taxing powers and, as noted by Stephan Kux, "any American town has a larger measure of independence and self-government than a Soviet republic."[19]

The formal structure of the Union of Soviet Socialist Republics was that of a federal state, but for all intents and purposes formal federalism was obviated by the centralized Communist party and bureaucracies. Nevertheless, the imagery of a federation and the statehood of the union republics created a nucleus of pluralist identity[20] that affected regime transition. By 1989 the democratic rhetoric of the Soviet Constitution had begun to haunt it: when republic leaders spoke of sovereignty they could point to formal constitutional guarantees such as Article 72, which proclaims that "each union republic retains the right freely to secede from the USSR." Soon, this right became the symbolic and concrete focus of republic relations with the center. Gorbachev countered independence claims with a stringent secession law, giving the all-union legislature the ultimate decision as to whether a republic could or could not secede.[21] His approach was bound to backfire, since according to scholars of comparative ethnopolitics "the best way for a government to prevent secession is a pledge not to resist it, accompanied by an offer of fair and effective power-sharing."[22] Although this does not always work, it is the best approach available. In the words of Estonian party chief Vaino Välias, the only hope for preventing republics from leaving the USSR was "to build the kind of union that no one would ever dream of leaving."[23]

The central authorities promised a new Union Treaty, yet the provisions fell short of what the individual republics claimed in their declarations of sovereignty.[24] More important, the center's approach to power sharing proved unacceptable to the republics, as consociational theory would have predicted. Rather than negotiating a document among all participants, the initial versions of the Union Treaty were written by central authorities and presented to republics for approval only. Yet democratic federalism assumes that the powers of the state are built from the bottom up. Typically, "republics" are sovereign except where powers have been ceded explicitly to the federal government. Extensive self-rule is a central principle of power sharing and it means that each territory rules itself in all matters, except those voluntarily turned over to the federal authorities. In contrast, the control model assumes that all powers inherently rest with central authorities, except for those powers that they deem fit to cede to federal subunits. Core issues of the constitutional division of power between the center and republics concern legislative power (including the power of taxation and budget allocation), judicial power, and executive power.

Despite yearlong promises of a restructuring of the Soviet federation, arrangements were slow in changing, including in the economic sphere where the Baltic republics were promised full autonomy as of 1 January 1990. This delay was due to the empire-saving impulses of central state bureaucracies as well as a failure to accept power-sharing principles in fact. Gorbachev promised a "free union of free peoples," but as Ukrainian leaders noted,[25] this is only possible if each republic first is accepted as independent and then voluntarily negotiates the terms for rejoining the union. There were contrasting presumptions about who was granting power to whom—whether the sovereign people of the republics were delegating some powers to a common government, or whether the federal government was ceding power to subunits. Republic leaders stressed the former, commonly expressed in formulas such as "fifteen (republics) plus zero (center)" or "nine plus zero." The central authorities were unwilling to start with a "zero" role in the formation of the new union and emphasized their own sovereign rights over the entire USSR. This proved to be a self-defeating policy.

Pluralist democracy recognizes the inalienable rights of minorities, including smaller nations. A majority cannot overrule the inalienable right of a minority through sheer numbers. Thus a nation's right to self-determination cannot be denied by the all-union legislature—as foreseen in the law on secession—or by an all-union referendum, as foreseen in the 17 March referendum on the preservation of the union.[26] As the example of Switzerland and other democratic multinational countries shows, a nation that joins with other nations to form a unified polity retains the right to decide essential questions by itself.

The balance of power was changed when leading Russian democrats joined the anticenter coalition of non-Russians. By mid-1990 Yeltsin was insisting that the central government recognize the full sovereignty of all republics, including the Russian Federation. As had Baltic leaders before him, Yeltsin defined sovereignty as the precedence of republic laws over all-union law. He proposed a loose confederation of republics based on voluntarily negotiated direct treaties and the delegation of just a few powers to a common government. Yet when the all-union authorities published their draft treaty in November 1990, he and other republic leaders were disenchanged. Further hopes were dashed during the winter of 1990–91 when Gorbachev supported the hard-liners and the bloody crackdown in the Baltics. Spring 1991 brought new treaty drafts, but even Russians increasingly identified the central authorities as the enemy of republic interests. As noted by one Russian commentator: "The Russian nation, as an ethnosocial organism, exists mostly within the boundaries of the RSFSR—she is interested in the sovereignty of Russia and in the escape of Russia from the diktat of the center."[27] Compromise was delayed because the republics felt that not enough powers were granted to them.[28] Increasingly, they passed their own laws and a system of competing sovereignties developed, with Lithuania declaring the restoration of full independence on 11 March 1990. Gorbachev reacted with dire threats and an economic blockade.

As noted in chapter 1, the nature of the process of forming a union affects the end result. If the process involves conciliatory negotiation and concessions by the larger partner, a consociational outcome is more credible and thus likely. The approach of the Soviet leadership created just the opposite effect. The credibility of a voluntary union of equals was undermined by a recurring pattern of interaction whereby each demand from a republic was met first by an angry rejection from the center, followed by a partial concession, soon to be challenged by some other central move.[29] Thus in 1990 the Supreme Soviet of the USSR unilaterally passed laws in direct conflict with the republics' declarations of sovereignty and laws on citizenship, state language, and economic relations between republics. It also passed a law delimiting the powers of the USSR and the republics.[30] A serious constitutional crisis arose as a result, but no mutually acceptable mechanism for conflict resolution was found. Instead the republics acted increasingly on their own.

While the legal standoff and increasingly self-assertive actions of the union republics promoted the disintegration of the USSR, the republics independently negotiated new ties with each other. This reintegration from the bottom up was negotiated in bilateral as well as multilateral meetings. For example, twelve republics sent envoys to Tallinn in April 1991 to work on an alternative Union Treaty in the absence of central authorities.[31] The leaders of republics engaging in such activity emphasized that sovereignty does not mean isolationism, but rather freedom of choice and the right to form autonomous ties with one another. The establishment of horizontal interrepublic ties was also crucial because the Soviet control system had precluded independent ties between the republics without central direction, according to the old notion of *divide et impera.*

By the summer of 1991 Gorbachev seemed to recognize that the only way to prevent total political deadlock was to negotiate a liberal Union Treaty with the republic governments.[32] Events escalated nevertheless, because the hard-liners in the Gorbachev government saw this as "the last straw" and staged a coup in August 1991. After the coup failed, union republic leaders pressed for complete independence and recognition as a basis for any new state-to-state ties. Effective power passed to the union republics, most poignantly in the case of the Russian republic and its president, Yeltsin.[33] By September 1991 the CPSU was disbanded and the USSR was dissolving, as one republic after another declared independence and the central authorities became increasingly unable to engage in decisive action. In December 1991 the USSR was formally disbanded and the Commonwealth of Independent States began to emerge. Yeltsin showed sensitivity to political symbolism in designating Minsk rather than Moscow as the capital of the new commonwealth. Early on it became clear that any new type of interrepublic common market, confederation, or cluster of regional federations could only flourish if its center remained weak and reliant on the voluntarily negotiated sharing of power by constitutent parts. Initial interrepublic activity, such as discussions on boundaries and new economic arrangements, demonstrated a new recognition that cohesion could be worked out only on the basis of bilateral or multilateral negotiation and consensus.[34]

Political Culture and Regime Change

Political culture is a twofold linchpin for our analysis. First, a consociational ethnopolitics requires political culture to have a distinct quality, which leads us to ask whether anything of this quality emerged during the transformation of the USSR. Second, since a major shift in political culture must proceed hand in hand with regime change, one needs to explain how such a shift could come about. I address this second issue after first arguing that in the late 1980s a new political culture developed among those people often referred to as "the democrats," while another segment of the Soviet population hung on to its old or slightly reformed version. This programmatic split was the most consequential development in Soviet politics during the transition from communism, even more so because it affected the dominant Russian nation especially deeply and led Russia to set an unprecedented democratic agenda that included the radical reform of the empire.

Political culture can be seen as a dynamic factor affecting the process of change, but only if one uses a definition that links a people's political cognition, emotion, evaluations, and values to concrete political structures and behavior.[35] In contrast, the anthropological definition of political culture focuses on constant underlying attitudinal patterns of peoples. The nonanthropological definition of political culture has been preferred by specialists on comparative communism, such as Kenneth Jowitt, who introduced the concept as a salient analytical-research focus for Marxist-Leninist regimes and argued that the study of political culture is most fruitful in connection with the study of political structure.[36] The Sovietologist Stephen White similarly defines political culture as "the relationship between political opportunities, political beliefs and political behavior."[37] This means that if political opportunities change, political beliefs and behavior are likely to change as well, and, extending this thought further, changing beliefs and behavior effect change in political opportunities and structures. The interaction goes both ways. Such a concept of political culture means that it provides "the connecting link between micro- and macro-politics."[38]

Applying this thinking to reforms of the Soviet regime suggests that once there was change in such core facets as party control over societal organization and the media, changes in political culture had to follow. The new democratic political culture emerged most strongly among the younger and more dynamic segment of the population. Its behavioral expressions included mass involvement in new political movements, electoral struggles, demonstrations, and strikes. Attitudinally, the emphasis shifted to a host of new values and beliefs. For our analysis, the most crucial shift was toward an acceptance of pluralism in every form, including territorially and ethnically based self-rule. Increasingly, decentralization of power was seen as a positive good, and this included both ethnicized and nonethnicized regionalism. By 1990 Russia's leaders clearly insisted on their state's sovereignty, and many Russians supported sovereignty for non-Russian republics. Yet while a growing segment of the people supported radical democratic restructuring, including the right to state independence, another segment continued to support an old-style autocratic polity led by a strong leader, state-controlled regulated economy, and Soviet internationalism. Because the latter agenda was increasingly defined as Sovietized Russianism, fewer and fewer non-Russians supported it, although there were notable exceptions such as that of the notorious "black" colonel, Viktors Alksnis.[39] The increasing ethnic polarization of the hard-liners stood out in stark contrast to the increasing ethnic pluralization of the democratic movement.

The credo of the democratic movement included the dictum that a nation that oppresses others cannot itself be free.[40] The new value system was reflected in events and surveys. One watershed indicator was an August 1990 survey by the All-Union Public Opinion Research Center showing "the collapse of imperial thinking," as described by the scholar presenting the data. Among other results, 31 to 55 percent of Russians in various republics supported republic secession.[41] Such findings were confirmed by other data, such as nearly half of Baltic Russians in 1990 voting for legislators who supported democracy and independence,[42] and results of the March 1991 Soviet referendum. Despite a widespread boycott by those opposing Gorbachev's vision of the union, the pro-union referenda failed or barely passed in major centers of the Russian democratic movement such as Moscow, Leningrad, Sverdlovsk, and the Kuzbass coal region.[43] When an all-Russia opinion poll shortly before the coup in August 1991 asked, "Which of society's problems do you find most menacing?" only 8 percent listed the "disintegration of the USSR," in contrast to the 69 percent listing "growing prices" and many more listing seven other categories of concerns.[44]

Two separate polls taken in the RSFSR in February 1991 showed the respondents divided fairly evenly between those stating that "the Baltic republics should be allowed to become independent states once again" (40 to 42 percent) and those saying that "these three republics are an inseparable part of the Soviet Union and must remain in it" (39 to 45 percent).[45] The people most strongly supporting self-rule for non-Russian nations were those who were more educated and younger in age. As Table 2.1 illustrates, the correlation between support for Baltic independence and higher education, as well as youth, is impressive.

Table 2.1
Baltic Independence and Residents of RSFSR

	Allow Independence (percent)	Remain in USSR (percent)	Don't Know/ No Answer (percent)
Total	42	39	18
Education			
Higher	63	23	14
Secondary	49	35	16
Grade 9 or less	28	50	22
Age			
16–24	58	31	11
25–39	51	34	15
40–49	39	40	21
50–59	32	43	25
60 or older	33	49	18

Source: All-Union Public Opinion Research Center random survey of 1,025 RSFSR residents between 9 and 19 February 1991; United States Information Agency Research Memorandum, 12 April 1991.

Ethnic Russians comprised more than 80 percent of respondents.

Other survey results revealed that in its last years Soviet politics was anything but a single-issue affair, and people showed increasing sophistication about links between problems, including links between ethnic issues and general politics. When in early 1990 the Moscow Center for the Study of Public Opinion asked 1,004 people (101 in Armenia, 313 in the Baltics, 385 in the RSFSR, and 205 in Ukraine) who was "primarily responsible" for the recent intensification of ethnic tensions in the USSR, respondents in all four regions blamed the central authorities and the existing political system far more often than they blamed the Russians or the indigenous nationalities of the republics.[46]

The perception of democratic movements in the non-Russian republics and those in the RSFSR that they were all in the same boat was a stimulus for unity. The new multiethnic coalition formed due to a common agenda, but also due to a common enemy and the trauma of crisis in the Soviet

Union. The well-known notion that domestic conflict decreases in the face of a common foreign enemy has been used by some theorists of comparative ethnicity to conclude that traumatic threats from within can also lead to constructive realignment in ethnic programs.[47] Expressions of political solidarity and coalition building existed between the democratic movements of the Baltics, Russia, Moldova, and other republics, and intensified when these movements faced Gorbachev's turn toward hard-line politics in late 1990. Yeltsin's expression of support for the Balts at the time of the military crackdown in Vilnius and Riga was symptomatic of this alliance, as was the support of the legislature of the RSFSR. It met in a special session and adopted a resolution repudiating the actions of the central Soviet government: "In our situation today, when the state is in a crisis situation, such an action of the central leadership can lead to dangerous consequences in all union republics and to future difficulties in establishing a voluntary union of sovereign states."[48] The Balts reciprocated by being the first to support Yeltsin and the Parliament of the RSFSR in August 1991. Although such moves had significant popular support, they also attest to the cooperation of elites, a requirement of consociational theory.

If a radical shift in political culture occurred among part of the population in the USSR, the question arises of how it came about. Western scholars, finding what they regard as surprisingly high levels of support for democratic values among Soviet citizens during this period, usually explain increasingly democratic attitudes by increased education and other consequences of modernization.[49] Although such developments clearly make a difference, the thrust of the argument here is that the primary explanation is political. Political culture changed in reaction to the loosening of traditional control mechanisms of the Communist regime. Once the transition was under way, change accelerated in a dynamic process whereby changing political structures influenced the emergence of new attitudes, and new attitudes initiated even more change in regime structures. We already noted the interaction with changing political institutions; and, as predicted by Carole Pateman, "The experience of participation itself will develop and foster the 'democratic' personality."[50]

Another explanation is linked to central events and trauma. Psychological distress due to seeing the old regime in a new light may be decisive, and so may focal events. Lucian W. Pye has noted that an intense "shock of failure is critical in weakening the legitimacy of authoritarian elites and in raising the consciousness of the public enough to cause the people to reflect on their country's troubles."[51] This shock was all the more intense in the Soviet Union where the regime had created artificial complacency through its control over public knowledge and debate. Glasnost changed all that. John Armstrong makes the same argument about a decisive shift in political culture among Russians and non-Russians alike and cites *Pravda* to support his point: "When you get right down to it, restructuring's great sin is that it really has chopped away at people's faith—in paradise, in a kind of religious and mystical expectation of a 'better future' that should justify everything."[52] Glasnost also eliminated the need for people to dissimulate about their true political preferences[53] and served as a catalyst of new values.

To this list one may add the impact of traumatic focal events. As Archie Brown has noted, a people's political memory is formed by major crises,[54] and the Soviet Union had quite a few of these in its last years. Besides traumatic crises of regime performance, such as Chernobyl and the economic decline, the regime discredited itself when police and special troops brutally attacked unarmed civilians in Tbilisi, Baku, Vilnius, and Riga. The dramatic impact of such focal events on public attitudes can be measured quantitatively. Thus although only 23 percent of non-Latvians in Latvia said that they supported the republic's independence-minded legislature in October 1990, 67 percent said so after the crackdown in January 1991.[55] A similar change of opinion in Leningrad concerning Baltic independence was reflected in polls conducted between September 1989 and January 1991. When asked whether they thought that force was necessary to prevent Baltic secession, 56 percent of Leningraders said "no" in September 1989, 65 and 66 percent in February and June 1990, and 87 percent in January 1991.[56] Clearly, the actual use of force in Lithuania and Latvia in January 1991 correlated with its increased rejection by Russian citizens.

Finally, in another traumatic event tanks confronted civilians in the streets of Moscow and Leningrad in August 1991, triggering a major shift in elite and mass political attitudes. Among other results, the trauma of the attempted coup was crucial in tipping the balance in favor of real sovereignty for union republics. Within days the Russian and Soviet governments accepted the restoration of Baltic independence and acknowledged that relations with the other republics had to be drastically reconstituted.[57]

Following the precedents already set by Yeltsin and his government, the focus shifted to direct negotiation between republics, and to new power-sharing institutions of the much-weakened central government. A new phase of regime transition had begun, with each republic focusing on changing its own political and economic system. Interrepublic relations had adopted a new quality, with individual republics emerging as independent states negotiating a loose confederation with joint defense and some form of a common market. If anything much is to come of this, the participants will more likely than not follow principles that closely resemble consociationalism.[58]

Conclusion

Paul Quirk notes that political scientists have paid insufficient attention to nonzero-sum policy conflicts that present opportunities for cooperation. He shows that a nation's capacity for cooperative resolution of policy conflict is linked to the structure of political institutions.[59] I extend this argument to ethnic politics. Many analysts underestimate the significance of political structures and culture on the chances of resolving ethnic conflict. Political regimes do make a difference. Specifically, I contrast the ethnic politics of a Soviet-style regime to theoretical consociationalism and the steps toward a ethnoplural arrangement during the disintegration of the USSR.

As an analyst examines the Soviet case, he or she cannot but ask questions about the role of the political regime in ethnic politics. Attention to regime structures and political culture adds a missing dimension to comparative ethnic studies, which all too often fail to identify the polity as a decisive variable and fail to explore the links between quests for regime change and quests for new ethnic arrangements. Neither the political system nor the ethnic system can be seen as an independent variable. In a case such as the Union of Soviet Socialist Republics, where territorially based nations are a social reality but the regime does not allow these nations to act on their interests, the quest for self-rule is bound to become a political force. This political quest was mostly latent as long as the old Soviet regime was stable, but as soon as it began to liberalize, the suppressed voice of nation-states— especially strong in the Baltic region—began to be heard. The quest of the nation-states soon won out in the politics of regime transition because its basic thrust coincided with the encompassing pluralist democratic goal of political decentralization in all spheres.

Autocratic political control in the Soviet Union rested on two pillars: a monopoly of control by the Communist party over all other political forces and a near-monopoly of control by central authorities over republics and lower-level bodies. Therefore, the move toward a democratic political system necessitated both the pluralization of political forces and the decentralization of the state and other institutions. The two dimensions of old-style control and the two dimensions of democratization were inextricably linked. And, because the Soviet Union was a multiethnic federal state, it was natural that republic and lower-level legislatures elected by the voters of specific territories would begin to claim to represent the interests of these territories, including ethnic interests.

As soon as the political reforms of the Gorbachev era led to the formation of autonomous political movements, legislatures, and other democratic institutions such as a free press, the quest for self-rule focused on the struggle for sovereignty at lower levels of government. In light of the nominal federalism of the USSR, it was not surprising that the initial demands came at the level of union republics, nor was it surprising that the Baltic republics spear-headed this movement because of their experience with independence and democracy in the interwar period. After its declaration of sovereignty in June 1990, the RSFSR joined the Balts in this leading role and in doing so emphasized that far-reaching decentralization is not a narrow ethnic issue, but rather is part and parcel of democratization.

During the crisis of the Soviet system the delegitimization of the old political order accompanied the delegitimization of old ethnic policies, and the quest for democracy was linked to the quest for ethnic power sharing. As the old regime changed, new structures and principles similar to consocia-tionalism began to emerge in the relations between union republics and their nations. The historical turning point was reached as Russia itself began to seek self-rule as a state and reached a new appreciation of group pluralism. The emergence and growth of a democratic political culture that included power-sharing ideas among a significant segment of the Russian population was a core factor in the transition from communism.

In large part, the democratic movement acted on the assumption that if it succeeded in dissolving the Soviet regime and establishing a truly new sys-tem, the rights of individuals, nations, and ethnic groups would be safe-guarded by democracy itself. In light of the record of some democracies in dealing with their minorities, some people might consider this assumption naive. It may be more appropriate to propose that democracy is a necessary but not a sufficient condition for ethnic conflict resolution.[60] As noted in the previous chapter and here, the type of political structures and culture can make a difference, and pluralist democracy appears to be better able to deal with certain types of multinationalism than democracies that are based on majority rule and the principles of liberal individualism. Provisions of electoral systems and other incentives for the moderation of policymakers also can make a difference.[61]

The principles of consociational democracy may prove important for political accommodation among the newly independent post-Soviet states. This means that any future union must base itself on the pluralism of autonomous groupings, held together by negotiated coalition agreements. This type of system does not "solve" the national question by making it disappear, but it does provide mechanisms for dealing with the issue. It also pays attention to the nurturing of a political culture that views the flourish-ing of every nation and ethnic group as a gain for the entire community. This is accomplished on the basis of equality and self-rule rather than pater-nalistic manipulation or control.

It is beyond the scope of this study to explore the evolving relations within the Commonwealth of Independent States since late 1991.[62] One central question concerns the strengthening of democratic values among all populations, especially the population of Russia. At the time of the breakup of the USSR, democratic institutions and cultures had developed unequally in various republics. Some of the republics that declared independence after the collapse of the August 1991 coup did so to protect the Communist system and the holders of power. It is unclear how successful such attempts will be in the long run. In either case, developments in Russia will remain a crucial determinant of politics in the entire region. The recent emergence of a democratic political culture among the younger and more educated segment of Russian citizens suggests that "new thinking" will prevail over old imperial impulses. Yet we must also remember that this shift in values was partly related to the perception that the democratic forces in the region of the former USSR had both common goals and a common enemy. The common enemy has been formally defeated, and this may lead some people to pick new quarrels. Yet there is also a paradoxical reason for hope, because the common enemy lives on in the remnants of old political institutions and in a painful legacy that will take years to overcome.

NOTES

1. Ian Lustick, "Stability in Deeply Divided Societies: Consociationalism versus Control," *World Politics* 31 (1979): 325–44.
2. Other theorists have used the terms "hegemonic" versus "accommodative" ethnic politics. See, for example, Myron Weiner, "Political Change: Asia, Africa, and the Middle East," in Myron Weiner and Samuel Huntington, eds., *Understanding Political Development* (Boston: Little, Brown, 1987), 45. David Laitin has examined the colonial hegemonic control model in Africa, in his "Hegemony and Religious Conflict: British Imperial Control and Political Cleavages in Yorubaland," in Peter B. Evans, Dietrich Rueschemeyer, and Theda Skocpol, eds., *Bringing the State Back In* (Cambridge: Cambridge University Press, 1985), 285–316.
3. Kenneth D. McRae, "Theories of Power-Sharing and Conflict Management," in Joseph V. Montville, ed., *Conflict and Peacemaking in Multiethnic Societies* (Lexington, Mass.: Lexington Books, 1990), 101.
4. Lustick, "Stability," 339.
5. Daniel H. Levine, "Paradigm Lost: Dependence to Democracy," *World Politics* 60 (April 1988): 388; Juan Linz, "Transitions to Democracy," *Washington Quarterly* (Summer 1990): 152.
6. Philippe C. Schmitter, "Modes of Interest Articulation and Models of Societal Change in Western Europe," *Comparative Political Studies* 10 (April 1977): 7–38.
7. Ted R. Gurr, "Persistence and Change in Political Systems, 1800–1971," *American Political Science Review* 68 (December 1974): 1482–1504.
8. S. Frederick Starr, "Voluntary Groups and Initiatives," in Anthony Jones and David E. Powell, eds., *Soviet Update, 1989–1990* (Boulder, Colo.: Westview Press, 1991), 105.
9. Prominent scholars and reform Communists such as Tatiana Zaslavskaia and Fiodor Burlatsky were among the first advocates of popular fronts; *New York Times*, 24 May 1988.
10. Starr, "Voluntary Groups and Initiatives," 97–116; Vladimir Brovkin, "Revolution from Below: Informal Political Associations in Russia 1988–1989," *Soviet Studies* 42 (April 1990): 233–57. Attempted cooptation and other regime policies are analyzed by Jim Butterfield and Marcia Weigle, "Unofficial Social Groups and Regime Response in the

Soviet Union," in Judith B. Sedaitis and Jim Butterfield, eds., *Perestroika from Below: Social Movements in the Soviet Union* (Boulder, Colo.: Westview Press, 1991), 175–95.

11. Vera Tolz, "Democrats Start Their Own Discussion of Russian National Problems," *Report on the USSR*, 30 March 1990; Roman Solchanyk, "The Changing Political Landscape in Ukraine," *Report on the USSR*, 14 June 1991; Victor Zaslavsky, "Nationalism and Democratic Transition in Postcommunist Societies," *Daedalus* 121 (Spring 1992): 97–121.

12. Alfred Erich Senn, "Toward Lithuanian Independence: Algirdas Brazauskas and the CPL," *Problems of Communism* (March–April 1990): 21–28.

13. *Izvestiia*, 10 December 1990, p. 3.

14. See David Marples, "The Communist Party of the Ukraine: A Fading Force?" *Report on the USSR*, 8 June 1990, pp. 21–22.

15. Dzintra Bungs, "Latvian Communist Party Splits," *Report on the USSR*, 27 April 1990, pp. 17–20.

16. *Izvestiia*, 18 April 1990, quoting the newspaper of the Baltic Military District, *Za Rodinu*.

17. *Latvijas Jaunatne*, 30 June 1990.

18. Paul Goble, "Central Asians Form Political Bloc," *Report on the USSR*, 13 July 1990, pp. 18–20.

19. Stephan Kux, "Soviet Federalism," *Problems of Communism* (March–April 1990): 1.

20. See also Teresa Rakowska-Harmstone, "The Dialectics of Nationalism in the USSR," *Problems of Communism* (May–June 1974): 1–22; Ian Bremmer and Ray Taras, eds., *Nations and Politics in the Soviet Successor States* (Cambridge: Cambridge University Press, 1993).

21. Article 20, "Law of Secession," *Pravda*, 7 April 1990.

22. Arend Lijphart, "The Power-Sharing Approach," in Montville, *Conflict and Peacemaking*, 494.

23. *Pravda*, 21 September 1989.

24. Draft of Union Treaty, *Pravda*, 24 November 1990; see also Ann Sheehy, "Moves to Draw Up New Union Treaty," *Report on the USSR*, 6 July 1990.

25. *Literaturnaia gazeta*, 15 November 1990.

26. For the two laws see Ann Sheehy, "Referendum on the Preservation of the Union," *Report on the USSR*, 15 February 1991, and Article 20, "Law of Secession," *Pravda*, 7 April 1990.

27. Sergei Arutiunov, "Mezhnatsional'nye konflikty," *Nezavisimaia gazeta*, 25 May 1991.

28. Ann Sheehy, "A Progress Report on the Union Treaty," *Report on the USSR*, 12 July 1991.

29. This is especially clear in interactions between the central government and the Baltic states. See the numerous excellent *Reports on the USSR* since January 1989.

30. *Izvestiia*, 16 April, 3 May, and 4 May 1990.

31. *Izvestiia*, 6 May 1991; see also Goble, "Central Asians Form Political Bloc"; Gytis Liulevicius, "Lithuania Signs Treaty with Russia," *Report on the USSR*, 23 August 1991. The signing of a treaty on economic and cultural matters between the Republic of Latvia and the RSFSR is reported in *Literatūra un Māksla*, 22 September 1990.

32. For the text of the Treaty on the Union of Sovereign States of 15 August 1991, see Charles F. Furtado, Jr., and Andrea Chandler, eds., *Perestroika in the Soviet Republics: Documents on the National Question* (Boulder, Colo.: Westview Press, 1992), 46–56.

33. Ann Sheehy, "Power Passes to the Republics," *Report on the USSR*, 13 September 1991.

34. Ibid.; *New York Times*, 15 November 1991.

35. Carole Pateman, "Political Culture, Political Structure and Political Change," *British Journal of Political Science* 1 (July 1971): 291–305.

36. Kenneth Jowitt, "An Organizational Approach to the Study of Political Culture in Marxist-Leninist Systems," *American Political Science Review* 63 (September 1974): 1171–91.

37. Stephen White, "Soviet Political Culture Reassessed," in Archie Brown, ed., *Political Culture and Communist Studies* (Armonk, N.Y.: Sharpe, 1985), 75.

38. Gabriel A. Almond and Sidney Verba, *The Civic Culture* (Boston: Little, Brown, 1965), 33.

39. For details see chapter 3.

40. Kathleen Mihalisko, " 'For Our Freedom and Yours,' Support among Slavs for Baltic Independence," *Report on the USSR*, 25 May 1990, pp. 17–19.

41. *Moskovskie novosti*, no. 41, 14 October 1990, p. 7. One year earlier a survey found that a significant segment (63.4 percent) of people in the RSFSR thought that they should above all "be concerned about the unity and cohesion of the USSR." *Ogonek*, no. 43 (October 1989): 4–5, reporting on a survey conducted by the USSR Academy of Sciences' All-Union Center for the Study of Public Opinion.

42. Rein Taagepera, "A Note on the March 1989 Elections in Estonia," *Soviet Studies* 42 (April 1990): 329–39; see also chapter 5.

43. Ann Sheehy, "The All-Union and RSFSR Referendums of March 17," *Report on the USSR*, 29 March 1991.

44. *Moscow News*, 22–29 September 1991, p. 5.

45. The first survey was undertaken by the Public Opinion Research Service Vox Populi and involved a random sample of 1,989 respondents. The second survey refers to an All-Union Public Opinion Research Center random sample of 1,025 RSFSR residents between 9 and 19 February 1991; United States Information Agency Research Memorandum, 12 April 1991; see also Public Opinion Research Service VP, *Mir mnenii i mneniia o mire*, 1991, no. 7, 1–5. Ethnic Russians made up over 80 percent of respondents. See also the methodological note in the Appendix.

46. Paul Goble, "Soviet Citizens Blame System for Ethnic Problems," *Report on the USSR*, 29 June 1990, p. 5.

47. Compare Donald L. Horowitz, "Making Moderation Pay: The Comparative Politics of Ethnic Conflict Management," in Montville, *Conflict and Peacemaking*, 452–75.

48. *Radio Rossiia*, 12 January 1991.

49. Jeffrey W. Hahn, "Continuity and Change in Russian Political Culture," *British Journal of Political Science* (October 1991): 393–421; James L. Gibson and Raymond M. Duch, "The Origins of Democratic Culture in the Soviet Union: Models of the Acquisition of Democratic Values," paper delivered at the meeting of the Midwest Political Science Association, Chicago, April 1992; Arthur H. Miller, William M. Reisinger, and Vicki L. Hesli, "Public Support for New Political Institutions in Russia, the Ukraine, and Lithuania," *Journal of Soviet Nationalities* 4 (Winter 1990–91): 82–106.

50. Carole Pateman, *Participation and Democratic Theory* (Cambridge: Cambridge University Press, 1970), 64.

51. Lucian W. Pye, "Political Science and the Crisis of Authoritarianism," *American Political Science Review* 84 (March 1990): 15.

52. *Pravda*, May 1990, quoted in John A. Armstrong, "Assessing the Soviet Nationalities Movements: A Critical Review," *Nationalities Papers* 19 (Spring 1991): 11.

53. Preference falsification in totalitarian systems is analyzed succinctly by Timur Kuran, "The Element of Surprise in the East European Revolution of 1989," *World Politics* 44, no. 1 (1991): 7–48.

54. Brown, *Political Culture and Communist Studies*, 100, 186.

55. Social Research Center of Latvia, *Social Review*, no. 1 (May 1991): 2; see also Figure 3.1.

56. Survey by the Leningrad Center for the Study and Forecast of Social Development, *Moscow News*, no. 5, 1991, p. 6.

57. See the texts of numerous speeches by political leaders at the extraordinary session of the Congress of People's Deputies as recorded by the *New York Times*, 27 August 1991 to 3 September 1991.

58. Numerous negotiations as reported in the *New York Times*, 21 August 1991 to 18 November 1991, and also reports in the Soviet press.

59. Paul J. Quirk, "The Cooperative Resolution of Policy Conflict," *American Political Science Review* 83 (September 1989): 905–21.

60. This formulation was used by Ashutosh Varshney in a seminar discussion at the Woodrow Wilson Center, July 1991.

61. Donald L. Horowitz, "Ethnic Conflict Management for Policymakers," in Montville, *Conflict and Peacemaking*, 115–32, especially 122–23.

62. But see Mark R. Beissinger, "The Deconstruction of the USSR and the Search for a Post-Soviet Community," *Problems of Communism* (November–December 1991): 27–35, especially 31–35; Ann Sheehy, "Commonwealth of Independent States: An Uneasy Compromise," *RFE/RL Research Report*, 10 January 1992. By late 1992 the Commonwealth of Independent States was fighting centrifugal forces. See Ann Sheehy, "The CIS: A Progress Report," *RFE/RL Research Report*, 25 September 1992, 1–6.

3

<hr style="width: 20%" />

Ethnic, State, and Regime Identities

It has become conventional wisdom that the nationalism of non-Russian nations was a major catalyst in the collapse of the Soviet state. Typically, the confrontation has been depicted as involving entire nations, such as the Lithuanians struggling against the Soviet central state. In fact, though, the political dynamic was more complex, especially in regard to the unique role of Russians and the newly emergent Russian state. Their role shows that ethnonational claims were just one of several factors undermining the old regime, and that these claims have to be analytically linked to broader political phenomena, especially the emergence of democratic forces.

Chapters 1 and 2 have focused on the relationship between two crucial variables in the transition from communism—the political system and the ethnic system. I have discussed the question of state independence as part and parcel of the general characteristics of these two systems. Yet once one shifts the level of analysis to the identities of individuals, further differentiations have to be made. The newly assertive political identity that caused the collapse of the Soviet Union consisted of three analytically distinct, though closely interrelated dimensions. The three dimensions are ethnic communal identity, identification with a territorial state, and identification with a political regime. The specific alignment between these three identities is the structural backbone of an ethnic politics and has to be analyzed as such. Yet individual identities and the patterns of alignment between identities are fluid, especially in times of regime transition and the emergence of new

42

states. Although this fluidity complicates analysis, it also makes it that much more interesting.

Social science has long argued that each individual has multiple identities, typically specifying occupation and class or social status, political outlook, gender, age, type of community resided in, and ethnicity. If one agrees that ethnic identity is one of many possible identities that can motivate political action, one has to ask how it interacts with the other identities in a given situation. Depending on the context, one or another identity may become more prominent, or new compromises may be reached. Thus the notion of the interplay of multiple political identities is a corollary of the theories emphasizing the contextuality of ethnicity. Ethnopolitical alignments change from one situation to another.[1] It has been argued that ethnic accommodation works best if a political regime or program is supported on the basis of the crosscutting of identities,[2] for example a multiethnic coalition that includes people from various occupational, ideological, and age groups. Whereas the crosscutting of cleavages is crucial for conflict resolution, their cumulative nature or the dominance of a single identity aggravates conflicts. Single-issue politics is rare, but it does happen that one issue, be it ethnicity or something else, becomes the only motivating force of a group of people. Similarily, it happens that several identities reinforce each other, if, for example, most people from one ethnic group have the same occupational identity or political beliefs. If so, it becomes more difficult to reach accommodation.

Multiple identities that crosscut in crucial ways played a major role in the breakup of the USSR. Ethnic nominalism, the simplistic ascription of ethnopolitical identity solely on the basis of ethnicity, is misleading. This is especially clear in the case of Russians, both those living in Russia and those in other republics. The contrast is exemplified by one Russian leader—Gorbachev—proposing the retention of a single Soviet state with a reformed Communist regime, and another Russian—Yeltsin—fighting for statehood for the union republics and democracy. Yet the contrast can be found among people of other nationalities as well. In the case of Latvia, most Latvians did identify with an independent and democratic state, but a small percentage consistently fought for the old regime and a Soviet identity, the most notorious being the coup-plotter Boris Pugo, the hard-line colonel Viktors Alksnis, and the first secretary of the Communist Party of Latvia (CPSU) Alfreds Rubiks. Rubiks expressed his loyalties clearly by stating, "I'm neither a Lett nor a Russian. I'm a Soviet."[3] In this remark, he was referring simultaneously to a type of national identity, to a state identity, and to allegiance to a political program. Rubiks never wavered in his loyalty to the three meanings of being Soviet, whereas many other "Soviets" underwent a deep crisis and shift of identity.

43

In chapter 2 I cited data on the changing political culture among a segment of the population of the former Soviet Union. Here my emphasis will be on shifts in territorial state identification and how it interacts with ethnic communal and political identification. As argued by Lucian W. Pye and Sidney Verba, identity is perhaps the most crucial belief forming political culture: "Of what political unit or units does the individual consider himself to be a member, and how deep and unambiguous is the sense of identification? By national identity I refer to the beliefs of individuals and the extent to which they consider themselves members of their nation-state."[4] The pattern in which this threefold identification with nation, state, and regime arranges itself is complex in theory, but in practice (fortunately for the democrats) it aligned rather clearly during the declining years of the Soviet Union. The people supporting the rights of nations and the independence of states were the same who fought to change the Soviet political regime, and vice versa—those who fought to retain the old regime were also those struggling against independence of union republics and the rights of nations. Once this struggle was decided in August 1991, new alignments between ethnic, state, and political identities began to emerge. One of the most difficult questions is how the fragile new democracies will deal with remaining unreformed "Soviets."

In sum, we have to analyze the complex relationship between individual identities as they are related to nations, states, and types of regimes. I deal with this threefold complexity by first discussing the relationship of states and nations, and then reintroducing the third dimension, that of regime.

Defining States and Nations

The Soviet crisis renewed many old questions, including that of the relationship between state, and nation, and smaller ethnic groupings. Some of the answers found during the crisis were similar to those encountered elsewhere, but some new twists also emerged. The most intriguing aspect is that as the nominally supranational Soviet identity collapsed, two types of new identities began to take its place: ethnically communal identities emerged side by side with multiethnic national identities focusing on territorial states. Roman Szporluk calls the latter "post-traditional nation states,"[5] but such states are nothing new, except that they usually take a longer time to form. As noted by Anthony D. Smith, the tension between civic-territorial nationalism and ethnic nationalism has meant that in multiethnic democracies it usually takes centuries for a common political culture to evolve. Smith argues that "it requires a special kind of territorial nationalism, namely with a strong 'civic' and participatory character, to achieve that balance [between ethnic identity and territorial nationalism]."[6] The trauma of the collapsing Soviet Union galvanized some new identities more quickly, especially those promoted by a broad democratic program such as that of the Popular Front of Latvia. Yet in light of the unusual context of the collapse of the old regime and the changing role of popular mass movements after the 1991 coup, it remains to be seen how permanent this shift is.

There are two definitions of a nation, one focusing on an ethnocultural community and the other focusing on a civic community. Under the first definition, Switzerland contains four nations, whereas under the second there is a single Swiss nation. Some analysts, such as Walker Connor, reject the use of the term "nation" in the latter sense as misleading and urge that it be reserved for ethnic communities, with civic communities clearly identified as states, be they mono- or multinational.[7] Yet the dual use of the term "nation" is bound to continue due to its history and because civic communities tend to develop a "national" identity over time, especially if the ethnopolitical arrangement is harmonious and if strong common civic values emerge and are nurtured by charismatic political leaders. Thus the founders of the Congress party in India presented the vision of a multiethnic democracy that respected Hindus and Muslims as separate religious communities united as a single civic nation of India, geographically defined.[8] The state of Czechoslovakia too was founded on the idea of a single political nation, consisting of two (linguistically similar) communal nations bound together by values and goals. This ideal was propagated by statesmen such as Tomás Masaryk, Edvard Beneš, and lately Václav Havel[9] and more or less accepted by individual Czechs and Slovaks—less by the latter. By 1993 tensions between the two territorially based communities led to a peaceful breakup of Czechoslovakia, but the point remains that a political union between Czechs and Slovaks has existed and continues to provide an alternative political identity.

History knows many instances when new states assisted the process of creating new nations,[10] although the reverse process is well known, too. The interactive relationship between state and nation is complicated because national and ethnic identity is based both on tangible communal traits and on a psychological sense of community. "The simplest statement that can be made about a nation is that it is a body of people who feel that they are a nation,"[11] and, though even tangible communal traits can change over time, this is especially true for the sense of community. With time and specific circumstance, the communal identification may shift toward a broader grouping or a narrower one. Until the 1960s, Western expectations about nation building—defined as "a massive shift of loyalties from the ascriptive group to the state"[12]—were overly optimistic, yet such shifts can occur. This is especially likely if individuals can retain several communal identities on different levels and if these identities are complementary rather than mutually exclusive. Thus a person living in Switzerland may consider herself as

Swiss-Italian, Swiss, and European, with each sense of community having its own connotations and becoming more or less relevant in specific contexts. "A person may have a different identification pattern for each ethnic identity which he may ascribe to himself or to others, and each ascription alternative may have a different salience at different moments."[13] This reminds us that ethnic identity embraces multiple levels and is strongly contextual.[14] From the point of view of the ethnopolitical democrat, the essential question to ask is how complementary collective identities are formed.

Since the eighteenth century there has been a tendency to associate the idea of the political state with national community.[15] This was linked to the democratic principle of the will of the people. Whereas before the French Revolution there was little connection between the state as a political unit and the nation as a cultural unit, the combination of these two elements in a single conception set in motion the history of the nation-state.[16] By the time of World War I, this conception was expressed in the principle of national self-determination, "the belief that each nation has a right to constitute an independent state and determine its own government."[17] President Woodrow Wilson saw this as a crucial democratic right and supported it by appealing to the peoples of the world over the heads of their governments. He became more cautious toward the end of World War I, when he noted that self-determination could clash with other principles such as those of historical or dynastic ties and economic or military interests.[18] Furthermore, the difficulty of defining cultural nations became more evident as increasingly many groups claimed the right to sovereignty. Although this impulse could be accommodated by ever more independent states arising in the world, as in fact they have throughout the postwar period, the more complex problem was that the lack of clear geographic and ethnic communal boundaries meant that many of the new states again included national minorities.

In the contemporary world only every fifth state[19] consists of a nation that is communally single; most states include several smaller or larger ethnic communities. The question is how each state deals with this configuration. Typically states aim to be more than purely civic communities and be a "national" community as well. The core question of ethnopolitics is how this national integration is promoted. Since few states acknowledge and accommodate their multinational or multiethnic nature, the potential for ethnic conflict is perennial.

Individuals of a majority nation living in states bearing the name of their group often feel that there is no "ethnic problem." And there is none—at least not for them, because their ethnic and civic communities overlap. Nevertheless, even majority groups have a consciousness of collective identity in regard to international relations of their state or when they go abroad as individual citizens. Crossing borders or otherwise coming into contact with persons of another ethnicity has long been seen as a crucial way of becoming aware of one's own identity.[20] The same kind of awareness is fostered when states give up their pretense of monoethnicity and make the effort to learn more about the ethnic minorities in their midst.

Analytically speaking, all people belong to at least two communities, the territorial civic community of the state and an ethnic community. Ideally the two identities are congruous in a monoethnic state, or are harmoniously arranged in a multiethnic state. If a state is built from several nations, it ideally represents a "community of communities." Yet if the interests and identities of two or more communities gathered in a single state are not harmonious, the search is on for new arrangements through either control or accommodation.[21] At that moment the question of type of political regime and its capacity for conflict resolution becomes paramount.

Like all politics, ethnic politics changes over time and is linked to numerous other political and socioeconomic factors. The mutability of ethnic politics means that the relationship of various ethnic communities toward the state can become more or less harmonious. In light of the statist argument presented previously, we argue that the state's (and regime's) policy makes a difference. Many comparative studies have explored this relationship in detail. Thus William Miles and David Rochefort show the strength of allegiance to the state among minorities in Sub-Saharan Africa,[22] and Juan Linz has shown the growth of a new Basque identity among recent migrants to that region. He notes that "identity . . . is not simply a reflection of descent, birth, or length of stay in the Basque country. The political and ideological climate to which different generations have been exposed is beyond doubt also strongly related to identity."[23] Or, in terms of previously introduced concepts, identity is related to political culture and sense of community. In sum, the identification with a territorial state can increase or decrease over time.

We now turn to an analysis of how the complexity of identity has affected Russians and Latvians. Their cases have been even more complicated than those found elsewhere because the breakup of the Soviet state coincided with the transition from communism. The issue of identification with the new state has been an issue of regime identification as well.

Nation, State, and Regime Identity: Patterns of Choice among Russians and Latvians

If we define citizens of the former USSR in terms of the territorial state that they identify with, the line of differentiation runs between individuals who identify with the boundaries of the old USSR and consequently have seen themselves—and continue to see themselves—as "Soviets," and others who identify with a smaller territory, typically a union republic. Many non-Russians have always had a problem of defining themselves as Soviets, but during the Gorbachev era increasingly many Russians redefined themselves as well. More and more, being "Soviet" was seen as foregoing national interests and democratic involvement in determining one's own affairs.[24] In addition, the Yeltsin forces began to provide the RSFSR with a separate identity through its own legislature and other autonomous institutions. As Russia began to insist on its own sovereignty, many Russians supported sovereignty for non-Russian republics. For most Russian democrats and some traditionalists, any territorial state larger than the RSFSR became discredited due to links to Communist Soviet identity. To be "anti-Soviet" meant to be both anti-Communist and anti-USSR.

Territorially speaking, many Russians living in the RSFSR identified increasingly with that republic (and sometimes with subregions, such as Siberia). In a similar process, Russians living in non-Russian republics increasingly had to decide whether they identified with that republic, the Soviet Union, or with Russia. As new states began to emerge, the question was phrased in terms of citizenship. Both subjective identification and citizenship questions became more complex after the USSR was dissolved in December 1991. The main problem was that although it was impossible to be a Soviet citizen without the Soviet Union, a significant number of Russians and some non-Russians continued to identify themselves as such. And, while some states such as Lithuania and Ukraine were generous in extending immediate citizenship to nearly everyone living on their territory,[25] other states such as Latvia and Estonia had difficulties due to the disproportional number of Russians and "Soviets" on their territory.

The differential self-identification with a territorial unit during and after the Soviet period is evident from surveys. In response to a question on what they considered to be their "motherland" in the late 1970s and early 1980s, 80 percent of Georgians and Uzbeks named their own republic, whereas Russians, regardless of where they lived, in most cases (70 percent or more) named the Soviet Union.[26] A December 1990 survey of 1,005 Russians living in eighteen cities in ten non-Russian republics asked, "Do you consider yourselves primarily a citizen of the Soviet Union or a citizen of the republic in which you live?" Most respondents said that they considered themselves citizens of the Soviet Union, with the highest percentages (77 to 88 percent) of those living in Central Asia saying so, and the lowest percentage (52 percent) of those living in Latvia. But even there, only 36 percent said that they considered themselves citizens of Latvia (another 15 percent replied that it was difficult to say). Clearly, identification with the republic was rather low. Nevertheless, many (65 percent in the case of Latvia) said that they would prefer to remain living there.[27] In another survey conducted in November 1991 after Latvia had restored its independence, 29 percent of Russian respondents stated that they considered Latvia to be their "homeland," 15 percent chose Russia, 27 percent the Soviet Union, and 29 percent responded that it was "difficult to say."[28] As Table 3.1 shows, many of the Russians and other non-Latvians who thought of Latvia as their homeland were people who themselves, or their families, had been citizens of Latvia at the time of its annexation in 1940.

In addition to having to rethink what constituted "their" state, Russians in various regions became involved in debates over their ethnic communal identity. In Russia the rival definitions of the nation were those of a more exclusively ethnic (*russkaia*) notion of nationhood and the more inclusive (*rossiskaia*) idea of citizenship of Russia/RSFSR.[29] In light of the emergence of other independent states it also became crucial to ask how Russians in Russia thought of their coethnics abroad, and how these people identified themselves. I discuss the latter issues in the case of Russians in Latvia.

The contrasting types of ethnopolitical identity among Russians in Latvia can be illustrated by the family of television journalist Sergejs Ancupovs, who has defined himself as a Russian who regards Latvia as his homeland and politically identifies with an independent and democratic Latvia (he speaks both Russian and Latvian). In this view, he is distinct from his mother, who is a Russian identifying herself with the Soviet state and the orthodox Communist political system.[30] Thus, even within a single family one finds differences in self-identification according to ethnic, state, and regime identity.

Table 3.1
"Homeland" of Non-Latvians, by Citizenship

| | | Citizen of Latvia[2] | |
"Homeland" Is[1]	Total (percent)	Yes (n = 147) (percent)	No (n = 309) (percent)
Latvia	28	42	21
USSR	28	27	30
Russia	13	5	17
Difficult to say	30	26	32

Source: Social Research Center of Latvia, November 1991. n = number.

[1]"When you say 'homeland' or 'fatherland' you usually think it to be. . . . "

[2]"Are you a citizen of the Republic of Latvia, or the descendant of a citizen?"

In assessing attitudes toward a territorial state, the question of sovereignty and independence is crucial. In the case of Latvia, survey data show distinctions according to the nationality of respondents as well as change over time. As Figure 3.1 illustrates, Latvians clearly have been much more supportive of Latvia's statehood than non-Latvians, but support also increased among the latter over time.

Other surveys and election results provide similar findings. In the March 1990 elections to the Supreme Soviet in Latvia about 30 to 40 percent of

FIGURE 3.1 Support for independence, inhabitants of Latvia (1989–91).

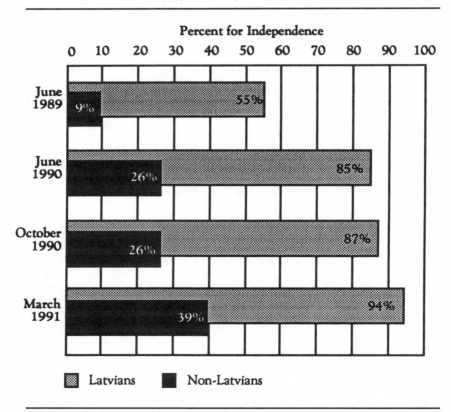

Source: Social Research Center of Latvia (see also Appendix).

non-Latvians voted for Popular Front candidates supporting independence. About 49 percent of non-Latvians supported independence in the advisory vote of March 1991.[31] A survey conducted in December 1990 revealed the profile of these individuals. Russians and other non-Latvians who have lived in Latvia relatively longer have been more supportive of independence: of those non-Latvians who have lived in Latvia since birth, 59 percent supported the view that "Latvia should be an independent state that bases its relations with the USSR on contractual agreements," 42 percent of those who had lived in Latvia for more than twenty years said the same, but only 30 percent of those who had lived there for a shorter period.[32] At the same time, younger people support independence for Latvia significantly more than older people. Figure A.1 in the Appendix illustrates that this correlation is consistent, except for a partial drop for those under twenty years of age.

Survey data also show the linkage between a proindependence stance and support for Yeltsin and the Popular Front in Latvia. As Table 3.2 illustrates, a clear preference for Latvia's independence was most strongly voiced by the non-Latvians with a high trust in Yeltsin. A similar correlation of political attitudes is evident from Tables A.1 and A.2 in the Appendix. Among non-Latvians living in Latvia, those who favored Latvia's independence also supported the Popular Front. Conversely, those non-Latvians who pre-

Table 3.2
Preferred Status for Latvia among Non-Latvians, by Trust in Yeltsin

| | Trust Yeltsin | | | |
Preference for Latvia	Mostly (n = 167) (percent)	Somewhat (n = 80) (percent)	Difficult to Say (n = 146) (percent)	No (n = 32) (percent)
Independence	32	27	22	9
Independent state within USSR as confederation	43	52	48	50
Part of USSR	20	12	14	31
Don't know	5	9	16	10

Source: Social Research Center of Latvia, September 1990. n = number.

ferred Latvia as part of the USSR were those who most strongly supported the Interfront, a political organization defending the preeminent role of the CPSU. Looking at the same data from the other side, one notes that respondents who opposed Yeltsin and supported the Interfront were also those most opposed to independence, that is, they were the most "Soviet" in the sense of being both pro-Communist and pro-USSR. Being Soviet meant identifying with a political system ensconced in the state territory of the entire USSR. Often political loyalty and interests were joined with the socioeconomic interests of working in the centrally controlled military-industrial complex or all-union institutions such as the CPSU, the military forces, and the KGB.

Contextual Constraints on Choice

People have multiple identities and interests, yet specific contexts limit the choices available to them. Often, a political situation presents only two options, while the actual preference grid is more complex in theory as well as in practice. The precise details of how multiple interests are reconciled are central to politics and political analysis. The outcome in a situation of limited choice can be beneficial if it binds people into a goal-oriented coalition, or it can be detrimental if people are forced into unwelcome coalitions or are left out of the political process altogether.

Game theorists have developed mathematical ways of expressing situations of choice and calculating optimal strategies. Here I only make the general point about the complexity of preferences and the necessity to make tactical and strategic choices in specific contexts. I also outline the pattern of choice as it emerged in Latvia during 1988–91. Similar choices involving ethnicity, territorial identification, and regime were pertinent throughout the former USSR.

In the last years of the Gorbachev era, citizens of the USSR were faced with a polarized choice between concrete political alternatives. The decisive choice was that between retaining the Communist regime and overturning it. There were more radical and more reformist individuals on both sides—Gorbachev, for example, being a reform Communist—but in the end there was no way to avoid the choice between just two options. Similarly, intermediate choices on state autonomy evaporated over time. By 1991 there was a clear juxtaposition between anti-independence and proindependence forces, and between those who supported the communal interests of specific nations less or more openly. In the previous chapters I argued that the coalition on both sides largely coalesced in principles; here my point is that even if individual values differed, there was little choice but to align with one or the other coalition. The one exception was to choose abstention from all political involvement, although even that has consequences, for example the indirect favoring of one candidate over another in an election.

During the final years of the USSR those Latvians and Russians who felt that all their values coincided were the happiest with the alliance they were put in: on the democratic side these were people who felt that opposition to the Soviet regime clearly coincided with support for independence and political pluralism, and that the latter was also the best way to support the interests of the Latvian and/or Russian nations. The contrasting view also was unequivocal—that a Communist Soviet Union, with Soviet internationalism, was the only way to proceed. Latvians who were pushed into the alliance with the democratic movement included some who were skeptical about its true principles, as well as others who feared that Yeltsin's support for independence was rhetorical, and that the interests of the Latvian nation demanded an uncompromising approach to the Russian-speaking settler population brought to Latvia by Soviet occupation forces.[33] When forced to choose, such as in the elections to the Supreme Soviet in March 1990, many people who held the latter conviction felt that they had to vote for the candidates of the Popular Front as the "lesser evil," although there were some who refused to vote altogether.[34] Similarly, not all the non-Latvians who had to choose between the Popular Front or the Interfront were happy with the lack of alternative choices, as is evident from the high percentage of "difficult to say" and "don't know" replies to survey questions.[35]

The actual strategic pattern of alignment among the three dimensions of identity in Russia and Latvia between 1988 and 1991 is illustrated in Figure 3.2. Those individuals who were forced into an alliance or who abstained in votes or surveys were the first to realign themselves once the opportunity presented itself. The possibility of realignment in the relative saliency of ethnic, state, and regime identities is dependent on political context. In this regard the most decisive change came after the failed coup attempt of August 1991, when independent states took the place of the Soviet Union and the old Communist party was outlawed. The internal differentiation among non-Communist forces became more pertinent, and differences in the interests of the Latvian and Russian states, as well as the Latvian nation and Russians in Latvia, became more evident. (This realignment is discussed in chapters 6 and 7.)

Identification by Self and Others

Ethnopolitical interaction depends on how people identify themselves and others. As noted, the categories used in identification are not just ethnic or communal, but also relate to territorial states and regimes. "None of the above" is another option in self-identification, especially prevalent among economic migrants following the motto *ubi bene ibi patria* (wherever life is

FIGURE 3.2 Alignment of political choices in Latvia and Russia, 1988–91.

ETHNIC AND REGIME IDENTITY
Ethnic Identity

Regime Identity	Latvian	Russian
Democratic non-Communist	Latvian non-Communist	Russian non-Communist
Communist (hard-line or reform)	Latvian Communist	Russian Communist

ETHNIC AND STATE IDENTITY
Ethnic Identity

State Identity	Latvian	Russian
Independent Latvia and Russia	Pro-independence Latvian	Pro-independence Latvian
Soviet Union	Anti-independence Latvian	Anti-independence Latvian

DIRECTION OF ALLIANCE

good, that is my country).[36] It is beyond the scope of this study to analyze this and other economic identities in full, yet they should be noted as relevant.

A primary question regarding identity is: Who does the identifying—is it the individual, or someone else? So far we have focused on data where individuals themselves chose their allegiance in surveys or elections. Yet it also matters how others in society identify a person, and whether any formal criteria for identification exist. Such identification can differ from self-identification.

During the Soviet period ethnic communal self-identification was reinforced by the practice of formally documenting the nationality of every person. In contradiction to the ideological tenet that a new historical community known as the "Soviet people" was developing, nominal national identity played a significant role both socially and in bureaucratic practice. In the USSR, the state's identification of the nationality of each individual was documented on virtually all official papers. Conversationally this was referred to as the "fifth point" since the item *natsional'nost'* typically appeared fifth after other standard items of personal identification such as name, gender, and year and place of birth. Nominal ethnic identification thus became a regulatory device used by the Soviet bureaucracy. Individuals could not choose their ethnicity, aside from children with parents of two different official nationalities, who were able to choose between the two. This nominal bureaucratic ethnic identification obviously reinforced people's perception of the relevance of their own ethnic identity and that of others.[37]

In Latvia identification has been simplest for Latvians. Living in their traditional homeland and able to use their language—although in limited ways[38]—most Latvians have had little difficulty identifying themselves as Latvians in the ethnic communal sense and being identified as such by others. Exceptions include individuals who come from mixed families or who themselves have intermarried,[39] and those whose families came to Latvia from the USSR after 1940. Politically, this latter group was prominent and privileged because they presented a pool of nominally Latvian people who were strongly loyal to the Soviet cause.[40] Mostly descendants of eighteenth- and nineteenth-century colonists to Russia or of Latvian Bolsheviks who remained in Russia after 1917, this population suffered greatly in the Stalinist purges, and few of the survivors dared to challenge the supreme wisdom of the Communist party. As is often the case with marginal people, many among these "Russian-Latvians" felt compelled to be super-loyal to the cause. Colonel Viktors Alksnis is a prime example. Alksnis learned Latvian when his grandmother—the widow of First Commander of Red Army Aviation Jēkabs Alksnis—took him to Latvia from Russia at the age of seven. Asked in 1992 whether he felt himself to be a Latvian, Alksnis answered, "No," adding that the Soviet army which he joined in 1968 "formed me as a Soviet man, and I do not see anything bad in that. I became a *rossianin*, which is not the same as a Russian. For me Liepāja [a city in Latvia] is Russia as well. A person belonging to Russia [*rossianin*] is a person who feels he belongs to a large state that has unified Uzbeks, Kirghiz, as well as Latvians."[41]

Apart from such Sovietized "Russian-Latvians," the overwhelming majority of Latvians clearly identified with an independent state of Latvia, as well as with a non-Communist regime. Self-identification and identification by others was more complicated for non-Latvians. We have already noted that a significant segment of the non-Latvians identified with an independent state of Latvia and a democratic regime, yet another part identified with the Soviet Union as a state and political system. In the politically charged environment of the late 1980s and early 1990s this division within the non-Latvian population, given the complexity of the interplay of threefold identities, has inevitably led to colloquial simplifications.

For some Latvians, being anti-Soviet is tantamount to being anti-Russian. For some others, such as the first chairman of the Popular Front of Latvia, Dainis Īvāns, good experiences with Russian democrats have led to tolerant attitudes toward all Russians in Latvia—as expressed, for example, in the willingness to extend immediate citizenship to them. Whereas Īvāns believes that this would strengthen Latvian democracy,[42] others argue that the naturalization of antidemocrats who fought the independence of Latvia on the side of Communist hard-liners is a sure way to undermine it. I return to these recent political dilemmas in chapters 6 and 7.

From 1988 onward the Popular Front of Latvia tried to induce as many Russians and others as possible to identify themselves with the interests of a democratic and independent Latvia. This was accomplished most easily among those non-Latvians who were citizens of the Republic of Latvia before its incorporation into the USSR in June 1940. Having had the personal or family experience of living in an independent Latvia, and having enjoyed rather generous cultural and political rights,[43] most non-Latvian citizens of this generation have identified with Latvia as a civic community. The Constitution of the Republic of Latvia adopted in 1922 speaks of a "nation of Latvia" proclaiming territory and citizenship as the basis for political state identity.[44] Thus citizenship in Latvia has never been reserved for ethnic Latvians only, and no serious political force has proposed that it be so in the future. This is important to point out in light of numerous mistaken reports that only ethnic Latvians are accepted as citizens.[45]

In chapter 7 I discuss in more detail the various positions about who is a citizen of Latvia, and who may apply to become one in the future. For the purposes of the discussion here, it is important to note that while some members of the non-Latvian population see Latvia as a civic community to which they wish to belong, and are accepted as belonging to it by most Latvians, another segment continues to identify with the defunct Soviet Union, or with Russia. In a survey conducted in spring 1990, 68 percent of non-Latvians said that they would remain in Latvia (but only just over half of them would adopt Latvian citizenship), 13 percent would move to the USSR, and 2 percent would go to other countries.[46] In September 1991 another survey of non-Latvians who were not already citizens of the Republic of Latvia found 44 percent saying that they would give up Soviet citizenship and try to become citizens of Latvia, 18 percent responding that they would keep Soviet citizenship and remain in Latvia, 27 percent replying "difficult to say," and the rest giving different or no answers.[47]

Thus Latvia has been confronted with the problem of a sizable internal population that has not identified with it as a territorial state and civic community. As long as these people identify with neighboring states such as Russia, Ukraine, or Belorussia, this problem can be tackled in interstate negotiations. The more difficult problem has been that the breakup of the USSR not only created new states and new regimes, but also left behind a resentful subgroup of people in Latvia and elsewhere that identifies with the old state and the old regime. The Soviets without the Soviet Union present a source of political instability.

In Latvia, the "Soviets" consist mostly of a Russian-speaking settler population that moved to Latvia in the postwar period. Many were sent to Latvia as representatives of central party or state institutions or to fill jobs in centrally controlled industries. Others migrated to Latvia for economic reasons, and a substantial group of Soviet officers chose to retire in Latvia because life there was made very attractive to them.[48] These individuals have difficulty adjusting to an independent and democratic Latvia because after losing the object of their identity, the Soviet Union, they now fear losing their privileges as the formerly dominant political, economic, and cultural elite.

The pro-Soviet forces in Latvia have also been identified as such by other political players in the country and this too makes their integration into any post-Soviet community more difficult—all the more because they actively fought against the independence of Latvia and sought the protection of the most hard-line forces in Moscow.[49] The alliance between Latvia's and Russia's hard-liners continued after the fateful events of 1991 and so did their common struggle for a reversal of history.

Ethnic group boundaries are fluid, and often ethnic groupings are aggregated or disaggregated, as is the case for Hispanics in the United States. Similarly there is the recent phenomenon of *russkoiazychnye*, "Russian-speakers," as an ethnic category in the former republics of the USSR. This identification by language is vague, but suggests that Russians and others who speak Russian form a common group of people. The political implication is that language matters more than origin, religion, or other traits in defining ethnopolitical identity. It is unclear whether "Russian-speakers" are monolingual, or whether this refers to the native language or most frequently used language. Either way the policy implication usually made is that the ability to speak only, or mostly, Russian in Latvia and elsewhere is an ethnic right that needs protection (see chapter 7).

For the smaller minorities of Latvia (see Table A.5 in the Appendix) the long-term practice of identification of ethnicity in documents means that members of all groupings identify ethnically to at least some degree. Many have also identified with Latvia as their state, and with a democratic regime. This tendency has been enhanced by recent policies of the democratic movements in Latvia. In contrast to Soviet practice, which largely ignored the cultural rights of nationalities living outside their traditional homeland (Russians being the exception), the Popular Front of Latvia during the national awakening worked to strengthen the ethnic identity of these groups and at the same time emphasized that their rights would be safeguarded in an independent state of Latvia. Programs were developed to allow Poles, Ukrainians, Jews, and other non-Latvians in Latvia to identify with their own respective nationality.[50] These efforts have been successful to a significant extent.[51]

The Politics of Identity Choice

The identity of an individual is composed from manifold subidentities defined in terms of social roles and class, ethnicity, geographic residence, age, gender, and so forth. Some of these identities are immutable—age, for example—but usually people have some choice in whether to belong to a category, be it occupational group or geographic location. Martin Heisler has emphasized that in modern Western democracies, ethnic identity often also is a matter of choice, that people have "considerable latitude in *choosing* the extent to which they assume or emphasize ethnic roles."[52] I would put the emphasis less on choice of ascriptive identity than on the need to make choices in the degree to which one or the other identity is emphasized in specific political and life situations. In the context of the threefold identification by ethnic community, state, and regime type, individuals and political movements can focus exclusively on one identity, or a mix of identities. The essence of political choice is precisely this type of decision, and the analyst has to determine whether a specific political program is aimed at creating a certain political system, a state, or is focusing on the interests of a nation or ethnic group. If the latter case prevails, it would be appropriate to call it nationalist, but a subsidiary question would be whether there is any preference in regard to regime type, be it democratic, authoritarian, or Communist. Another subsidiary question is whether the nation is defined in exclusive ethnic terms or whether it is based on a territorial principle.

I have argued in chapters 1 and 2 that once the primary choice of regime type is made, certain consequences for ethnic politics follow, because it is difficult, for example, to reconcile democracy with an ethnic control system. Conversely, it is difficult to reconcile an authoritarian system with significant ethnic power sharing, although some states such as Malaysia come close. When an individual or political movement is primarily interested in state independence, there is usually considerable choice as to regime type, but in the transition from communism in the Soviet Union, claims for independence went hand in hand with claims for democratic government. Once union republics attained independence in late 1991, it was up to the new polities to determine how democratic they would become.

In chronological terms one can say that during the initial phase of transition from communism the democratization of the regime was the dominant issue being fought over, and the independence of republics was a part of regime change. Once the central Soviet Communist regime was overturned in the fall of 1991, a new political phase began. Now the new post-Communist states had to define the meaning of independence and democracy in relation to each other and in internal political struggles. In this second phase of democratic transition the questions of identity in regard to ethnic community, state, and regime have been reformulated and it will take time for clear answers to emerge.

Conclusion

Ethnic nominalism, the ascription of ethnopolitical identity to whole groups, is misleading. People have multiple identities, which are differently interpreted by individuals, and one has to analyze how they align in various contexts. The alignment of identities determines a polity's ethnopolitics. Ethnic accommodation works best if a program is supported by people on the basis of several of their identities. If a certain context urges a political alliance, compromises may be made for the sake of the cohesiveness of a political movement. Although ethnic conflict is mitigated by the overlap of several identities, it increases if people are pushed toward a single identity or toward an involuntary alignment due to lack of choice.

The three identities focused on here are ethnic community, territorial state, and political regime. During the perestroika period, multiethnic coalitions focused on the question of regime type. This focus coincided with identification with the sovereign states of Russia and Latvia, since the creation of democratic regimes required a move away from the hypercentralism of the USSR. The agenda focusing on regime change and state sovereignty also appeared to be the best guarantee for the preservation of ethnic communal identities. Nevertheless, the Popular Front of Latvia engaged in a compromise during 1988–91 by emphasizing an inclusive territorial conception of membership in the "national" community. After independence was restored in August 1991 and the common goal with the democratic forces in Russia to bring down the Communist regime had been achieved, it was to be expected that the alignment of forces would change.[53]

The definition of the state interests of Russia and Latvia became an issue, and so did the conception of "nation" in both countries. The new Russian Federation became more circumspect about its attitudes toward the "loss" of the union republics and the need to protect Russians outside of Russia. Rather than emphasizing the alliance with democrats in the non-Russian republics against the center, Russia's primary focus moved toward assuaging nationalist challenges within Russia.[54]

Once both Russia and Latvia had established independence and were moving toward democracy, the question about each state's identity and definition of citizenship shifted to the forefront of political debate. In Latvia, a broad definition of the nation encompassing everyone residing on the territory of the state was challenged by forces emphasizing that citizenship in a state could only be given to people who identify with that state and its form of government. How could the independent and democratic state of Latvia give citizenship to people who had actively fought against her independence and democratic regime?[55] The main issue became what to do with "Soviets" without the Soviet Union, and what the status of citizens of Russia and other new states would be if they continued to reside in Latvia. Russia for its part began to develop its own views on the latter question, although with some inconsistencies (see chapters 6 and 7).

We have identified three types of political and national identity that played a role in the precoup era, and they continue to play a role, although in a new alignment, during the postcoup era. There are individuals who identify themselves politically as democrats and anti-Communists, and others who are their Communist and "Soviet" opponents, and then there are people who take positions somewhere in between or are politically apathetic. In ethnic communal terms, the clearest identification exists for Latvians and longtime local minorities that identify themselves as Latvian Russians, Jews, Poles, or Gypsies.[56] A subgroup of postwar migrants to Latvia are in the process of becoming similar locally acclimatized "ethnics" who would retain their Russian, Ukrainian, or other identity, while at the same time acquiring Latvian language skills and other ethnic traits linked to the environment they live in. Yet another subgroup of people has no inclination of such acclimatizing and remain Russian-speaking "Soviets," or people who identify with an ethnic community outside of Latvia, for example Russians in Russia. And last but not least, there is the question of identification in terms of the territorial state of Latvia. Again, Latvians and the historical minorities of Latvia have the clearest identification with "their" state of which they are citizens. A subgroup of postwar immigrants also identifies with this state and is eager to become its loyal citizens. Finally, there is a third subgroup, people who remain Soviets in their loyalties or who would choose to be citizens of Russia or another of the new states.

Although these differential identities and loyalties existed throughout the Soviet era, the collapse of the USSR and the transition from communism has made the contrasts more evident and politically salient. In addition, the process of transition to new regimes and new states has meant that new collective identities are formed and old ones are reinforced. After discussing attitudinal differences and change in this chapter, we next focus on the organizational and behavioral dimension. In the next two chapters I discuss the role of political mobilization and group formation in the emergence of new polities, states, and nations.

NOTES

1. Nelson Kasfir, "Explaining Ethnic Political Participation," *World Politics* 31 (April 1979): 365, 371–73.
2. Robert J. Thompson and Joseph R. Rudolph, Jr., "Ethnic Politics and Public Policy in Western Societies: A Framework for Comparative Analysis," in Dennis L. Thompson and Dov Ronen, eds., *Ethnicity, Politics, and Development* (Boulder, Colo.: Lynne Rienner, 1986), 32.
3. *Moscow News*, no. 8, 1991, p. 11; Rubiks was born in Latvia and is Latvian according to the ethnic category on his passport.
4. Lucian W. Pye and Sidney Verba, *Political Culture and Political Development* (Princeton: Princeton University Press, 1965), 529.
5. Roman Solchanyk, "Roman Szporluk and Valerii Tishkov Talk about the National Question," *Report on the USSR*, 1 June 1990, 21.
6. Anthony D. Smith, "Ethnic Identity and Territorial Nationalism in Comparative Perspective," in Alexander J. Motyl, ed., *Thinking Theoretically about Soviet Nationalities* (New York: Columbia University Press, 1992), 61.
7. Walker Connor, "Ethnonationalism," in Myron Weiner and Samuel P. Huntington, eds., *Understanding Political Development* (Boston: Little, Brown, 1987), 196–219.
8. Comments by Ashutosh Varshney, Woodrow Wilson Center Ethnic Cluster Group meeting, 31 July 1992; see also Ashutosh Varshney, "India, Pakistan, and Kashmir," *Asian Survey* 31 (November 1991): 997–1019.
9. Václav Havel, *Summer Meditations*, trans. Paul Wilson (New York: Knopf, 1992).
10. Uri Ra'anan, "The Nation-State Fallacy," in Joseph V. Montville, ed., *Conflict and Peacemaking in Multiethnic Societies* (Lexington, Mass.: Lexington Books, 1990), 13.
11. Rupert Emerson, *From Empire to Nation: The Rise to Self-Assertion of Asian and African Peoples* (Cambridge, Mass.: Harvard University Press, 1960), 102.
12. Donald L. Horowitz, *Ethnic Groups in Conflict* (Berkeley: University of California Press, 1985), 568.
13. Daniel Glaser, "Dynamics of Ethnic Identification," *American Sociological Review* 23 (February 1958): 31.

14. See also Donald L. Horowitz, "Ethnic Identity," in Nathan Glazer and Daniel P. Moynihan, eds., *Ethnicity: Theory and Experience* (Cambridge, Mass.: Harvard University Press, 1975), 118; also Rasma Karklins, *Ethnic Relations in the USSR: The Perspective from Below* (London and Boston: Allen and Unwin, 1986).
15. Alfred Cobban, *The Nation-State and National Self-Determination* (New York: Crowell, 1970), 32.
16. Ibid., 35. See also discussion in chapter 1.
17. Ibid., 39.
18. K. R. Minogue, *Nationalism* (Baltimore: Penguin, 1967), 137.
19. Gunnar P. Nielsson, "States and 'Nation-Groups,' a Global Taxonomy," in Edward A. Tiryakian and Ronald Rogowski, eds., *New Nationalisms of the Developed West: Toward Explanation* (Boston: Allen and Unwin, 1985), 27–56.
20. Frederick Barth, ed., *Ethnic Groups and Boundaries: The Social Organization of Culture Differences* (London: Allen and Unwin, 1969); Karl W. Deutsch, *Nationalism and Social Communication*, 2d ed. (Cambridge, Mass.: MIT Press, 1966).
21. See also John Darby, "Northern Ireland: The Persistence and Limitations of Violence," in Montville, *Conflict and Peacemaking*, 157.
22. William F. S. Miles and David A. Rochefort, "Nationalism versus Ethnic Identity in Sub-Saharan Africa," *American Political Science Review* 85 (June 1991): 393–403.
23. Juan Linz, "From Primordialism to Nationalism," in Tiryakian and Rogowski, *New Nationalisms*, 229.
24. See also Roman Solchanyk, "Ukraine, the (Former) Center, Russia, and 'Russia'," *Studies in Comparative Communism* 25 (March 1992): 31–45.
25. See Saulius Girnius, "The Lithuanian Citizenship Law," *Report on the USSR*, 27 September 1991, 21.
26. Leokida Drobizheva, "Perestroika and the Ethnic Consciousness of Russians," in Gail W. Lapidus and Victor Zaslavsky, with Philip Goldman, eds., *From Union to Commonwealth: Nationalism and Separatism in the Soviet Republics* (Cambridge: Cambridge University Press, 1992), 101.
27. The total comes to 103 percent; data are from "Study on Russians in the Union Republics," All-Union Public Opinion Research Center, Moscow, December 1990, cited by Klaus Segbers, "Migration and Refugee Movements from the USSR: Causes and Prospects," *Report on the USSR*, 15 November 1991, 12. For other results of this interesting study see L. D. Gudkov, "Attitudes toward Russians in the Union Republics," unpublished study by the All-Union Public Opinion Research Center, translated in *Russian Social Science Review* 34 (January–February 1993): 52–69.
28. Social Research Center of Latvia; see the methodological note in the Appendix.
29. Ronald G. Suny, "Rethinking Soviet Studies: Bringing the Non-Russians Back In," paper presented at Soviet Studies Workshop, Woodrow Wilson Center, 24 July 1992, 36; also Solchanyk, "Ukraine," entire.
30. *Diena*, 1 March 1991, weekend section.
31. It is difficult to be more exact because the percentages depend on voter turnout by nationality and this statistic is unavailable. More details are presented in chapter 5 and Table 5.2.
32. Survey conducted by sociological section at the Supreme Council of Latvia in December 1990, random sample of 1,675 people throughout Latvia. Cited in *Latvijas Jaunatne*, 29 December 1990, 2.
33. Numerous articles in the informal press of Latvia, especially *Junda*, *Neatkarība*, and *Pilsonis*.
34. Ibid.
35. See for example, Table 3.2. A lengthy article in the Moscow journal *Sobesednik* based on interviews with Russians in Latvia in May 1990 notes ambivalence among many: "Considerable numbers of Latvia's Russian-speaking population have today really found themselves out of it, as it were: They are not on the same track as the Interfront, seemingly, nor are they in complete harmony with the People's Front." *Sobesednik*, no. 21 (May 1990): 5; quoted in *FBIS-SOV*, 9 July 1990, 35.

36. A prominent journalist in Latvia, Aleksejs Grigorievs, has argued that no real Russian community exists in Latvia and is being artificially defined as such by Latvian nationalists. He has complained that everyone is being pushed into identifying with a certain nationality, even if people prefer not to—"There could be groups that do not take on any ethnic identity." Presentation at Conference on Ethnicity and Democratization, Riga, 19–21 May 1992.
37. For more details on Soviet practice and on choices made by teenagers of dual parentage, see Karklins, *Ethnic Relations*, chap. 1.
38. See chapters 6 and 7.
39. Karklins, *Ethnic Relations*, chap. 1.
40. Ādolfs Šilde, "The Role of Russian-Latvians in the Sovietization of Latvia," *Journal of Baltic Studies* 18 (Summer 1987): 191–200; Egil Levits, "The Development of Legal Relations between the Communist Party of Latvia and the Communist Party of the Soviet Union," in Dietrich A. Loeber et al., *Ruling Communist Parties and Their Status Under Law* (Dordrecht, Boston, Lancaster: Martinus Nijhoff, 1986), 57–74; Rolf Ekmanis, *Latvian Literature under the Soviets 1940-1975* (Belmont, Mass.: Nordland, 1978).
41. Interview with Viktors Alksnis, *Diena*, 27 March 1992.
42. Press reports and author's interview with Īvāns, May 1992.
43. Ethnic minorities were granted numerous cultural rights and significant practical political leverage and powers; see Zigurds L. Zile, "The Legal Framework of Minorities' Policies in Latvia: Background, Constitution, and the League of Nations," *Journal of Baltic Studies* 11 (1980): 3–24; Michael Garleff, "Ethnic Minorities in the Estonian and Latvian Parliaments: The Politics of Coalition," in V. Stanley Vardys and Romuald Misiunas, eds., *The Baltic States in Peace and War 1917-1945* (University Park: Pennsylvania State University Press, 1978), 81–94; Temira Pachmuss, "Russian Culture in the Baltic States and Finland, 1920-1940," *Journal of Baltic Studies* 16 (Winter 1985): 383–98.
44. K. Dišlers, *Latvijas valsts varas orgāni un viņu funkcijas* (Riga: Tieslietu Ministrija, 1925), 7.
45. For example, Irina Litvinova, "Who Will Receive Citizenship," *Izvestiia*, 26 April 1990, 3; *Current Digest of the Soviet Press* 42, no. 17 (1990): 28.
46. *Izvestiia*, 1 May 1990, as translated in *FBIS-SOV*, 1 May 1990; the survey was conducted by the Sociologists' Association of Latvia and involved twenty-four thousand questionnaires. For a survey of Russian opinion based on the local Russian language press, see V. Volkov, "Obzor russkoiazychnoi pressy Latvii po problemam mezhnatsional'nykh otnoshenii za 1986–1992 gody," *Latvijas Zinātņu Akadēmijas Vēstis*, no. 5 (1993): 12–16.
47. Social Research Center of Latvia survey of September 1991, summary in *Atmoda*, 29 October 1991; see also Table 7.1. Before the collapse of the USSR many loyal "Soviets" explicitly rejected the idea of being citizens of Latvia.Thus a letter to the editor of a Communist party newspaper notes that "while it was somehow possible to feel ourselves as citizens of the USSR, it is hardly possible to feel this way in regard to the republic." *Jūrmalas Rīts*, 2–8 July 1991, 1.
48. Since 1945 more than 55,000 retired Soviet officers have settled in Latvia, mainly in Riga. Together with their families they total approximately 180,000 people. The process of settling retired officers intensified between 1986–88 as a result of housing policies pursued by the municipal leadership at the time. Unpublished materials compiled by the Commission on Human and National Rights Questions, Supreme Council of Republic of Latvia, 14 April 1992; see also chapter 6.
49. See chapters 6 and 7 for further discussion.
50. For a programmatic statement see, for example, *Jelgavas Ziņotājs*, 13 February 1990.
51. As early as September 1989 a Jewish school for four hundred students was opened in Riga; its language of instruction is Yiddish, but courses in Hebrew, Latvian, Russian, English, and German are given as well. *Skolotāju avīze*, 6 September 1989, 3.
52. Martin O. Heisler, "Ethnicity and Ethnic Relations in the Modern West," in Montville, *Conflict and Peacemaking*, 25.
53. This passage follows the theoretical points made by Adam Przeworski, "Democracy as a Contingent Outcome of Conflicts," in Jon Elster and Rune Slagstad, eds., *Constitutionalism and Democracy* (Cambridge: Cambridge University Press, 1988), 63–64.

54.   See Solchanyk, "Ukraine," entire; and chapters 6 and 7.
55.   Author's interviews with various political activists in Latvia; see also chapter 7.
56.   For demographic data see Table A.3 in the Appendix.

4

⟫·◇·⟪

Building Democracy from Below: Civil Society and Ethnicity

The literature on the transition to democracy emphasizes the role of civil society as a precondition—and characteristic—of democracy. Yet how can civil society emerge in a nondemocratic system? Specifically, how can it emerge in a Soviet-type system that deliberately limits social autonomy?[1] Two propositions are advanced in this chapter. First, communal ties provide an informal network that can form the nucleus of a nascent civil society. Second, ethnicity and the symbols of self-rule express common goals that can form the basis for mobilizing civic activity and a political culture of solidarity and participation. This culture is crucial for the solidification of social movements into civil society. Most propositions about civil society emphasize autonomous structures, but here congruent values are highlighted as well.

For theorists of democracy like Tocqueville, the free play of social forces is even more important for democracy than institutionalized political organizations.[2] Most analysts of recent transitions to democracy in various parts of the world make a similar point when noting the significance of civil society. Thus Samuel Huntington advances the thesis that a differentiated social structure is a necessary precondition of democracy. He mentions relatively autonomous social classes, regional groups, occupational groups, and ethnic and religious groups as providing the basis for the limitation of state power, hence for the control of the state by society, and hence for democratic political institutions as the most effective means of exercising that control.[3] Typically, civil society is defined as groups independent of state tutelage and control,[4] and as "the arenas, movements, and organizations for expressing and advancing manifold social interests."[5] As the analysts note, even limited social pluralism is crucial for a successful transition to democracy, because it creates alternative institutions and leaders.[6]

Although all definitions of civil society emphasize the articulation of its interests by society independently of the state,[7] some make the stronger claim that civil society is the institutionalization of the people's will determining governmental policy. In this perspective government is the servant of popular will and its institutional expression, in contrast to the reform Communist view that democracy is an instrument of popular mobilization for strengthening the links of citizens to the state. The contrast between an instrumental and essential view of democracy was at the core of controversies between perestroika "from above" and the perspective of grass-roots democrats, for whom civil society had meaning only if it is built "from below." Paradoxically, the tension between the two approaches in Latvia proved to be a source of dynamic political change as it triggered ever more debate and societal initiatives.

How does civil society emerge and what sort of social groups form its basis? Unfortunately, many theorists only speak about the need for nonstate social organizations without going into specifics. Some analysts focus on the role of socioeconomic groups. In the case of Taiwan's transition to democracy, the emergence of an economically and socially independent middle class is seen to have been a crucial step toward societal emancipation,[8] a conclusion that harks back to older theories about the role of the bourgeoisie in the emergence of popular democracy. Yet other groups can be equally important. Many analysts have noted the crucial roles of the independent labor union *Solidarnošc* and the Catholic church in Poland's transition from communism.[9] Theorists in Poland and Czechoslovakia developed the notion of a parallel polis built from below and gradually replacing official power structures.[10] It appears that any type of pluralism can contribute to the formation of civil society. Huntington even refers to the role of the caste system in India or a strong aristocracy in highly developed feudalism.[11] He sees ethnic and religious groups as one building block of civil society; here I go further and argue that ethnic pluralism can act as a substitute for other forms of social pluralism if the latter has been deliberately suppressed. Or, to use more traditional concepts of social science, if *Gesellschaft* is too weak, *Gemeinschaft* can take its place.[12]

One reason for the potential power of communal identities is that they are tenacious. Even if communal identities and ties are weakened by a regime's social engineering, as they were in the former Soviet Union, they retain symbolic and emotional power that can be mobilized in certain contexts. As noted by Donald Horowitz, "In times of rapid change, ethnic ties can provide a basis for interpersonal trust and affection"[13] and thus provide a building block of social organization.[14] In a similar vein, it has been argued that "political transition, because it sets institutions in flux, places a premium on whatever cultural guidelines might be at hand as a device for reducing confusion."[15] This argument has been developed further in the case of Spain, where the dearth of secondary associations did not signify an absence of social activity, but rather their equivalent presence in primary ties, that is face-to-face linkages, often between kin.[16] In addition, ethnic communal identities refer to the collective identity and rights of "the people" and thus are conceptually close to the notions underlying democracy and civil society.

The Baltic states provide an example of how ethnicity and memories of independent statehood can play a constructive role during an era of transition. Most new social movements and mass activities fused a reliance on the symbols of national identity and state independence with a broad agenda of democratic reform. One example concerns the League of Women of Latvia who took on no lesser a foe than the Soviet military establishment in fighting for the rights of draftees. Other examples include the environmental clubs, the Association of Politically Repressed People, and the Popular Front of Latvia. Groups such as the National Independence Movement of Latvia focused on statehood and the rights of the Latvian nation, and in doing so went beyond symbolism and formulated political goals for public life. They emphasized that group pluralism and a participatory political culture could become genuine only by addressing the source of their suppression in the past, namely the CPSU's and Soviet Union's policies against Latvia.[17]

When a political regime suppresses free speech and the expression of alternative political goals, symbols take on a special role. Symbols are a subtle form of communication with tremendous suggestive and emotional power. Besides expressing common goals, symbols can have an organizing function. In Latvia the anniversary days of crucial dates in the nation's political history played such an organizing role by providing an automatic schedule for popular demonstrations (see also chapter 5). The national flag, anthem, and other attributes of the interwar state were additional symbols of patriotism attaining new significance beginning in 1986. So were the Freedom Monument in the center of Riga and other historically significant locations that provided obvious settings for opposition gatherings and demonstrations.[18] Religion and folk traditions provided additional means of cohesion and communication, crucial resources for the mobilization of social movements, as noted by Sidney Tarrow, Charles Tilly, and others.[19]

In chapters 1 and 2 I conceptualized the democratization of the Soviet regime as revolving around both the horizontal and the vertical rearrangement of power. Whereas the emergence of autonomous mass movements in Latvia devolved power horizontally from party institutions, decentralization brought a vertical redistribution of power to Latvia from central Soviet authorities. Thus, in addition to the emergence of civil society through grass-roots movements, civil society was promoted by the emancipation of state-sponsored associations from the center. The Writers' Union of Latvia is a good case in point. It called a meeting with other artistic unions in June 1988 and produced a broad agenda for emancipation from the central bureaucracies in Moscow as well as from the tutelage of the CPSU.[20] Within a year, most professional and social organizations in Latvia had declared themselves independent from the all-union Soviet hierarchies.[21]

Under conditions of Soviet hypercentralism the autonomization of republic institutions and the articulation of regional interests signified more democratic political participation. Rather than discussing this development in more detail, however, I focus here on the emergence of altogether new grass-roots social movements. It is beyond the scope of this study to discuss to what extent true civil society can be created from the "restructuring" of state- and party-controlled institutions, except to note that a credibility gap emerges in those cases where the leading cadre remains the same and the legacy of old-time structures and patterns of behavior remains strong.[22]

In this chapter I focus on the organizational emergence of grass-roots movements; the broad repertoire of other democratic activism that emerged in the "era of awakening"[23] is analyzed in-depth in chapter 5. Here and there, I highlight the links between democracy building and the awakening of a twofold national identity—the identity of Latvians as an ethnonational community and as an ethnoplural civic nation.

The Emergence of Grass-Roots Social Movements in Latvia

For democracy to work, political participation must become self-generated. A new kind of political activism from below emerged in 1987 in Latvia and began to flourish by 1988 and 1989. The activity of grass-roots movements was notable throughout the USSR, but Baltic groupings often served as models to be copied elsewhere. The Lithuanians, Latvians, and Estonians also triggered impulses in each other with regard to specific forms of popular activism, be they mass demonstrations, petition drives, or support for draft avoidance. During the various phases of the struggle for independence, one or the other of the three Baltic states moved to the forefront in initiating challenges to Soviet rule. Although in later years Latvia often followed the lead of Estonia or Lithuania, it led in developing activist grass-roots movements in 1986, most notably with the Helsinki 86 group and the Environmental Protection Club.

THE PIONEER GROUPS

The first steps are the most difficult. The pioneers of grass-roots activism in Latvia had to create new forms of social organization in addition to overcoming psychological barriers of apathy and fear created during Soviet rule. National cultural traditions as well as political symbols from the history of the Latvian nation became important catalysts for achieving this.

Among cultural traditions two stand out as significant for the rebirth of national identity in Latvia. For one, Latvian folksongs and folklore have always constituted the basis of the sense of beauty and meaning of being Latvian. In the 1980s folk music ensembles and individual enthusiasts began to revive these traditions. They were so successful that people began to refer to events in Latvia as "the singing revolution." The link between civic and folkloristic identity was highly evident during the Baltica 88 folk festival in Riga in July 1988. Flags of independent Latvia, Estonia, and Lithuania were featured prominently, and the *New York Times*, commenting on the mass choral participation, described the festival as "an exuberant nationalist rally."[24]

The other core aspect of a constructive traditional Latvian identity has been the deep appreciation of nature and the duty to preserve one's history and beautify one's environment. Although this can be done individually, there is a tradition of *talkas*, of neighbors joining together to help each other or work on communal projects. This tradition was revived in the mid-1980s by small informal groups and the Environmental Protection Club which organized activities to save old churches and historical memorials. Between 1984 and early 1988 more than one hundred *talkas* were conducted by enthusiasts;[25] according to the goal of the Environmental Protection Club these *talkas* were intended "to activate citizens for practical work to preserve their environment and monuments."[26] The club also mobilized people against environmentally destructive government projects such as a hydroelectric dam in 1986 and the Riga metro in 1988. Both projects were stopped. In September 1988 ten thousand people demonstrated at places along the Baltic Sea to protest pollution there. By March 1989 the club boasted some thirty-five hundred members, mostly young people, but there were many more informal supporters.[27]

The political history of the reform era in Latvia started when workers in Liepāja founded the Helsinki 86 human rights group in 1986. Its most significant political contribution was to raise the issue of Latvia's political past as an independent state and as a victim of Soviet oppression, which it did by issuing statements and marking politically significant holidays at symbolic places. The high point of the group's activity came on 14 June 1987 when, despite the arrest of its leaders,[28] the group organized several thousand demonstrators to march to the Freedom Monument in Riga, lay flowers, and give short speeches. Although the monument itself and its inscription "For Fatherland and Freedom" symbolize the aspirations of the Republic of Latvia, 14 June marks the darkest day for Latvia in recent memory, being the day when thousands of citizens were brutally torn from their homes and deported to Siberia in 1941. Although other demonstrations were to follow—most notably those marking the signing of the Hitler-Stalin pact on 23 August 1939 and the anniversary of the declaration of Latvia's independence on 18 November 1918—this first large-scale demonstration was the spark that ignited further activities. The demonstrators set a precedent by declaring their views without fear in the face of arrests and other repression, and they also set a precedent for success because news of the demonstration spread like wildfire.[29] The Helsinki 86 movement was started by blue-collar workers, but they were soon joined by other activists, including several prominent dissidents. This served as an auspicious reminder that throughout the dark years of Soviet oppression small groups of dissidents had been pioneers at self-organization and had paid for it dearly by being sent to Soviet labor camps or mental hospitals.[30] The death in April 1988 of the most outstanding Latvian dissident, Gunārs Astra, who had spent nineteen years in Soviet prisons, provided a tragic rallying point for people inspired by his uncompromising stand. Between eight and ten thousand people participated in his funeral[31] and joined in filling his grave with handfuls of soil. But the event's message extended beyond symbolism as people talked about Astra's work and repeated his courageous speech from his last trial in 1983, where he protested the oppression of Latvian culture and rights and stated, "I know that these times will pass like a bad nightmare passes."[32]

The late 1980s became known as the "awakening" of the Latvian nation. Parallel to the awakening in the ethnocultural and political spheres, religious freedom became a central issue in the emergence of civil society in Latvia in 1987. The Soviet regime denied churches the right to conduct their own affairs and one of its means of doing so was the Council for Religious Affairs in Moscow and its local subsidiaries. A confrontation between the Council for Religious Affairs in Latvia and a religious rights movement headed by young Lutheran pastors became a catalyst for change both within the religious sphere and in society as a whole.

The religious rights movement began in 1983 with a spiritual revival among a group of pastors and lecturers at the Lutheran Theological Seminary, but by early 1987 it included a clash with the state and the subservient leadership of the Lutheran Church of Latvia. The crisis was precipitated when the state's commissioner for religious affairs denied a license to one young pastor and then revoked the license of another pastor, Modris Plāte, who had come to the defense of his young colleague. Without the state's license, the work of the pastors was illegal. Although the church leadership went along with this pressure, the young clergymen refused to do so and continued their pastoral work. They were supported by two dozen other clergymen and Pastor Plāte's congregation in Kuldīga, where he was immensely popular due to his innovative services, Bible study courses, concerts of religious music, and renovation of the church. The human rights group Helsinki 86 also sent protests on this issue to the signatory states of the Helsinki Agreement.[33]

Strengthening the tradition of symbolically important dates, Pastor Plāte and fourteen of his supporters in the Lutheran Church of Latvia founded the Rebirth and Renewal group on 14 June 1987. Its aim was "to defend openly the right of Latvians to lead a Christian life,"[34] to revise the Law on Religious Associations in the Latvian SSR, and to strengthen democratic processes within the church. Among the issues raised were religious instruction for children, legal rights for the church, access to state radio and television, publication of more religious literature, the authorization of religious activities in hospitals and old people's homes, and alternative military service for religious believers. The group's activities were met by repression from the church leadership and state authorities. The members of Rebirth and Renewal fought back in sermons and by issuing public appeals. In early 1988 the group scored a partial victory when repression against it stopped and the Lutheran Church in Latvia underwent some reform.[35] Yet its main victory was that of having contributed to the emergence of a genuinely democratic society where people, on their own, stand up for their beliefs and rights.

THE LEAGUE OF WOMEN

In Latvia one of the most impressive success stories of grass-roots activism and civil disobedience involves the League of Women's struggle against abuses committed by the Soviet military forces. It is a prime example of fostering civil society by challenging an imposing state institution to observe the rights of individual citizens. By its insistent and innovative emphasis on law and human rights, the league also contributed to the strengthening of a new democratic political culture. As the survey data later in this chapter show, the league soon became one of the most highly regarded social organizations in Latvia. It made its mark by undertaking concrete work and taking risks. In the words of the chairwoman of the league, "the men talked about nonviolent resistance, but we engaged in it."[36]

The League of Women of Latvia emerged in early 1989 as a movement in defense of the rights of draftees. Individual young men had resisted being drafted into the Soviet military before 1989, and some had urged the creation of alternatives to military service, but it took the league to launch a concerted effort. The movement emerged when women, at first mostly mothers of draft-age boys, saw the need to protect their sons from illegal acts of the Soviet military. The immediate issues raised were the mistreatment of soldiers and the need for an alternative service option, but the broader issue concerned the unacceptability of Balts being drafted into the army of an occupying power.

The activities of the League of Women were focused at the grass-roots level to provide concrete help for individual soldiers. The Soviet army has a tradition of brutally hazing new recruits,[37] but as the Baltic efforts to regain independence accelerated, mistreatment of draftees from the Baltics—both native and Russian—increased noticeably. The league took on the responsibility of documenting and preventing instances of brutal mistreatment that included murder. If mistreatment was suspected, the women first made every effort to speak to the immediate superiors of the soldiers, seeking redress through official Soviet army channels. Sometimes these efforts met with success. More often than not, however, appeals had to be made to higher officials or to legal authorities. The league co-opted numerous lawyers and medical personnel and worked in Latvia and various regions of the USSR to prove mistreatment and defend draftees against unjustified charges. When soldiers were returned to their parents in closed zinc coffins, the league members insisted on opening the coffins and ordering an independent medical examination to document their case.

As conditions in the USSR deteriorated, more and more young men deserted from the Soviet military or evaded the draft altogether. The league worked in their defense and established a network of safe houses for hiding these boys. Families and individual volunteers all across Latvia joined in. At the height of their activities between 1990 and summer 1991 there was a core of more than five hundred volunteers,[38] with many more unknown persons helping in individual cases. Due to the nature of the work, illegal according to Soviet law, many of these people remained anonymous.[39]

The activists in Latvia pioneered resistance to abuses in the Soviet military, but soon women all over the USSR joined the effort. The grass-roots activity targeted the ethos of the Soviet army and conditions within it. Following the example of the League of Women in Latvia, groups in other regions documented dozens of instances of physical and psychological abuse.[40] Cooperation across the Soviet Union was good and the league assisted both Latvian and non-Latvian soldiers who had been drafted from Latvia, as well as others who showed up in Latvia, regardless of their ethnicity. Truck drivers were told to be on the lookout for lost and helpless deserters trying to hide in the countryside. Drivers brought dozens of young

Ukrainians, Uzbeks, and others to the league, which then hid them with the help of the underground network of Latvian families.

The league also worked for legislative change and was the primary force behind the law on alternative service to the draft passed in Latvia on 1 March 1990.[41] The first version of the law allowed alternative service only for reasons of religious or pacifist conviction, but amendments passed on 15 May and 2 October 1990 broadened this provision. Young men selecting alternative service mostly performed low-paid but much needed work as orderlies in hospitals and first-aid stations,[42] and later could serve their time in many branches of the economy. Even though alternative service was legal according to Latvian law, representatives of the Soviet military often hounded the young men, leaving to the league the task of helping them and documenting their cases.

In addition to providing support for draft-age men and involvement in legislative advocacy, the league focused on gathering information and presenting it to the government, mass media, and international human rights organizations. It also organized public meetings in support of draft resisters. Some six thousand people attended one such meeting on 11 January 1991. They were addressed by Marina Kostenecka, a Russian living in Latvia, who argued that the draft-resistance movement in Latvia had natural allies in Russia where many mothers also did not want their sons to serve in the army.[43]

League activists were primarily women, in part because the movement was founded by mothers of abused soldiers, but also because men were seen as being more vulnerable to retaliation. Most men in Latvia had served in the Soviet armed forces and could be recalled to active service or otherwise harassed more easily than women. The women activists also felt that they had the psychological and moral upper hand when dealing with Soviet military authorities. Many officers did not know how to react to assertive women confronting them in such unexpected ways.[44]

Although the league made no distinctions among those it aided, its activists were predominantly Latvians. In part this can be explained by differential attitudes toward service in the Soviet military evident from various surveys. When asked in early 1990 whether Latvians should serve in the armed forces of the USSR, only 7 percent of Latvian respondents said "yes" compared with 48 percent of non-Latvians; 31 percent of non-Latvians said "no" compared with 85 percent of Latvians.[45] In addition, the director of the league noted that Russian women had difficulty with the idea of nonstate organizations and that even those Russian mothers who turned to the league for help tended to interact with the league as if it were an official institution rather than a volunteer group. By 1991 the league helped mostly Russian soldiers who had been drafted from Latvia, because few Latvians remained in the Soviet armed forces. After the regaining of independence, when no one was drafted into the Soviet army from Latvia but the army remained stationed there, the league continued to assist mistreated Russian soldiers seeking its help. It also turned its attention to the young men joining the nascent armed forces of Latvia.

In retrospect the draft-resistance movement appears more significant than has been acknowledged so far. It dared to challenge a pillar of Soviet power, the armed forces, and it did so by emphasizing legality, nonviolence, and civic responsibility. If the values of civil society are solidarity and voluntary work on the behalf of others, then the League of Women made a huge contribution to the building of such a society both in Latvia and beyond its borders. It demanded that the Soviet military authorities be held account-able for their actions and put them on the moral defensive by relying on civility, legal procedure, and public awareness as their means of action. It demonstrated that dedicated efforts of citizens joining together in a cause could make a difference. Although the movement was started by individ-uals, these initiatives soon gained mass support[46] and led to legislative action. Even though draft resisters pointed out Latvian laws on alternative service and the Geneva Convention of 1949 concerning the illegality of drafting in occupied territories, their resistance was deemed illegal and penalized by Soviet authorities. Soviet draft boards and newspapers used threatening language[47] and staged raids to look for draft-age men not com-plying with their orders.

One could even say that the draft issue changed the course of history when the Soviet Ministry of Defense announced on 7 January 1991 that it was sending elite paratroop units to Latvia and Lithuania to arrest draft resisters and deserters.[48] When countered by civil disobedience, the units attacked civilians in Vilnius and later in Riga. In doing so they in effect signed the death warrant of the USSR because popular revulsion against the crackdowns was so widespread that the old regime lost its last threads of legitimacy, leading to its formal defeat in the course of the August 1991 putsch attempt.

THE NATIONAL INDEPENDENCE MOVEMENT OF LATVIA

As its name indicates, the National Independence Movement of Latvia was characterized by an emphasis on independence and national goals and its greatest achievement was that it raised these issues at a time when others were ambivalent and fearful. In July 1988 dozens of people who had previ-ously worked in the political underground or in nascent social movements joined together publicly to found the new movement. Immediately its core aim was defined as the restoration of the independence of the Republic of Latvia founded in 1918.[49] The emphasis on the restoration of the Latvian state rather than the creation of a new sovereignty (as initially proposed by the Popular Front) was seen as crucial for making a clear legal claim against Soviet occupation and its consequences. Emphasizing continuity with the interwar democracy was also seen as basic for restoring national pride and a consciousness of the value of self-rule among the Latvian people.[50]

The Independence Movement immediately became the target of attacks by hard-line Communists and the Soviet press.[51] Administrative harassment was used to try to prevent meetings, and in early 1989 the authorities tried to find pretexts for a legal ban, but were outmaneuvered by the movement's swift adjustment of ambiguous articles in its statutes. The movement soon became an impressive organizational force with local branches all over Latvia. The number of registered members grew from six hundred in late July 1988 to eleven thousand by November 1989. The membership included many people from rural areas and with blue-collar backgrounds, some of whom had been denied higher levels of formal education because of their allegedly anti-Soviet outlook or activities. Compared with the Popular Front, the Independence Movement included significantly fewer establishment intellectuals.[52]

Aside from adopting an unwavering stand for the restoration of the Republic of Latvia, the Independence Movement focused on informing people about historical and political facts hidden by the propaganda machine of the CPSU. As far as its limited means permitted, the movement funded lectures, pamphlets, and its own newspaper. In 1989 it sponsored an international conference about the consequences of the secret protocols of the Hitler-Stalin pact of August 1939.[53] Independence Movement leaders such as the composer Imants Kalniņš were among the first to give voice to the frustration of countless Latvians at their intolerable ethnic situation. One example mentioned was the Soviet policy on residence permits that encouraged retired Soviet officers and others to settle in Riga to the point that Latvians had been turned into a minority of about 30 percent of Riga's population.[54] When raising issues like these, the movement was careful to place the blame on Soviet policymakers rather than the individuals affected. Thus the Council of the Independence Movement adopted a statement saying: "Our enemy is not other states and nations, but the power apparatus of the CPSU that has subjugated other states and nations."[55] All of this served as a stimulus for public dialogue and the crystallization of new policy options.

The Independence Movement organized numerous activities such as the picketing of the Soviet nuclear radar base at Skrunda in July 1989 and later, and the registration of citizens.[56] Organizationally the movement retained a separate existence, yet it was open to cooperation with other movements, most notably the Citizens' Committees as well as the Popular Front. Cooperation was especially close in rural localities with few politically active individuals.

CITIZENS' COMMITTEES

Another innovative strategy of political mobilization that came to the fore in 1989 was the creation of Citizens' Committees. The idea was to create independent political structures, legally rooted in the citizenry of the Republic of Latvia, parallel to the institutions of the Soviet Socialist Republic of Latvia then undergoing restructuring. The idea first arose in Estonia, but by April 1989 the National Independence Movement of Latvia, the Environmental Protection Club, Helsinki 86, and the Radical Groups of the Popular Front joined to form a coordination center for citizen registration. Legal citizens were defined as people who were citizens of the Republic of Latvia on the day of the Soviet invasion (17 June 1940), and their descendants. When critics argued that insisting on legal citizenship alone would aggravate ethnic relations with recent immigrants, the movement responded by allowing people who wished to become citizens to register as citizen candidates. Citizens' Committees were formed, and in April 1990 "a congress of the legal representatives of the Republic of Latvia, the citizens of Latvia" was elected. The movement emphasized that all politics would come to naught unless it was based on the recognition that Latvia had been illegally occupied in June 1940 and that the consequences of this occupation had to be dealt with. Aside from the value of legal continuity,[57] the emphasis on citizenship was also seen as the only way to gain fair representation of the interests of Latvians as a nation.[58]

Movement leaders emphasized international law and the fact that the United States and most other democracies of the world regarded the annexation of the Baltic states to be illegal and had retained de jure recognition of them.[59] The Citizens' Congress also pointed to tenets of international law such as the Geneva Convention of 1949 on Occupied Territories, which outlaws deliberate colonization and other practices.[60] Therefore, congress members argued, only citizens and their descendants could decide the future of Latvia. Rejecting the Soviet system outright, the Citizens' Movement argued that a gradual transformation of the Soviet system from within was impossible and any compromise with it immoral. The attempt to use perestroika to gain sovereignty step by step in confrontation with Moscow was seen as doomed to failure. Even worse, it was seen as being based on the hidden agenda of reform Communists to undermine true independence and popular power. Therefore the citizens of Latvia had a duty to create their own representation and struggle for the reconstitution of their legal state.[61]

At first the Citizens' Committees were highly successful and established an impressive grass-roots registration drive. Thousands of citizens registered, even though the movement was denied access to official media and had to rely on limited exposure in the informal press, local initiatives by word of mouth, and people going from door to door. In July 1989 the Supreme Soviet of the Latvian SSR passed a decree calling the Citizens' Committees illegal and initiating administrative measures to halt their activities.[62] Nevertheless, the movement prospered. In April 1990 some 707,000 people who had registered as citizens and 29,000 citizen candidates voted for representatives to the Citizens' Congress. Its first session convened on 30 April 1990 and elected a fifty-member Committee of Latvia as a standing body.

After its success at building popular representative structures from below and fostering mass consciousness of legal issues—certainly a part of a civil society—the Citizens' Movement failed to play a significant role in subsequent political events. It was much less influential than the parallel movement in Estonia, where the Citizens' Congress and the Popular Front found ways to cooperate despite principled antagonisms.[63] In Latvia both sides chose a confrontational position. Some Popular Front leaders accused the Citizens' Movement of being radical and bound to provoke a crackdown by Moscow. For their part the Citizens' Committees were wary of any compromise with the Popular Front's strategy of gaining control of Latvia's Soviet structures in order to transform them. Thus they criticized the elections to the Supreme Soviet on March 1990 as "illegal and undemocratic, because they are occurring in the presence of the occupying army, with the participation of its soldiers and the citizens of the occupying state."[64] Although many people sympathized with this critique, most supporters of the Citizens' Movement nevertheless went to the ballot box because they felt that in a situation of little choice an election boycott would in effect strengthen the pro-Moscow forces.

The Popular Front succeeded in gaining a majority in the Supreme Soviet of Latvia, which on 4 May 1990 proclaimed a transition period toward full independence. The Citizens' Congress continued to claim exclusive political legitimacy,[65] but in practice had become little more than a watchdog committee. Internal strife weakened the citizens' alternative power structures over time,[66] but their long-term success was that of having galvanized popular concern about the issue of legality and legitimacy.

POPULAR FRONT OF LATVIA
The Popular Front has played many roles in the transition from a Soviet regime in Latvia. Here I discuss its role as a social movement contributing to the strengthening of civil society; in the next chapter I analyze its role as a catalyst of mass political mobilization and in the taking over of legislative power through electoral victories.

By early 1988 numerous grass-roots groupings ranging from musical ensembles and environmental clubs to political and religious movements had emerged. The Popular Front of Latvia (PFL) was founded as an umbrella organization for these "informal groups," but it soon took on the role of a national political movement. It was ambivalent in nature because it emerged partly as a genuine coalition of grass-roots groups and partly as a creation of perestroika from above. This dualistic origin led to internal tensions and indecisiveness regarding what goals to pursue.

The first initiative for the formation of a popular front came from below, when seventeen activists from the environmental movement, the human rights group Helsinki 86, clergy, and others signed an appeal to that effect in mid-1988. Yet the leader of the Writers' Union, Jānis Peters, along with other establishment intellectuals quickly moved to take charge. The first president of the Popular Front, Dainis Īvāns, later had this to say about the founding document: "The first variant was signed in the name of Helsinki 86 and other informal groups. My signature was also there. But evidently someone did not like the surnames and organizations listed under the invitation. Hence a 'new' document was published—in reality the same text with the signatures of different people."[67] The new activists included reform Communists eager to co-opt the mass movements and win their support for perestroika. As noted earlier, the idea of popular fronts, or "popular movements for perestroika" as they were called in Ukraine, Lithuania, and elsewhere, found support in reformist forces within the CPSU eager to engage the populace as a force of change. This was emphasized in a statement of the Bureau of the Latvian Communist Party Central Committee in late September 1988, yet the same statement pointedly noted that some of the groups within the front "include elements that are evoking justifiable concern among the republic's working people."[68]

Rein Taagepera has argued that the conjunction of three interests led to the founding of popular fronts in the Baltic: Moscow had an interest in promoting limited reform in the republics; the republic governments were interested in preventing a radicalization of the population; and the emerging alternative elite was interested in finding a means to enter into a dialogue with the authorities.[69] The last aspect explains why the National Independence Movement of Latvia and other groups joined in the Popular Front after tough negotiations.[70] Yet, despite compromise, an unease persisted between the more radical wing of the PFL and people who had made their careers within the Communist party. Patriots of the Republic of Latvia especially objected that the PFL's first program spoke of "sovereignty" for the Latvian Soviet Socialist Republic rather than the restoration of the independent Republic of Latvia.[71] Paradoxically, such criticism strengthened the Popular Front because it made it more acceptable to reformers within the regime while at the same time pushing the PFL to adopt a clear pro-independence stand at its second congress in 1989.[72]

By spring 1989 the Popular Front of Latvia registered 230,000 members[73] out of a total population of 2.7 million. It became a strong voice for democratic reform and Latvian independence, with the initial emphasis being on economic and political autonomy within the USSR. Among the issues raised were ecological devastation, continuing disregard by Soviet authorities of human and civil rights, and longstanding ethnic problems. Among the latter, the PFL raised national concerns of Latvians as well as those of ethnic minorities. Two of the initial problems raised in regard to the Latvian nation were the diminution of the Latvian language in public life and the tremendous demographic imbalance due to uncontrolled immigration of non-Latvians. The census of 1989 showed that Latvians had become a minority in all cities and were close to becoming so in the country as a whole.[74] While raising these issues, the Popular Front rejected accusations by the Interfront that it was nationalist, arguing instead that one is a true internationalist only if one respects both one's own nation's and other nations' right to self-determination, cultural expression, and identity.[75]

In light of this approach the Popular Front sponsored the cultural revival of ethnic minorities in Latvia. It was part of Soviet nationality policy in Latvia to ignore the cultural rights of smaller extraterritorial ethnic groups; the PFL reversed this policy. It initiated the establishment of the first Jewish secondary school in postwar USSR, soon to be followed by other minority schools.[76] It also supported the formation of minority cultural centers and the founding of twenty-two cultural societies, including those supporting a revival of Russian culture and the Orthodox church.[77] It was the front's philosophy that multiculturalism and its expression in autonomous institutions was a means of promoting civil society. The Popular Front of Latvia has been especially supportive of Jewish cultural aspirations The weekly paper of the Latvian writers' and artists' union devoted an entire issue to Latvian Jewry.[78] In a 1990 interview Ruta Marjaša, a member of the board of the Jewish Cultural Society and a deputy in the Supreme Council, emphasized that Jews in Latvia were enjoying more cultural freedom, respect, and general rights than Jews in Moscow or Leningrad.[79]

The Popular Front worked deliberately to promote ethnic conciliation. One symbolic indication is that the PFL chose its name so as to reflect territory (that is, Latvia), rather than ethnicity. The front sponsored inter-ethnic dialogue through special discussion groups such as the Civic Harmony roundtable in Riga that outlined links between political democratization, market reform, and ethnic harmony.[80] A network of lecturers was set up to speak to non-Latvian audiences. The second chairman of the Popular Front, the Lithuanian Romualdas Ražukas, emphasized that the front had to explain the path toward independence to non-Latvians and that democrats from Russia should be invited to assist in this.[81] Seeing democratization in Latvia as linked with the democratization of the USSR was a hallmark of Popular Front politics. The PFL believed that direct exchanges with grass-roots movements all over the USSR were needed to promote democracy and better ethnic relations. In a typical initiative in July 1990 it established contact with the striking coal miners of the Kuzbass. A delegation of journalists returned with an extensive report on the situation there and also arranged a visit of Kuzbass miners to Latvia for the express purpose of meeting with Russians to explain their views.[82] In the same month thirty-six delegates representing some fifteen informal organizations in Moscow visited Latvia in order to inform non-Latvian audiences of developments in Russia.[83] The exchange of democratizing influences also included the participation of democrats from Latvia in the all-union legislature and the distribution of their own liberal media such as *Sovetskaia molodezh*, the Russian-language edition of the Popular Front weekly *Atmoda*, and others.[84]

The Popular Front not only established close ties to non-Latvian democrats inside and outside Latvia, it also provoked the founding of its political counterpart, the International Front of Workers of the Latvian SSR, or Interfront. Founded in October 1988, Interfront was dedicated to the defense of socialism and the unity of the USSR and emphasized the leading role of the CPSU.[85] In early 1990 an Interfront leader claimed that the organization had three hundred thousand members, including "maybe 12 percent" Latvians.[86] As a defender of the status quo and a close ally of official power structures, this group did little to promote civil society, except to galvanize activism among people frightened of its possible success.

OTHER GROUPS AND PARTIES

Although many non-Latvians participated in the movements discussed so far, some groups were founded primarily to represent the interests of Russians and "Russian-speakers." As early as summer 1988, the Balto-Slavic Society for Cultural Development and Cooperation was founded under the aegis of Russian, Belorussian, and Ukrainian cultural centers. Initiatives toward the formation of the Russian Community of Latvia emerged in the fall of 1991; it soon published its own newspaper and founded the private Technical University.[87] In spring 1992 Russians who were citizens of the interwar Latvian state formed the Economic Association of Russian Citizens of Latvia, which was primarily aimed at regaining property owned before incorporation in the USSR. According to its chairman, Vladimir Sorochin, the new association represented the interests of approximately two hundred thousand people in Latvia. Sorochin rejected the notion that all Russian-speakers were represented by Interfront, alluding to his group's special loyalty to the Republic of Latvia.[88]

Independent trade unions have always been one of the forms of civic association most resented by Leninist party functionaries. When Latvian workers began to organize their own unions in the fall of 1989, orthodox communists reacted with alarm, noting that "the creation of the LWU [Latvian Workers' Union] along lines similar to the Polish 'Solidarity' must ring alarm bells for trade union functionaries and republican trade union leaders."[89] Yet this did not deter the organizers. Another important civic group was the Association of Politically Repressed People, which represented individuals who had paid dearly for their political convictions and demanded that this would happen "never again."[90] The year 1990 also brought a proliferation of autonomous professional societies, economic enterprises, and political parties. In short, civil society was well on its way.

Who Supports What Groups?

For civil society to emerge it is not enough to have its institutions emerge; the populace has to identify with them and extend to them its active support. In the late 1980s surveys became a fashionable measure of public opinion in Latvia. Although it is difficult to establish in detail how reliable and valid individual surveys are, they appear to be useful in their overall thrust,[91] not least because they coincide with other data, such as electoral results and membership information.

As various surveys and membership data indicate, support for the building of civil society in Latvia has been stronger among the Latvian than the non-Latvian population. The gap first became evident from a survey conducted in November 1989 showing 51 percent of Latvian respondents saying that "informal groups help find ways to solve the problems of our republic," whereas 63 percent of non-Latvians stated that informal groups "only engage in extremist activities" (see Table A.3 in the Appendix). The survey also revealed differential exposure to informal groups, as the percentage of non-Latvians "making use of meetings and activities of informal groups to gain information about topical issues in the life of our republic"[92] was significantly lower than that among Latvians. In addition the differential involvement with the informal groups can be explained by the ethnic communal and civic symbolism involved. More Latvians than non-Latvians identified with the symbols of Latvia's independence, whereas many postwar settlers believed the Communist critique of "bourgeois" Latvia. In addition, most postwar settlers came to Latvia as individuals and as a result have had fewer communal, religious, or historical ties to build upon in the formation of civil society. Those organizations that did emerge with time, such as Interfront, did not evolve from the community itself, but were instituted by the Communist party. As Table 4.1 indicates, they never achieved a level of popular support comparable to that of the genuine grass-roots movements.

Table 4.1 also illustrates that Latvians and non-Latvians differ in the intensity of their support for various organizations, but one should note that a sizable segment of the non-Latvian population has supported movements focusing on Latvia. This should be no surprise to social scientists, who have

Table 4.1
Support for Political Movements, by Nationality

Latvians Supporting Political Movements

Movements	Sept. 1990 (n = 411) (percent)	June 1991 (n = 491) (percent)	Sept. 1991 (n = 448) (percent)
Popular Front	84	83	76
Environmental Protection Club	77	—	—
League of Women	75	76	67
Independence Movement	55	56	33
Cultural Societies	67	—	—
Citizens' Congress	—	16	—
Interfront	3	3	—

Russians and Others Supporting Political Movements

Movements	Sept. 1990 (n = 429) (percent)	June 1991 (n = 449) (percent)	Sept. 1991 (n = 384) (percent)
Popular Front	42	43	24
Environmental Protection Club	46	—	—
League of Women	32	36	25
Independence Movement	10	13	3
Cultural Societies	47	—	—
Citizens' Congress	—	3	—
Interfront	27	22	—

Source: Social Research Center of Latvia. n = number; — = data not available.

long known that single-issue politics is rare and that people typically have a variety of political interests and beliefs. Ideally, a political organization will represent multiple goals, and compromise on the basis of crosscutting loyalties will come into play. For example, ideally a Russian supporter of the Popular Front of Latvia supports its political, economic, and ethnic programs in their entirety, but he or she may also support the Popular Front even if only to support its overall political and economic goals. Whatever the reasons, there was a basis for a political coalition between Latvian-oriented movements and the non-Latvian populace.

After nationality, age stands out next in prominence among factors affecting differential support for various social movements. As Table 4.2 illustrates, the generational gap is especially wide in regard to support for the Popular Front and Interfront, most poignantly so among non-Latvians. Among young Russians and the category "others," support for the PFL is significantly higher than for the Interfront, whereas the reverse is true for the older generation. This huge age gap in political attitudes of Russians is consistent with the findings of most sociological surveys undertaken since the 1980s, for example the surveys reported in Table 2.1.[93]

As also indicated by Table 4.1, support for all of the movements decreased somewhat between September 1990 and 1991. Other data on the development of these and other grass-roots movements since the restoration of Latvia's independence in August 1991 confirm the trend toward decreased activism and popular enthusiasm for such movements. A detailed analysis of this development is beyond the scope of this volume, but a preliminary explanation is suggested by analysts of transitions to democracy. As these analysts have emphasized, one should differentiate between the phase of a regime's breakdown, the phase of transition to democracy, and the subsequent phase of the stabilization of a new political system.[94] The politics of each phase is distinctive. During the transitional phase the activism of grass-roots movements is crucial for undercutting the nondemocratic structures of the old regime and for galvanizing the emergence of a civil society. Once this goal is achieved and a new regime is formally instituted, new political institutions such as traditional political parties, interest groups, and a democratically elected parliament should take the lead in representing the popular will. This does not mean that there is no room for grass-roots movements. Even stable democracies require impulses "from below" to remain vital, but popular movements lack the primary democratizing role that they have during the transition phase and therefore fade into the background.

Conclusion

A civil society, democracy at the grass roots, and a participatory political culture are crucial for the transition from a Communist system. Yet these

Table 4.2
Support for Political Movements, by Nationality and Age
(September 1990)

	Latvians (n = 411)			
Age	Popular Front (percent)	Independence Movement (percent)	Cultural Societies (percent)	Interfront (percent)
Under 21	95	74	79	0
21–30	85	57	64	2
31–40	84	59	64	2
41–50	79	47	66	4
51–60	90	48	70	9
61 and older	79	59	72	6
	Russians and Others (n = 429)			
Age	Popular Front (percent)	Independence Movement (percent)	Cultural Societies (percent)	Interfront (percent)
Under 21	55	23	54	23
21–30	47	12	42	16
31–40	43	11	47	22
41–50	44	8	47	23
51–60	34	8	53	38
61 and older	29	8	51	52

Source: Social Research Center of Latvia. n = number.

qualifications are difficult to achieve in a context where the opposite values have been promoted for years by the system that is to be overcome. The "leading role" of the Communist party meant more than a patronizing usurpation of the right to social and political initiative; it in effect criminalized all alternative initiatives. Any autonomous grouping was seen as a threat to the regime and efforts were made to squash it. Therefore the emergence of group pluralism in Latvia and elsewhere in the late 1980s was nothing less than a revolutionary development. Although reform policies from above opened the door for this change, it was carried forward by many small groups taking advantage of the opportunity presented and creating an irresistible momentum for change. The interplay of various political forces and the adjustment of agendas over time mark when democratic politics begin to exist. In this sense the turning point in Latvia came in 1988 with the founding of the Popular Front as a coalition movement between autonomous pioneer groups and party reformists.

The Latvian case illustrates democratic self-organization from below and shows how ethnic identity and issues formed a driving force in a close symbiosis with concern over the environment, human and civil rights, religious freedom, and defense against abuses of state power. Once the fear induced by years of political terror began to dissipate, autonomous social and political activity flourished. In Latvia, this quest for democracy was closely tied to a reassertion of ethnic communal identity and patriotism for the Republic of Latvia. The symbols of national identity and the interwar state emerged as catalysts for the rejection of the symbols and reality of Soviet rule. Although anyone can organize a demonstration to commemorate the victims of Stalinist terror, such a demonstration becomes politically more potent when held, as it was in Latvia, at the Latvian equivalent of the Statue of Liberty—the Freedom Monument in the center of Riga. This joining of civic and national messages was the spark that, on 14 June 1987, ignited the commitment of an entire nation for years to come.

NOTES

1. Intermediary groups have been seen as bulwarks against totalitarianism by many, for example William Kornhauser, *The Politics of Mass Society* (Glencoe, Ill.: Free Press, 1959).
2. Alexis de Toqueville, *Democracy in America*, ed. J. P. Mayer and Max Lerner (New York: Harper and Row, 1966).
3. Samuel P. Huntington, "Will More Countries Become Democratic?" *Political Science Quarterly* 99, no. 2 (Summer 1984): 203.
4. Daniel H. Levine, "Paradigm Lost: Dependence to Democracy," *World Politics* 40 (April 1988): 388.
5. Tun-jen Cheng, "Democratizing the Quasi-Leninist Regime in Taiwan," *World Politics* (July 1989): 471.
6. Juan Linz, "Transitions to Democracy," *Washington Quarterly* (Summer 1990): 152.
7. George Schöpflin, "Post-communism: Constructing New Democracies in Central Europe," *International Affairs* 67, no. 2 (1991): 241; Levine, "Paradigm Lost," 388.
8. Cheng, "Democratizing"; on the role of the middle class see also Barrington Moore, Jr., *Social Origins of Dictatorship and Democracy* (Boston: Beacon Press, 1986), especially 418.
9. Hania M. Fedorowicz, "Civil Society in Poland: Laboratory for Democratization in Central Europe," *Plural Societies* 21 (1990): 155–76.
10. See Václav Havel et al., *The Power of the Powerless* (Armonk, N.Y.: Sharpe, 1985), and the special issue on Poland in *Telos* 47 (1981).
11. Huntington, "Will More Countries Become Democratic?" 203.
12. See Rasma Karklins, *Ethnic Relations in the USSR: The Perspective from Below* (London and Boston: Allen and Unwin, 1986), chap. 7.
13. Donald L. Horowitz, "How to Begin Thinking Comparatively about Soviet Ethnic Problems," in Alexander J. Motyl, ed., *Thinking Theoretically about Soviet Nationalities* (New York: Columbia University Press, 1992), 10.

14. Horowitz, "How to Begin Thinking Comparatively," 11.
15. Peter McDonough, Samuel H. Barnes, and Antonio Lopez Pina, "Authority and Association: Spanish Democracy in Comparative Perspective," *Journal of Politics* 46 (August 1984): 654.
16. McDonough et al., "Authority and Association," 660.
17. Movement programs and other primary documents.
18. For analysis of a similar role played by marketplaces and anniversary dates in East Central Europe, see Rasma Karklins and Roger Petersen, "The Calculus of Protesters and Regimes: Eastern Europe 1989," *Journal of Politics* (August 1993): 588–614.
19. Sidney Tarrow, "'Aiming at a Moving Target': Social Science and the Recent Rebellions in Eastern Europe," *PS: Political Science & Politics* 24 (1991): 12–20; Charles Tilly, *From Mobilization to Revolution* (Englewood Cliffs, N.J.: Prentice-Hall, 1978).
20. Texts of all speeches in *Literatūra un Māksla*, 10 and 17 June, and 1 and 9 July 1988.
21. For example, the Cultural Fund of Latvia declared independence from the All-Union Cultural Fund in May 1989.
22. There is a popular saying about turncoats (in Latvian, literally "turning one's fur around") that has been used in numerous debates. In Latvia, young people appear to be especially cynical about the true democratic transformation of previously Soviet- and Moscow-controlled institutions. Author's observations on six research trips to Latvia between March 1990 and May 1993.
23. The notion of awakening referred back to similar historical events in the nineteenth century. See Andrejs Plakans, "The Latvians," in Edward C. Thaden, ed., *Russification in the Baltic Provinces and Finland, 1855–1914* (Princeton, Princeton: University Press, 1981), 207–86.
24. *New York Times*, 13 July 1988.
25. *Staburags*, journal of the Environmental Protection Club, 1988, no. 1: 8; some events were of a humorously symbolic nature, such as the "funeral" given to a traditional wooden building by cultural activists. "Bēres bez kapračiem," *Padomju Jaunatne*, 12 January 1988.
26. Article 2 of the statutes of the Environmental Protection Club of Latvia, *Staburags* 1988, no. 1: 5.
27. Interview with the chairman of the Environmental Protection Club, A. Ulme, *Cīņa*, 7 March 1989, 4. Nils Muiznieks, "The Daugavpils Hydro Station and Glasnost in Latvia," *Journal of Baltic Studies* 18 (Spring 1987): 63–70. On the debate about the Riga metro, see *Padomju Jaunatne*, 20 February 1988.
28. One of the leaders, L. Grantiņš, was sentenced to six months ordinary regime labor camp for supposedly avoiding reserve military duty. Other leaders were harassed and detained for shorter periods. *USSR News Brief* 1987, no. 11-12: 4–5.
29. Various press reports, especially *Christian Science Monitor*, 27 August 1987; also Egil Levits, "Lettland unter sowjetischer Herrschaft, Die politische Entwicklung 1940–1989," in Boris Meissner, ed., *Die Baltischen Nationen: Estland, Lettland, Litauen* (Cologne: Markus, 1990), especially 146–47.
30. Ādolfs Šilde, *Resistance Movement in Latvia* (Stockholm: The Latvian National Foundation, 1972); Ludmilla Alexeyeva, *Soviet Dissent: Contemporary Movements for National, Religious, and Human Rights* (Middletown, Conn.: Wesleyan University Press, 1985); S. P. de Boer, E. J. Driessen, and H. L. Verhaar, eds., *Biographical Dictionary of the Dissidents in the Soviet Union, 1956–1975* (The Hague: Martinus Nijhoff, 1982).
31. *Chronology of Events in Estonia, Latvia, and Lithuania in 1988*, Baltic Appeal to the United Nations (New York: n.p., n.d.), 3–4.
32. Pāvils Brūvers, "Gunārs Astra," in *Latvija Šodien* (Rockville, Md.: World Federation of Free Latvians, 1988), 30–31; Astra's famous speech of 1983 was published in *Atmoda*, 3 April 1989, 3.
33. Marite Sapiets, "'Rebirth and Renewal' in the Latvian Lutheran Church," *Religion in Communist Lands* 6 (Autumn 1988): 237–49.
34. Ibid., 242.

35. Ibid., 242–43 and 248–49.
36. Personal interview with Anita Stankēviča, 17 May 1992; for similar statements see interview with her in *Atmoda*, 10 September 1991, 11.
37. Cases of brutal hazing and desertion are described in *Atmoda*, 25 September 1989. See also Teresa Rakowska-Harmstone, "Baltic Nationalism and the Soviet Armed Forces," *Journal of Baltic Studies* 17 (Fall 1986): 191; Stephen M. Meyer, "How the Threat (and the Coup) Collapsed," *International Security* 16 (Winter 1991–92): 22.
38. By then other groups were beginning to organize, most prominent of these being the "Geneva 49" group of draft-resisters. *Neatkarība*, 23 March 1990, 3.
39. Personal interview with Stankēviča, 17 May 1992, and interview with her in *Atmoda*, 10 September 1991, 11.
40. See Rosamund Shreeves, "Mothers against the Draft: Women's Activism in the USSR," *Report on the USSR*, 21 September 1990, 3–8.
41. Text in *Cīņa*, 15 March 1990.
42. See *Moscow News*, 1991, no. 28.
43. *Laiks*, 16 January 1991, 5.
44. Personal interview with Stankēviča.
45. *Atmoda*, 26 June 1990, 11. Survey conducted between 17 and 22 May 1990, stratified random sample of 834 respondents. A joint Soviet-American survey conducted in December 1989 also found ethnicity to be a powerful shaper of political attitudes. One difference is in the attitude toward the Soviet army: when asked whether the Soviet army "always," "sometimes," or "never" acted in their interests, 29 percent of Russian respondents said "always" but no Balts thought so, 39 percent of Russians said "sometimes" compared with 17 percent of Balts, and 12 percent of Russians said "never" compared with an overwhelming 72 percent of Balts. Ellen Mickiewicz, "Ethnicity and Support: Findings from a Soviet-American Public Opinion Poll," *Journal of Soviet Nationalities* (Spring 1990): 140–47.
46. See Table 4.2.
47. For example, *Sovetskaia Latviia*, 1 November 1989, and *Krasnaia zvezda*, 13 April 1990, stated that draft evaders in Latvia were irresponsible simpletons who would end up behind bars.
48. *New York Times*, 9 January 1991.
49. *Neatkarība*, no. 1 (September 1988), 2–3.
50. Interviews with leaders of the movement and information from various publications.
51. Levits, "Lettland," 156.
52. *Neatkarība*, no. 1 (September 1988); author's interviews with the first chairman of the Independence Movement, Eduards Berklāvs, and administrative staff.
53. *Literatūra un Māksla*, 26 August 1989.
54. Imants Kalniņš, "Cita internacionalisma nav," speech at the founding congress of the Popular Front, 9 October 1988.
55. Statement of the Council of the National Independence Movement of Latvia (LNNK), 28 November 1989, *Informācijas Lapa* 1989, no. 44.
56. LNNK activists who participated in a Catholic celebration in Aglona registered eight hundred citizens. *LatNIA, Informatīvais Ziņotājs*, 24 August 1989.
57. *Atmoda*, 17 July 1989, p. 5.
58. See Latvijas TF Radikālās Apvienības Neatkarīgs Izdevums, *18. novembris*, no. 2 (1989), pp. 1–2; Aigars Jirgens, "Pilsoņu Kongress un Latvijas Republika," *Neatkarība*, 19 January 1989, 1; *Neatkarība*, 30 March 1990.
59. See William J. H. Hough III, "The Annexation of the Baltic States and Its Effect on the Development of Law Prohibiting Forcible Seizure of Territory," *New York Law School Journal of International and Comparative Law* 6 (Winter 1985); Boris Meissner, *Die Sowjetunion, die Baltischen Staaten und das Völkerrecht* (Cologne: Politik und Wirtschaft, 1956).
60. The text of the convention was published several times, for example in *Atmoda*, 7 August 1989, 5.

61. Author's interviews, and numerous speeches and documents of the Citizens' Congress, for example *Atmoda*, 31 July 1989, 1.
62. See *Izvestiia*, 13 July 1989, p. 13; Nils Muiznieks, "The Committee of Latvia: An Alternative Parliament?" *Report on the USSR*, 318/90, 20 July 1990, 29.
63. See Juri Luik, "Intellectuals and Their Two Paths to Restoring Civil Society in Estonia," in Zbigniew Rau, ed., *The Reemergence of Civil Society in Eastern Europe and the Soviet Union* (Boulder, Colo.: Westview Press, 1991), especially 90; Riina Kionka, "The Estonian Citizens' Committee: An Opposition Movement of a Different Complexion," *Report on the USSR*, 9 February 1990.
64. *Atmoda*, 13 February 1990.
65. One leader of the movement argued that only the Soviets had real power and everything else was a sham and self-delusion. Visvaldis Lācis, *Latvijas Jaunatne*, 4 July 1990, p. 1.
66. Agnis Balodis, *Atmoda*, 16 May 1991, p. 4; see also Muiznieks, "The Committee of Latvia: An Alternative Parliament?" 30.
67. *Jūrmala*, 20 October 1988, as cited in Juris Dreifelds, "Latvian National Rebirth," *Problems of Communism* (July-August 1989): 84; a very similar statement by Ivāns appeared in *Atmoda*, 2 October 1990, p. 8.
68. *Sovetskaia Latviia*, 1 October 1988, p. 2.
69. Rein Taagepera, "Estonia's Road to Independence," *Problems of Communism* (November-December 1989): 11-26. See also analysis of co-optation and other regime policies by Jim Butterfield and Marcia Weigle, "Unofficial Social Groups and Regime Response in the Soviet Union," in Judith B. Sedaitis and Jim Butterfield, eds., *Perestroika from Below: Social Movements in the Soviet Union* (Boulder, Colo.: Westview Press, 1991), 175-95.
70. Levits, "Lettland," 149.
71. See the statutes and program of the Popular Front of Latvia, *Rīgas Balss*, 17 and 19 October 1988; also *Sovetskaia Latviia*, 19 October 1988.
72. See the statutes and program of the Popular Front of Latvia as printed in *Atmoda*, 11 September 1989.
73. *Padomju Jaunatne*, 14 March 1989, p. 1.
74. For closer demographic analysis, see chapter 6 and Table 6.1.
75. See, for example, Viktors Daugmalis, "Homo Sovieticus un starpnacionālo attiecību problēma," *Literatūra un Māksla*, 9 December 1989.
76. See chapter 7.
77. For a full listing of societies see Aleksei Glubotskii, *Strany Baltii: Politicheskie partii i organizatsii* (Moscow: Panorama, 1992), 26-27; support for the groups is indicated in Tables 4.1 and 4.2.
78. *Literatūra un Māksla*, 25 November 1988.
79. *Atmoda*, 2 October 1990, p. 4; also, during a December 1989 congress in Moscow, 352 representatives of Jewish communities from all over the Soviet Union were surveyed and asked, "Do you believe that in your place of residence anti-Semitism with expressions of vandalism, cruelty, and violence could occur in the near future?" The highest response rate for "no" (60 percent) was registered for the three Baltic republics. Although 24 percent thought that such occurrences were possible in the Baltics, the percentage was much higher elsewhere: 54 percent in Moldavia, 67 percent in Belorussia, and 72 and 94 percent in Moscow and Leningrad, respectively. *Kultūras forums* 1990, no. 1: 6.
80. See a declaration by Civic Harmony in *Rīgas Balss*, 21 February 1990, p. 1.
81. *Atmoda*, 26 June 1990.
82. *Atmoda*, 7 August 1990.
83. *Latvijas Jaunatne*, 12 July 1990.
84. Russian-language newspapers and journals from Latvia were widely sought after by liberals throughout the Soviet Union. The Russian-language Latvian youth journal *Sovetskaia molodezh* increased its circulation from 139,000 to 325,000 between 1987 and 1988. Dreifelds, "Latvian National Rebirth," 91.
85. Glubotskii, *Strany Baltii*, 30.
86. *Sovetskaia Rossiia*, 24 February 1990, 2d ed., p. 3, as quoted in *FBIS-SOV-90-043*, 5 March 1990.

87. Glubotskii, *Strany Baltii*, 27, 40.
88. *Diena*, 13 February 1992.
89. *Sovetskaia Latviia*, 12 September 1989, p. 3.
90. Statutes of the organization and various issues of their newspaper, *Avīzīte*.
91. See the methodological note in the Appendix.
92. Original survey questions, see source listing for Table A.3.
93. The generational gap is also evident in the findings of the Soviet Interview Project conducted among emigrants in the early 1980s. See Rasma Karklins, "Soviet Elections Revisited: The Significance of Voter Abstention in Non-Competitive Voting," *American Political Science Review* 80 (June 1986): 449–69; James R. Millar, ed., *Politics, Work, and Daily Life in the USSR: A Survey of Former Soviet Citizens* (Cambridge: Cambridge University Press, 1987).
94. See, for example, Peter H. Smith, "Crisis and Democracy in Latin America," *World Politics* 43 (July 1991): 616.

5

⟹•◆•⟸

Mass Events and Elections as Catalysts of Democracy

B eginning in 1987 the Baltic states witnessed a wave of mass demonstrations and rallies that has few parallels in comparative political
history. In Latvia alone, thousands of people participated month after
month in numerous oppositional activities. Although this political participation was unprecedented in its intensity and scope, it was also innovative in
its broad repertoire, which included demonstrations and rallies, pickets and
petition-drives, congresses and roundtables, high turnout at elections and
plebiscites, and civil resistance to armed attacks. All of this undermined the
old regime while at the same time shaping the attitudinal and structural
preconditions of a new polity. How was such mass mobilization possible and
what did it mean?

Analysts of the transition to democracy focus on the origin and development of political opposition,[1] especially mass movements. In the preceding
chapter we discussed the emergence of social movements; here we focus on the
emergence and growth of mass activism. Adam Przeworski sees the formation
of autonomous organizations as crucial and states that "the campaign for
democracy must assume a mass character. Mass Movement is needed as a
means of pressure, and the street becomes the chief arena of expression in the
early stages, when no other channel exists."[2] He and others define large-scale
popular mobilization as a crucial component of the opening and eventual fall
of authoritarian regimes.[3] The experience in Latvia confirms this thesis and
shows the links between mass mobilization and institution building, especially

through elections. Moreover, the Latvian case highlights two motive forces of political mobilization, the expression of suppressed ethnic and civic identity and the reaction to past and present repression.

The Latvian experience also lends support to the thesis of the democratic-transitions literature positing that preconditions for change are often less crucial than the dynamics of the process of change.[4] Each new event in a string of interactions creates new and frequently unexpected outcomes. Recent writings on protest similarly analyze it not as a single event or several separate events, but rather as a process of strategic interaction.[5] The focus is on the dynamics of change as a process that unfolds in a certain sequence. Timing matters, as well.[6] As protesters gain initial successes and new coalitions of actors emerge, so does new power—protesters feel confident enough to make demands, and established elites become less sure of their right and ability to rule (see later in chapter for detailed discussion).

Political change is better explained by focusing on the action and interaction between masses and established power-holders than by the traditional Sovietological emphasis on institutions. Communist regimes were effective at the institutional organization of power, leading many democrats to despair of the possibility of change. Yet events in Eastern Europe in the fall of 1989 and the more protracted transformation in the USSR showed that new political power can be developed through innovative mass activism from below. Participation in itself is necessary if a democratic regime is to exist, but it is also a means for political change. Once mass activism begins, each new demonstration or petition drive urges the reform process along by changing the balance of power between popular forces and the regime. This chain reaction parallels the "political opportunity structure" model of transition from authoritarianism presented by Sidney Tarrow:

> Expanded political opportunities during waves of mobilization have effects at the citizen, group and elite levels: expanding the space within which ordinary citizens perceive that they can legitimately make claims; providing new opportunities for organizers to build movements with which to attract the support of these citizens and for existing movement organizations to increase their support; and offering new opportunities for elites *within* the polity to expand their influence and achieve their policy goals. It is the interaction among these elements that moves the cycle along from one phase to the next and determines its outcome.[7]

Even though popular demonstrations are crucial in democratic transitions, they may not suffice to change a regime. According to Juan Linz, it is not enough for disorganized people to demonstrate, because they "may be unable to negotiate a transfer or sharing of power, or processes to achieve such a goal, and may be pushed to intransigent positions, and, thus, their efforts will end if not in revolutions, then in repression."[8] This is why even the limited social pluralism of authoritarian regimes is so crucial for the transition to democracy: it creates alternative political groupings and leaders to take on the responsibility of governing. Alternative power elites may also emerge during a prolonged period of regime crisis[9] when the old elite experiments with reform and the opposition gains room to maneuver. This was the prevailing pattern in the declining Soviet Union and Latvia. As outlined in the preceding chapter, regime liberalization after 1986 allowed the self-organization of civil society from below. Emerging alternative groupings used the new semifree elections to catalyze popular mobilization and to strengthen themselves organizationally.

Elections bring forth alternative leaders, and electoral campaigns galvanize civic participation. Comparative experience serves as a surprisingly good guide to events in Latvia and the USSR. As noted in regard to new democracies in Latin America, "The intensity of electoral campaigns and voter participation throughout the 1980s, often conducted under hazardous conditions, indicates a remarkable willingness on the part of ordinary citizens to utilize ballots to express preferences, settle conflicts, and confer authority on leaders."[10]

In Latvia, the most decisive campaign was the March 1990 election to the republic's Supreme Soviet, won by the Popular Front coalition. In addition, the nonbinding plebiscite on Latvia's independence in March 1991 added legitimacy to the cause and served as another mobilizing exercise. Voter turnout and support for Latvia's independence reached an all-time high, in part due to revulsion toward the hard-line crackdown by Soviet forces just a few weeks earlier. This backlash phenomenon illustrates the theoretical proposition about new politics and power emerging from interaction between the populace and the regime, a proposition I expand on later in this chapter.

New popular assertiveness and power was even more evident in the widespread civil resistance to the January 1991 pro-Soviet coup attempts by the National Salvation Committees in Latvia and Lithuania. The putschists were supported by Soviet troops and special police, yet they were thwarted by the determination of thousands of unarmed citizens who formed human barriers around media centers and parliamentary buildings. Nonviolent civil resistance proved to be an effective expression of popular will and commitment to self-determination. It changed the political balance of power by laying bare the inappropriateness of regime violence. It discredited the coup-makers in the Baltics as well as their hard-line backers in Moscow. I discuss this event at the end of the chapter, but first outline the tide of political demonstrations and the mobilizing role of electoral campaigns.

Demonstrations and Mass Rallies

Between 1987 and 1991 a pattern of political demonstrations emerged in Latvia that was characterized by growing numbers of participants as well as an effective expression of popular will and power. The mass demonstrations did not lead to a swift change of political regime as they did in Eastern Europe in the fall of 1989, but eventually they achieved the same goal. They were effective in delegitimizing the Soviet regime and at the same time presenting an image of "the people" taking charge of their political fate. The keys to this effectiveness were the scope of demonstrations, their impressive organization, their peaceful and determined message, and a keen sense of advantage in interactions with the regime.

First, regarding the scope of demonstrations, the sheer number of participants was noteworthy from any perspective, and even more so when compared with population size. Whereas the first mass protest on 14 June 1987 involved between three to five thousand people, about one hundred thousand protested on the same date one year later. The 23 August 1988 rally in Riga had thirty to fifty thousand participants, and several demonstrations in 1989 and 1990 involved from a quarter to a half million people.[11] The total population of Latvia in 1989 was 2.7 million, of whom about 1.4 million were Latvians. Clearly, a large segment of the populace participated in the demonstrations.

The most impressive example of the Baltic popular will capturing world attention occurred on 23 August 1989. Between one and two million Estonians, Latvians, and Lithuanians joined hands and formed a human chain across the Baltic states to protest the consequences of the Hitler-Stalin pact on their nations. While protesting the continued impact of this infamous pact on its fiftieth anniversary, the Balts standing in this human chain also expressed their commitment to restoring their independent states. Known as the demonstration of the "Baltic Way," this human chain became a watershed in Baltic self-assertion. It was psychologically liberating and expressed a new political commitment, much like the first visit of Pope John Paul II to Poland in 1979.[12] As in Poland, the experience of being able to carry out without incident such a mass event also boosted organizational self-confidence. Bringing together so many people in a coordinated effort meant overcoming numerous problems of communication, transport, and order, and all of it was done efficiently.[13]

This and other demonstrations carried two kinds of messages. One was the explicit message stated by speakers and written on placards. The dominant demands were for an end to Soviet occupation and the restoration of Baltic independence and democracy. The other message was in the nature of the demonstrations themselves, that is, that these goals were to be attained peacefully and in a constructive manner. The protests deliberately emphasized peacefulness and aimed at building a sense of community and purpose among participants. The symbolism of people linking hands across the three Baltic countries is a prime illustration of this intent. Other symbolic actions involved moments of silence, the laying of flowers, and singing. A Swedish journalist had this comment about the 12 March 1989 demonstration in Riga: "The strongest impression of today's rally . . . was not the speakers, the flags, and the placards, but the calm and dignity with which the hundred of thousands of Latvians assembled listened to their new leaders and sang their old beloved songs."[14] A few days later, on 25 March 1989, between a quarter and half a million people from all over Latvia marched through the streets of Riga to mark the date in 1949 when tens of thousands of their countrypeople were forcibly deported to the labor camps of the Soviet Union. As recorded in the *New York Times*,

> In keeping with the Popular Front's tactic of restraint to avoid provoking the Russians, when the marchers stopped at the headquarters of the K.G.B., the Soviet security police, they stood in silence, their banners lowered. "It was raining and people were crying, but their silence was a much more powerful demonstration of our power than if they shouted," Mr. Ivans said.[15]

Comparative analysts too have argued that the restraint and nonviolence of the Baltic mobilization against Soviet rule showed strategical acumen and was one reason for its success.[16] The discipline of various demonstrations encouraged people to participate and discredited the Soviet depiction of them as a threat to public peace. The Soviet authorities reacted especially badly to the "hands across the Baltic" demonstration of August 1989. On 26 August the Central Committee of the CPSU accused the Balts of nationalist hysteria and threatened to roll in with tanks.[17] When Baltic opposition leaders repudiated this accusation, there was silence from the Kremlin followed by conciliatory statements.

As noted earlier, it is helpful to think of a series of protests as an interactive process. There is interaction between one demonstration and the next, and also between each demonstration and the authorities. Although most rallies in Latvia conveyed a positive message urging political change, many were reactive to past and present regime repression. The marking of anniversaries of the Hitler-Stalin pact or of the genocidal deportations of thousands of people to Siberia dramatized the illegitimacy of Soviet rule in Latvia. Other rallies were called in response to repressive moves by contemporary authorities. When the procuracy of Soviet Latvia tried to outlaw the Independence Movement, between 100,000 and 250,000 people demonstrated in protest on 12 March 1989. And, as will be noted later at greater length, when Soviet forces instituted a crackdown in January 1991 hundreds of thousands protested at rallies and by manning improvised street barricades.

The experience of January 1991 also illustrates that as the wave of mass activism became stronger in Latvia, repression became more and more costly and counterproductive. Although repressive moves against the first protests in 1987 and 1988 frightened some potential protesters away from participating, protesters felt more secure as their numbers grew and the legitimacy of their efforts increased. This enhanced self-assurance among demonstrators grew relative to the decreasing self-confidence of the regime. A similar process is noted by Giuseppe Di Palma in a discussion of events in Eastern Europe during 1989. He speaks of the loss of confidence of the established regimes and notes that it is reconfirmed by the activism of the populace: "Popular mobilization tended to *confirm* communist regimes in their belief that they had lost the right to rule—and hence to repress."[18]

In discussing the unprecedented rise of mass activism in Latvia one also needs to examine the resources and motives of the participants, two issues prominently featured in social science literature on collective action. Charles Tilly defines collective action as "joint action in pursuit of common goals"[19] and highlights the problem of resource mobilization. How do people know when a rally will be held, and where, and how do they get there? In Latvia, these issues were most significant for the first protests when resources were balanced unequally between protesters and the regime. The communication of schedules was facilitated by a knowledge of political anniversaries: 25 March and 14 June mark the dates of mass deportations to Siberia, 23 August marks the date of the Hitler-Stalin pact, and 18 November marks Latvia's Independence Day. Other dates symbolizing Latvia's independence or the introduction of Soviet rule are 17 June (Latvia is occupied in 1940), 21 July (Latvia is made a Soviet republic in 1940), 13 August (the Constitution of the Republic of Latvia is passed in 1922). As for the place of rallies, symbolic memorials and the urban architecture of Riga provided obvious settings: the Freedom Monument and Brethren's Cemetery, the large square around Riga's cathedral, and the open spaces by the banks of the Daugava River. Holding meetings on recurring dates and at the same locations helped resolve organizational and communication problems.

As for motives, the marking of politically symbolic anniversaries in itself expressed a rejection of the Soviet regime by participants as well as their commitment to Latvia's independence and democracy. Yet although this group motive was clear, the collective action literature notes that we have to explain why individuals participate in such events, especially if a danger of retribution exists.[20] Participation in the initial demonstrations in 1987 and 1988 certainly was dangerous, although by then the regime used repression in a more calculating manner than it had in the past. The simple answer is that courageous individuals placed the common good above their individual benefit and were willing to suffer if necessary. In addition, interaction within social groups motivates people to participate or abstain from demonstrations. Various studies have shown that membership in groups has a positive influence on collective political action. Friends or colleagues act as reference groups and thus motivate each other.[21] This process is even more pronounced in the case of collective action with an ethnic dimension, because by definition ethnic goals refer to group interests rather than individual interests. Although in the final analysis individuals decide whether or not to participate in a given demonstration, ethnic and other face-to-face groups influence their decision.[22] This was most significant in the later period of protest, when peer pressure greatly encouraged participation in these mass events. Increasingly, participation in rallies became a form of pleasurable social interaction, for example when local groups of the Popular Front of Latvia sent busloads of people to Lithuania at the time of Gorbachev's visit in January 1990. Furthermore, as the tide of protests rose higher, each event was accompanied by domestic and international media exposure, reinforcing the motives for participation.

Petitions and Pickets

The mobilization of popular will in Latvia also involved the signing of petitions, the passing of resolutions at workplaces, and picketing. Petition drives produced impressive numbers of signatures. In the course of a newspaper debate in the fall of 1988 about the need to establish Latvian as the state language of Latvia, more than three hundred thousand people signed their names to letters and appeals supporting such a policy.[23] Also in the fall of 1988, nearly a million people in Latvia signed petitions against proposed changes to the Soviet Constitution and electoral law, fearing that the changes would restrict rather than expand democratic and republic rights. The effort was spearheaded by the Popular Front, and similar efforts were undertaken in Estonia and Lithuania. The petitions were addressed to Soviet authorities in Moscow, but meetings were also held with Latvia's deputies to the Soviet legislature to persuade them to support the move. The Baltic deputies did carry the initiative forward, in modified form, but had little impact in the Supreme Soviet of the USSR.[24] Although the lack of success in Moscow could be interpreted as a failure of initiatives from below, the lack of responsiveness of Soviet state bodies ultimately reinforced Baltic determination to restore independence.

In a similar campaign in late 1990, the Popular Front of Latvia collected one million signatures opposing the new Union Treaty formulated by central Soviet authorities.[25] Smaller petition drives were organized on various occasions.

Mass activism in Latvia also included individual and organized picketing. Numerous pickets were held beginning in 1988. Members of Helsinki 86, the Independence Movement, and the Environmental Protection Club picketed the City Council of Riga for several days in November 1988 demanding that the Latvian national flag be displayed on the tower of Riga Castle. They were successful. In March 1989 the Independence Movement organized several pickets against press censorship.[26] Many pickets established themselves in front of Soviet draft boards throughout 1989 and later. One newspaper account described the picketing this way: "Some people pin homemade posters with inscriptions, drawings, and photographs, covered in polyethylene [as protection] against the rain, to their clothes; others hang them around their necks; yet others simply hold them in their hands."[27] In May 1991 peaceful picketers in front of the Political Education Building of the Communist party asked that it be converted to a youth center.[28] These sorts of activities differed in detail, but their common denominator was the taking of the initiative from below and the focus on democratic and patriotic issues crucial to Latvia's political transformation.

Citizen initiatives are important in any polity, but they were especially crucial for the gradual transition from the old Communist system, which considered any self-organized political expression to be a criminal offense.[29] Each event in the chain of mass activism weakened the old regime and at the same time strengthened the confidence of people that they could have a political effect.

National Emancipation through Elections

As comparative studies show, elections can accelerate regime change. When authoritarian regimes engage in liberalization they often hold semicompetitive contests to bolster their legitimacy. Yet regimes also face the dilemma that "when an election is held to consecrate a regime, it must be credible; yet to assure that it does not result in a transfer of power, it must be controlled."[30] Often this balancing act fails and a true transition to democracy begins, as was the case in the Soviet Union. In the Baltic states and western Russia in particular, elections became catalysts of self-generated mass participation in the selection of candidates, debates about issues, and bringing the vote out. Elections provided another means for expressing popular will, not just as a means of selecting representatives, but in staging new mass events. On the eve of the 18 March 1990 election in Latvia, about a quarter million people came to a rally in Riga with flags, flowers, and homemade placards.[31]

Voter turnout in the March 1990 elections was 81.3 percent,[32] a high popular involvement in any comparative perspective. The no-choice elections of the Soviet period had typically claimed that 99.9 percent of voters supported the single candidate on the ballot, and they also claimed a 99.9 percent voter turnout. Analysis shows that actual turnout was much lower[33] and sociological surveys undertaken in Latvia in May and June 1989 revealed that in the past, 33 percent of voters had their vote cast by a family member or someone else, and that 7 percent had avoided voting altogether. The surveys also showed that the election results of the first semifree elections to the all-union legislature in March 1989 were seen as very satisfactory by 13 percent of Latvian voters and by 5 percent of non-Latvians, as partly satisfactory by 80 percent of Latvians and 56 percent of non-Latvians, and as nonsatisfactory by 5 percent Latvians and some 34 percent of non-Latvians.[34] In the March 1989 elections independent groupings for the first time could contest candidates put forward by the CPSU and its affiliates. In Latvia, the result was a victory for democrats since fifteen of the new deputies were associated with the Popular Front, while another seven were considered conservatives.[35] Candidates put forward by grass-roots movements gained more victories in elections to local councils held in late 1989.

Apart from an unexpectedly intense voter involvement, the elections of 1989 gave the first tangible indication that a considerable segment of non-Latvians supported Popular Front candidates. In the December 1989 elections to the City Council of Riga, where two-thirds of the population is non-Latvian, Popular Front candidates won half the seats.[36] As will be noted later, this tendency was even more evident in elections to the republic's Supreme Soviet in 1990. The electoral platform of the Popular Front of Latvia specified that it wanted to restore Latvia as an independent state with broad-ranging cultural rights for non-Latvian minorities.[37] It emphasized the need for radical renewal in all spheres, for a democratic political system, radical economic reform, and social transformation. Since the Popular Front was a coalition, the choice put before the electorate was bipolar, with the pro-Moscow Communist Party of Latvia (CPL) and its satellites at the opposite pole. Yet the election platform of the CPL was couched in moderate rhetoric[38] and more uncertainty was added by overlapping organizational affiliations.

As noted, the transition from the Soviet single-party system to a plurality of groups and parties is a core aspect of the democratization of the former USSR. But this is a gradual process. At the time of the March 1990 elections to the Supreme Soviet of Latvia, nothing resembling a Western-style party system existed. The Popular Front brought together a variety of groups such as the Environmental Protection Club, the Independence Movement, the League of Women, and others. It also had unaffiliated individual supporters and cooperated with the reformist wing of the Communist party. The latter fact was confusing to voters because the reformists only split from the Communist Party of Latvia after the March 1990 election had occurred (see chapter 2). Most candidates had multiple organizational loyalties. As summarized in Table 5.1, the Popular Front sponsored its own candidates as well as reformist members of the CPL, and the CPL sponsored orthodox Communists as well as some with additional affiliations, such as the Interfront or Latvia's Union of Agricultural Workers. The ambivalent institutional affiliations of many candidates meant that voters could not vote for clearly

Table 5.1
Supreme Soviet Elections and Organizational Affiliation

Membership	Candidates	Deputies
Popular Front of Latvia (PFL) only	47	33
Communist Party of Latvia (CPL) only	155	58
PFL and CPL	54	32
PFL and other	52	34
CPL and other	26	7
Other	5	4

Source: *Atmoda*, 10 April 1990, p. 3. This list is incomplete since run-off elections were held on later dates. In the final tally, 131 of 201 deputies were affiliated with the Popular Front, 11 were independent, and 59 joined the opposition Equal Rights faction (data provided by the Press Center of the Supreme Council of the Republic of Latvia, 11 February 1991).

defined programs and parties, but rather chose between reform candidates broadly defined and candidates supporting the status quo. The lack of clear programmatic or organizational commitments of deputies was to become a problem in the legislature once it was elected. The Popular Front faction in Parliament was at its most united on 4 May 1990, when voting for a transition period to full restoration of Latvia's independence. After that, factionalization gradually increased and it became increasingly difficult for any group of deputies to get legislation passed.[39]

As the high number of candidates affiliated solely with the Communist party suggests, the CPSU branch in Latvia still had considerable organizational capacities in 1990. The electoral victory of the Popular Front had to be fought for in an intense electoral campaign with an unequal distribution of resources. The entrenched monopoly over communications by the Communist party meant that media access for the Popular Front was limited, especially for more radical candidates.[40] The Communist old guard also used its bureaucratic power. One of the most notorious cases was the denial of former political prisoner Ints Cālītis's right to register as a candidate because, due to his imprisonment in a Russian labor camp, he did not satisfy the election law's requirement of living in Latvia for the ten years before the election.[41] The distribution of organizational resources between establishment candidates and their opponents was even more unequal. In many smaller towns and the countryside, Communist functionaries had ruled like feudal lords and were able to deny campaigners access to public facilities. This was the experience of the leader of the Independence Movement,

Eduards Berklāvs, who nevertheless won 62 percent of the vote in the Madona district after campaigning intensely by going door to door and organizing small meetings at workplaces, drugstores, and libraries.[42] Although the efforts of individual candidates made a difference, so did the dedication and enthusiasm of their campaign workers. With little technical support, the campaign centers of the Popular Front managed to put together a strong effort showing organizational ability, strategic thinking, and a lot of hard work, including door-to-door canvassing.[43]

The candidate lists presented by the Popular Front and the Communist party showed some ethnic polarization, with Latvians being overrepresented in the Popular Front and underrepresented in the list of "others" (see Table A.4 in the Appendix). The converse was true as well: Russians and other eastern Slavs dominated in the list sponsored by the orthodox Communists and were underrepresented in the Popular Front (see Table A.4 and also the population statistics in Table A.5). Latvian Poles, Jews, and "others" were overrepresented among the candidates of the Popular Front, illustrating its deliberate support for smaller minorities. Yet the Popular Front's candidate selection followed ethnic lines more than did the actual voting. It is misleading to focus on the sociopolitical background of candidates without linking it to the profile of voters overall and in specific districts. A comparison of census data and election outcomes shows that between 20 and 30 percent of non-Latvians voted for Popular Front candidates, whether they were Latvians or not. In Riga, for example, census data show a majority of non-Latvians in all 69 election districts, yet Popular Front candidates won in 30 districts. Exact data cannot be provided because the ethnicity of voters was not recorded at the polls, and estimates are difficult because though most of the 201 election districts in Latvia had two opposing candidates, 30 districts had more than two candidates, yet 50 districts had only one candidate (36 Popular Front, 14 solely CPL).[44] The latter situation was the result of insufficient time for preparation and the procedural difficulties of registering candidates.

An unusual aspect of Soviet-era elections in Latvia was the participation of Soviet military personnel, determined by Article 2 of the Election Law stating that "soldiers serving on the territory of Latvia may vote or be elected regardless of whether they are citizens of the Latvian SSR or of how long they have served in the Latvian SSR."[45] Many Latvians saw this as a mockery of the democratic process, and commentators cited Lenin's Decree on Peace, which states that elections can only be free when held without the presence of occupying troops.[46] Because the number of Soviet troops in Latvia was considered a state secret, it is unknown how many Soviet military personnel voted, but the Popular Front of Latvia estimates that it was well above one hundred thousand. This figure must be compared with the total electorate of slightly under two million. The ballots cast by Soviet troops were decisive in seven districts and cost the leader of the Polish Cultural Society in Latvia, Ita Kozakēviča, election by 150 votes.[47]

It is also noteworthy that fifty-seven of the candidates to the Supreme Soviet were active members of the Soviet armed forces.[48] A score of them were elected by the pro-Soviet segment of the electorate and joined the legislature without feeling the need to demobilize. After Latvia declared the restoration of independence in August 1991 they were asked either to demobilize from the Soviet military or to face losing their mandate; most chose demobilization.[49]

The Plebiscite of March 1991

In a republicwide advisory poll on 3 March 1991 voters in Latvia were asked, "Are you for a democratic and independent Republic of Latvia?" The response was strongly affirmative. Of the registered voters, 87.6 percent participated, and of these 73.6 percent voted "yes," 24.7 percent voted "no," and the rest (1.7 percent) cast invalid ballots.[50] Since the nationality of voters was not registered at the polling stations, one cannot determine the exact percentage of non-Latvians voting for independence, but estimates show that it was higher than expected. Guided by sociological surveys, the organizers of the plebiscite anticipated that between 30 and 40 percent of non-Latvian voters would support the measure, and initial calculations assumed that this expectation was fulfilled.[51] Yet analysis of the number of votes in comparison with census data shows that the percentage of non-Latvians nationwide casting "yes" ballots was around 49 percent, with another 47 percent casting "no" ballots (Table 5.2).[52]

Other results of the plebiscite also indicate that support for independence was very high among Latvians, quite high among non-Latvians, and that political participation, as expressed by turnout rates, was also very high. In the March 1991 poll all permanent residents of Latvia were eligible to cast a ballot, despite protests by the Citizens' Congress arguing that only legal citizens of Latvia should be allowed to vote.[53] Since Soviet soldiers on active duty in Latvia were not registered as permanent residents, they were barred from voting. The Communist Party of Latvia and other pro-Moscow organizations urged their supporters to go to the polls and vote "no" or invalidate their ballot.[54] Nevertheless, turning out for the vote was a sign of support, as indicated by the very high turnout rate in most towns and rural districts of Latvia, which are predominantly Latvian and overwhelmingly supported independence. The average turnout in cities was about 80 percent.[55] The lowest turnout (63.4 percent) was in the city of Daugavpils in the southeastern corner of Latvia. In Daugavpils only 13 percent of the inhabitants are Latvian and at the time of the poll the city was governed by a staunchly

Table 5.2
Poll on Latvia's Independence, 3 March 1991

	Total "Yes" Vote[1] (percent)	Latvians in Population[2] (percent)	Voter Turnout[1] (percent)	Total Number Registered Voters[1]	Estimated Number of Non-Latvians Voting "Yes"[3]	Estimate of Non-Latvians Voting "No"[4] (percent)
Latvia	73.7	52	87.6	1,902,802	49% (381,577)	47
Riga	60.7	36.5	84.4	660,634	42% (132,277)	58
Jelgava[5]	70	50	87.1	52,818	45% (10,084)	51.7
Daugavpils	51.3	13	63.4	92,716	42% (19,833)	48
Towns and rural districts	85.9	69.4	93.1	906,259	67.4% (187,015)	29.7

Sources:
[1] Dzintra Bungs, "Voting Patterns in the Latvian Independence Poll," *Report on the USSR*, 22 March 1991, tables 1 and 2.
[2] Census of January 1989, see Table 6.1.
[3] Calculation based on assumptions that a) the percentage of Latvians and others among the registered voters is the same as among the census population; b) voter turnout among Latvians was 90 percent; c) "yes" vote among Latvians was 95 percent.
[4] Based on total number of negative votes, minus 5 percent of "no" vote for Latvian voters casting ballots.
[5] The data on four other cities are omitted for the sake of brevity.

pro-Soviet old guard. It is thus impressive that even there a majority (51.3 percent) of those voters who did go to the polls cast their ballots for "a democratic and independent Republic of Latvia." Clearly, a large segment of non-Latvians voted "yes," probably many of them members of families who had been citizens of Latvia in the interwar period.

The high percentage of non-Latvians casting ballots in favor of an independent and democratic Latvia also can be explained by the timing of the poll. It was held after the turn toward hard-line Communist politics in Moscow in October 1990 and after the January 1991 Baltic crackdown by Soviet troops. As noted before, both survey data and reports indicate that these events spurred support for democratic and proindependence forces everywhere (see chapters 2 and 3). Such findings support the argument of this study that the quality of ethnic politics is linked to the broader political context.

The 3 March 1991 poll on independence in Latvia was conducted as a counterpoint and alternative to the 17 March all-union referendum organized by Soviet authorities eager to preserve the Soviet Union. Gorbachev hoped that the referendum would halt the devolution of power away from the center. Because it was stated that the unionwide outcome would be binding everywhere, irrespective of results in individual republics, opposition forces all over the USSR deemed it unconstitutional. Six republic governments refused to hold the referendum,[56] typically organizing alternative pollings, as in Latvia. In protest, pro-Soviet forces in Latvia and Moscow decided to organize the all-union referendum through "labor collectives and public organizations, including associations of labor collectives, the international front of working people, and the 'Soyuz' deputy group."[57] Even the pro-Soviet minority faction leader of Latvia's legislature was against the referendum, due to inopportune timing,[58] by which he presumably meant popular anger at the January crackdown.

Despite energetic campaigning by pro-Soviet forces, participation in the all-union referendum in Latvia was low. The organizers claimed that "about 500,000 persons"—approximately one-fourth of the registered voters—had cast ballots.[59] The actual outcome is uncertain because referendum sponsors instituted few procedural checks about who could vote. One reporter received invitations to vote in three districts, and when she proceeded to cast ballots found she could do so in five districts.[60] In accordance with Soviet electoral practice, a special polling place was set up on the platform of the Riga train station and announcements were made on incoming trains encouraging every traveler to stop and vote.[61]

Nevertheless, the claim by the all-union referendum organizers in Latvia that half a million persons voted for the Soviet federation and thus against Latvia's independence is close to the mark. In the 3 March poll, a total of

411,374 persons cast votes saying "no" to "a democratic and independent Republic of Latvia" (see Table 5.2). As the analysis of these votes shows, these respondents were mostly non-Latvians in the larger cities and in the Daugavpils region. They acted in direct opposition to the many non-Latvians in the same areas (and elsewhere) voting for independence. This split among the non-Latvian population of Latvia in regard to their political identification is one of the most intriguing aspects of ethnopolitics both in Latvia and in comparative perspective. It illustrates how misleading it is to use purely nominal categories to pinpoint political allegiances of ethnic groupings.

Counterdemonstrations

The anti-independence forces not only expressed their views only at the ballot box but also staged demonstrations and supported coup attempts by the self-declared All-Latvia National Salvation Committee in January and August 1991. The links between putschists in Latvia and hard-line forces in Moscow are discussed in chapter 6. Here it should be emphasized that most activities of the pro-Soviet forces were organized by traditional Soviet power holders rather than the participants themselves. The organizational core of the hard-liners consisted of the Communist Party of Latvia (CPSU platform), Soviet military and police personnel, the Interfront, and spokespeople for certain "labor collectives." A Popular Front deputy, Andrējs Pantelējevs, has noted that the anti-independence protests in spring 1990 had little to do with ethnicity or social interests per se, but were linked to the defense of power positions, especially by the established military-industrial complex. He also noted that demonstrations were being organized by the Baltic Military District.[62]

In the traditional Soviet political system, self-organized protest meetings or demonstrations were harshly repressed as expressions of anti-Soviet dissent. The Communist party, of course, sponsored rallies and street marches on Soviet holidays such as the anniversary of the October Revolution. Some of this orchestrated political participation continued throughout the perestroika period, and some new events were organized by the Interfront in response to the activities of the Popular Front of Latvia. Yet their turnout typically was low in comparison.[63] One such meeting occurred on 8 May 1990, after a Soviet military parade in Riga marking the forty-fifth anniversary of the end of World War II. About twenty thousand people, mostly Russians, met at the Soviet Victory Monument and listened to speakers berate Parliament for its declaration of independence.[64] In addition, the first secretary of the Communist party denounced plans to restore the "bourgeois republic of Latvia" and called for loyalty to the Soviet cause.[65]

Other protests were more ominous. A few days later, an aggressive pro-Soviet group gathered in front of the Parliament Building on 15 May 1990.

104

The demonstration was triggered by the legislature's debate over a law about alternatives to service in the Soviet military and funding for the military draft. Red Army helicopters dropped anti-independence leaflets while hundreds of protesters, most of them Soviet military personnel in uniform, tried to force themselves into the building. They were stopped in part by counter-demonstrators from the Popular Front. The diametrically opposed views of the two groups were audible, as the anti-independence group chanted "Soviet Union" and the Popular Front people responded with chants of "A Free Latvia!"[66]

Pro-Soviet forces mobilized support for the military crackdown in January 1991. On 15 January the Interfront in Riga held a rally where several hundred thousand participants were expected. Many fewer came,[67] but the All-Latvia National Salvation Committee used the occasion to declare that it was taking over power in Latvia. On 17 January a pro-Soviet strike committee accused Latvia of "sliding into a brown-tinged totalitarian and bourgeois regime," and declared a strike "aimed at preserving the USSR."[68]

Following Soviet tradition, some workers' collectives passed unanimous declarations addressed to the leadership of the Communist party. *Pravda* on 21 January 1991 published a telegram sent by "the collective" of the Riga Electric Lamp Factory to Gorbachev, stating among other things that they "recognize the authority of the All-Latvia National Salvation Committee as the only authority in the republic that defends the interests of all segments of the population," "demand that the government of the Latvian Republic resign and the republic parliament be dissolved as an antipopular body," and "demand that Comrade Gorbachev . . . ensure the enforcement of laws and the USSR Constitution to protect human rights in the Baltic republics."[69] Furthermore, *Pravda* stated that "the collective of the Riga Electric Lamp Factory unanimously condemns the separatist activity of B. N. Yeltsin . . . which is contributing to the exacerbation of the explosive situation in the Baltic republics."[70] Other protests and strikes in May 1991 were organized by a Baltic Strike Committee "on behalf of the labor collectives of forty-two enterprises and organizations."[71]

Civil Resistance against Armed Crackdown

On 7 January 1991, the Soviet Ministry of Defense announced that it was sending elite paratroop units to the Baltics and other republics to arrest draft resisters and deserters. Although the West saw this as "amounting to intimidation" of independent-minded republic governments,[72] it was also a show of force in support of local antigovernmental forces. Already on 6 December 1990, the self-appointed All-Latvia National Salvation Committee, headed by leaders of the Communist party, had sent a request to Gorbachev to "institute Presidential Rule" in Latvia.[73] They cited numerous complaints of how the authorities in Latvia disregarded Soviet laws and the Constitution of the USSR.[74] Clearly, the confrontation was between the hard-line forces supporting Soviet rule and residents supporting the rule of Latvia's Parliament and government. On 13 January 1991, the day of the armed attack in Vilnius, the pro-Soviet Communist Party of Latvia decided that power should be assumed by the Salvation Committee. Twenty-one deputies of the orthodox Communist faction of the legislature of Latvia participated in the meeting of the Central Committee making this decision.[75]

As soon as the first indications of a violent coup attempt appeared in Latvia, the Popular Front began issuing calls for nonviolent civil resistance. Initial preparations were made in December 1990, and some nonviolent resistance was offered when troops of the Soviet Ministry of Interior took over the Press Center in Riga on 7 January 1991.[76] Immediately after it became known that Soviet troops had started a violent crackdown in Lithuania, the vice-chairman of Latvia's legislature, Dainis Īvāns, appealed over the radio for people to defend the Parliament Building, as well as to attend a mass protest in the early afternoon of 13 January, a Sunday. Hundreds of thousands of people came to what probably was the largest mass demonstration ever held in Riga.[77] The rally proceeded under the slogan "We shall not yield to the dictate of the occupier." At the same time many more people gathered around the Parliament and other governmental buildings to help ward off attacks by Soviet forces.[78]

Numerous calls for nonviolent resistance continued throughout the next week. In addition to residents of the capital, tens of thousands of people from other parts of Latvia came to Riga to participate in self-organized defense activities. Fearing attacks against the Parliament and other buildings, people erected barricades and formed human chains around them. Some people from the countryside came with trucks and tractors, carrying materials for barricades, and others came individually or by the busload to guard the barricades.[79] Many others engaged in support efforts such as bringing food and warm drinks to those staying out on the barricades day and night.

On 20 January 1991, the special "black beret" police forces of the Soviet Ministry of Interior staged an attack on Latvia's Ministry of Interior, killing five people, two of them famous filmmakers killed while capturing the event on film.[80] No further violent actions were taken, although Soviet tanks continued to meander through the streets for several days thereafter. The unexpectedly strong resistance by unarmed civilians in Vilnius and Riga and the support extended to them by Yeltsin and other Russian democrats stopped further attacks.[81] The dramatic display of opposition received worldwide attention and embarrassed the Soviet Union. Gorbachev and other Soviet leaders tried unsuccessfully to blame the victims for the attacks. As noted by a journalist,

The attempt to display the Baltic peoples as violent provocateurs seems particularly inane in light of their hard-earned reputation for dogged civil resistance during their long attempt to regain independence. In fact, the Balts' strength appears to be in their meekness, and this is what they are brandishing now on their rag-tag ramparts at the Gorbachev Government.[82]

The failure of repression is discussed in detail later, but clearly the non-violent activism of large numbers of people was a core component. This activism is unthinkable without the preceding waves of mobilization in various activities since 1987. The rallying of people in support of the nascent democratic and independent institutions of the Latvian polity in January 1991 was the culmination of a prolonged process of popular mobilization.

The January events also acted as a catalyst for further support of Latvian statehood. The increased support for independence is especially noticeable among non-Latvians, as noted in the survey results summarized in Figure 3.1 and in results of the 3 March 1991 nonbinding plebiscite (Table 5.2). The solidarity created by the nonviolent resistance to the Soviet crackdown strengthened identification with Latvia as a civic and national community, as also attested by numerous individual reports. A student in charge of Russian-language broadcasts in Riga concluded from listeners' calls that "the attitude of Russians toward the republic and the Latvian language has changed."[83] The Belorussian writer Olesh Adamovich urged Balts to recognize that the Russian-speaking population in their midst also hated the Soviet system and preferred a "bourgeois economy."[84] The Russian-language newspaper of the Popular Front of Latvia emphasized that of the five victims in the attack on Latvia's Ministry of Interior, one was Russian and another was Belorussian.[85] It was also emphasized that hard-line authorities in Moscow were trying to use the situation of Russians in the Baltics as a pretext for its policies. Thus the Russian Cultural Society in Latvia held a meeting on 3 February 1991 to protest such manipulations against the legal government and Parliament. The meeting specifically rejected the claims made by the Salvation Committee that the rights of Russians in Latvia were endangered.[86] In sum, the violent policies of hard-line Soviet forces in January 1991 backfired in more ways than one. Although this situation decided the fate of Latvia, it was equally if not more significant for the fate of the Soviet Union. In many ways, the events of January 1991 were a dress rehearsal for the unsuccessful Moscow coup of August 1991.

The Failure of Repression

Nondemocratic systems rely on repression to keep power. Surprisingly, writings on the democratization of authoritarian systems say little about changes in coercion. Such an omission is particularly unjustifiable in the analysis of a Soviet-style system. One cannot discuss the emergence of mass political participation without analyzing its interaction with changes in state repression. To respond to this issue we first have to examine the nature of coercion.

Coercion in the USSR has always relied on more than naked force. Even before Gorbachev, the established habits of fear began disappearing due to generational change and new policies.[87] But the social psychology of terror was dealt a decisive blow by glasnost and by the inconsistent use of limited repression during the perestroika period. First, coercion was delegitimized by the public repudiation of Stalinist crimes against humanity. Public exposure of the extent of state-sponsored horrors, including the opening of mass graves, defused the image that somehow the victims were guilty after all. It created a Soviet version of the "never again" motto expressed by survivors of the Holocaust. Without this new attitude people might have reacted differently once the regime reverted to repression on some occasions. Moreover, if glasnost had not discredited state violence against citizens, the regime would have felt more sanguine about reverting to it.

Coercive power involves institutional expressions such as media censorship and police powers, but primarily it manipulates people's behavior through the use of threats. This sociopsychological dimension makes coercion more fragile than it is often believed to be. If people no longer fear the consequences they are threatened with, or disbelieve that they will occur, coercion is undermined. In addition, the inconsistent use of repression tends to be counterproductive.[88] Theorists of protest have noted that the effect of repression is linked to the expectations of participants. When people decide whether to protest they are influenced by the precedents of the regime's use of repression,[89] and this means that the effect of repression changes over time. At the beginning of perestroika, experience told potential protesters that they could expect intensive repression. The participants in the first demonstrations were highly motivated people taking a huge risk. But the dynamics changed as soon as the initial protests were not met with repression as in the past. Protesters gradually felt more and more assured that the same would be true the next time, and consequently more and more people demonstrated. If repression is used at such a late stage, it is likely to backfire.

The "boomerang effect" of limited regime violence occurs because once thousands of people are in the streets, police brutality against a few of them is a weak deterrent and any remaining deterrent effect is more than counterbalanced by the catalytic effect of regime violence: because protesters have come to expect that the regime will not use repression, they feel betrayed when it does occur and so protest even more. Those standing at the sidelines are drawn into escalating protests precisely because of the regime's repression. The delegitimation of regime violence is especially effective if the protesters themselves are clearly nonviolent.[90]

This theoretical logic is supported by events in the USSR and Latvia. Until the mid-1980s police and legal repression was used instantly if even minor dissent was expressed.[91] By mid-1988 most unofficial demonstrations could proceed unhindered. Yet some protesters were harassed, arrested, or attacked. The most brutal instance occurred in Tbilisi in April 1989, when scores of peaceful demonstrators, most of them women, were killed. Public outrage ensued and escalated calls for radical democratization. The use of Soviet internal troops in Baku in January 1990 was more difficult to assess, but it too undermined the regime's power to engage repressive activities as Russian mothers began to protest the use of their sons in such situations.[92] The turning point in the effectiveness of the regime's repressive powers came with the January 1991 crackdown in the Baltic states, when people risked their lives in resistance and thousands demonstrated in support all over the Soviet Union.

"People power" was demonstrated in Moscow as well, especially in the March 1991 showdown between Yeltsin supporters and Gorbachev. Even though Gorbachev banned a rally in support of Yeltsin and brought in countless troops, huge crowds still gathered. In the end, no force was used, and the threat of force backfired politically. As noted by *Izvestiia*, the authorities "demonstrate not power, of course, but powerlessness, fear before their own people, an inability and even unwillingness to talk with them."[93]

The lesson of the Baltic events and the Moscow demonstrations was twofold: mass protest in defense of democratic institutions could deter armed units and could make hard-liners back down from repression. As we know, both these lessons were repeated during the coup in August 1991.[94] Indeed, one wonders why the hard-liners had not learned anything. Apparently this was because hard-line elites who had used violence against challengers of their power in the past assessed its utility as being high,[95] and the physical trappings of power were still in place. But though little had changed in the physical means of repression between 1987 and August 1991, its usefulness had declined. As noted, coercive power is to a large extent psychological, and it is reciprocal in that the outcome is affected by the actions of the repressors as well as those of the repressed. The new reality of mass protest, despite a show of armed force, undermined the regime's confidence. Regime actors, like protesters, are influenced by calculations of future political outcomes. As Mancur Olson has pointed out, dictatorships are inherently fragile because they rest on the perceptions of their guards and administrators. If these perceptions suddenly change, the officials will cease to carry out orders: "If the cadre observe a moment of vacillation, an incident of impotence, a division of leadership, or even a collapse of analogous regimes, all the power of an imposing regime can vanish in the night air."[96]

More than anything, this explains the collapse of the hard-line coup in August 1991. Initially, there was a lack of clear orders to the security forces, who consequently waited to see which way events would turn. Once it became apparent that the coup had little support, the potential repressors increasingly refused to follow orders.[97] This was the truly revolutionary event signaling the end of the old regime, but it was only the final step in an interactive process between regime and protest actors that had begun years earlier.

Conclusion

Civil society, nations, and states are based on collective identities, prompting us to inquire how such identities are formed. In Latvia mobilization in the form of demonstrations, petitions, elections, and resistance to repression played a pivotal role in the forging of a civic and national community that in turn became the basis for the restoration of statehood. No single aspect was by itself sufficient to serve as the basis for this community. Ethnic and state national identity was significant, but as noted by Nelson Kasfir,

> Shared perception permits, but does not necessarily create, sufficient social solidarity to turn individuals assigned to an ethnic category into an active ethnic group. Even then, the likelihood of social solidarity being channeled into participation depends on the opportunities created by the specific political situation.[98]

These opportunities were created by a political opening from above and creative initiatives from below. An interactive process was triggered whereby the old regime was increasingly delegitimized and new structures emerged in its stead. Between 1987 and 1991 the tide of popular political participation rose gradually but consistently, outmaneuvering attempts of control by both hard-liners and regime reformers.

As noted, there were systemic reasons why the attempts by hard-liners to stop the tide of mass activism by repression were doomed to fail. The interaction between elite reformers and grass-roots initiatives, however, was more complicated. The initial demonstrations in Latvia originated from below, as did many pickets and the civil resistance in January 1991. Beginning in 1988, elite reformers tried to channel mass activism by initiating rallies and framing the electoral and plebiscite campaigns, yet here too popular participation often went beyond expectations. On balance, this interaction between the elite and mass level of politics appears to have been decisive for the eventual success of democratization and the restoration of statehood. As noted in the theoretical literature cited in the introduction to this chapter, spontaneous mass demonstrations alone often fail to lead to institutional change. Elite reforms, on the other hand, face the danger of falling short of decisive change. In Latvia we see a creative synthesis of grass-roots and elite efforts.

This experience conforms to Sidney Tarrow's theoretical statement that "it is from the interaction among collective action, social movements, and movement organizations that modern protest systems gain their most dynamic potential."[99] In addition, mass activism often went beyond mere protest and played a constructive institution-building role, most notably in the elections of March 1990.

As in Russia, elections in Latvia became true schools for democracy by fostering civic participation and creating an institutional alternative in a formerly closed political system. And, because electoral politics is by its nature linked to specific territories, it was to be expected that issues concerning the Latvian nation and state would play a prominent role. In addition, the electoral debates and choice between candidates contributed to a shift of political culture toward a more participatory and democratic mode.

The self-organization of the Latvian people between 1987 and 1991 was amazingly quick, complete, and nonviolent. The direct involvement in the building of democracy from below through unprecedented mass activism had immediate effects on the balance of power and shaped a new political culture. Participation in mass protests was extremely effective in delegitimizing the old regime and at the same time strengthened the identity of Latvia as a civil society, nation, and state. It is crucial to note that this identity was only partly created anew and that many of the popular initiatives invoked the link to interwar Latvia. As noted in this chapter and in chapter 4, the symbols of the interwar Republic of Latvia as well as its constitutional makeup and record as a self-governing state served as catalysts of popular mobilization. Knowledge of the precedent of statehood, nationhood, and experience as a parliamentary democracy[100] made the activities aimed at their restoration both credible and legitimate. This precedent also improved the chances of success. As the writings on transitions to democracy emphasize, it is much easier to make such a transition if a country has had previous experience with democracy.[101]

In Latvia's case the other side of this experience with independent statehood was witnessing its destruction by the Soviet occupation in 1940. Thus the mass demonstrations were galvanized by the dates marking "black days" in Latvia's recent political history, such as the signing of the Hitler-Stalin pact and the genocidal deportations of Latvia's citizens to Siberia. The protests against these acts had a twofold nature in that they dramatized the illegitimacy of both the Communist regime and the rule by the Soviet Union. "Soviet" rule was rejected as a political system and as rule by an aggressive neighboring state. In this regard the transition politics in Latvia, Lithuania, and Estonia differed from democratization in Ukraine or Russia and their focus on internal transformation. In Latvia and the two other Baltic states, transition from Soviet rule meant both the construction of an alternative politics and liberation from foreign dominance. It is this second dimension of emancipation that we turn to in the next chapter.

NOTES

1. Tun-jen Cheng, "Democratizing the Quasi-Leninist Regime in Taiwan," *World Politics* (July 1989): 474; also Daniel H. Levine, "Paradigm Lost: Dependence to Democracy," *World Politics* 40 (April 1988): 337–94.
2. Adam Przeworski, "Democracy as a Contingent Outcome of Conflicts," in Jon Elster and Rune Slagstad, eds., *Constitutionalism and Democracy* (Cambridge: Cambridge University Press, 1988), 72–73.
3. Levine, "Paradigm Lost," 384.
4. Ibid.; Dankwart A. Rustow, "Transitions to Democracy: Toward a Dynamic Model," *Comparative Politics* 2 (April 1970): 337–63.
5. Rasma Karklins and Roger Petersen, "The Calculus of Protesters and Regimes: Eastern Europe 1989," *Journal of Politics* (August 1993): 588–614; James DeNardo, *Power in Numbers: The Political Strategy of Protest and Rebellion* (Princeton, N.J.: Princeton University Press, 1985).
6. See Susan Olzak, "Analysis of Events in the Study of Collective Action," *Annual Review of Sociology* 1989, no. 15: 119–41.
7. Sidney Tarrow, " 'Aiming at a Moving Target': Social Science and the Recent Rebellions in Eastern Europe," *PS: Political Science & Politics* 24 (1991): 15.
8. Juan Linz, "Transitions to Democracy," *Washington Quarterly* (Summer 1990): 152.
9. Ibid.
10. Peter H. Smith, "Crisis and Democracy in Latin America," *World Politics* 43 (July 1991): 621.
11. See *Le Monde*, 25 August 1988, p. 7, and other newspaper reports from the scene; also Olgerts Eglitis, *Nonviolent Action in the Liberation of Latvia*, monograph series no. 5 (Cambridge, Mass.: The Albert Einstein Institution, 1993), 14.
12. See *Telos* 47 (1981), special issue on Poland.
13. See numerous articles in the Baltic and international press, for example the *New York Times*, 24 August 1989.
14. *Stockholm Domestic Service*, 12 March 1989, as translated in *FBIS-SOV-89-047*, 13 March 1989, 44.
15. *New York Times*, 23 April 1989, 14.
16. Hank Johnston, "The Comparative Study of Nationalism: Six Pivotal Themes from the Baltic States," *Journal of Baltic Studies* 23 (Summer 1992): 100.
17. *Pravda*, 27 August 1989, 1.
18. Giuseppe Di Palma, "Legitimation from the Top to Civil Society: Politico-Cultural Change in Eastern Europe," *World Politics* (October 1991): 75.
19. Charles Tilly, *From Mobilization to Revolution* (Englewood Cliffs, N.J.: Prentice-Hall, 1978), 84. For a good summary of the protest literature and how it relates to ethnicity, see Maurice Pinard and Richard Hamilton, "Motivational Dimensions in the Quebec Independence Movement: A Test of a New Model," in Kurt Lang and Gladys Engel Lang, eds., *Research in Social Movements, Conflicts and Change*, vol. 9 (Greenwich, Conn.: JAI Press, 1986), 226–28.
20. Mancur Olson, *The Logic of Collective Action* (Cambridge, Mass.: Harvard University Press, 1965), passim.
21. Karklins and Petersen, "Calculus of Protesters," 590–93.
22. Sidney Tarrow, *Struggle, Politics, and Reform: Collective Action, Social Movements, and Cycles of Protest* (Ithaca: Cornell University, Center for International Studies, Occasional Paper no. 21, 1989), 13; also Olzak, "Collective Action."
23. *Literatūra un Māksla*, 5 October 1988, 2.
24. Baltic Area Situation Report/1, *Radio Free Europe Research*, 5 January 1989, 1–7.
25. *Atmoda*, 20 December 1990.

26. *LNNK Informācijas Lapa*, no. 7, 1989.
27. *Sovetskaia Latviia*, 21 April 1989, 2.
28. *Rīgas Balss*, 15 May 1991, 1.
29. See Articles 90 and 170 of the Criminal Code of the USSR; for examples of activities prosecuted under these articles, see S. P. de Boer, E. J. Driessen, and H. L. Verhaar, eds., *Biographical Dictionary of the Dissidents in the Soviet Union, 1956-1975* (The Hague: Martinus Nijhoff, 1982); Ludmilla Alexeyeva, *Soviet Dissent: Contemporary Movements for National, Religious, and Human Rights* (Middletown, Conn.: Wesleyan University Press, 1985).
30. Paul W. Drake and Eduardo Silva, eds., Introduction to *Elections and Democratization in Latin America, 1980-1985* (San Diego: University of California Press, 1986), 3.
31. Author's on-site observation.
32. Statistics of Election Center of the Popular Front of Latvia.
33. See Rasma Karklins, "Soviet Elections Revisited: The Significance of Voter Abstention in Non-Competitive Voting," *American Political Science Review* 80 (June 1986): 449-69.
34. Brigita Zepa and Aldis Pauliņš, "Kas sadalīja vēlētāju balsis," *Cīna*, 7 October 1989.
35. Dzintra Bungs, "A Victory for Reformers in Estonia and Latvia," *Report on the USSR*, 28 April 1989, 15-17.
36. Data of Election Center of the Popular Front.
37. *Rīgas Balss*, 14 February 1990.
38. *Cīna*, 25 January 1990.
39. Author's observation at legislative sessions and discussions with deputies.
40. Author's interviews with numerous candidates, March 1990.
41. *Rīgas Balss*, 12 March 1990. With great difficulty Cālītis managed to get registered at the last moment and won his district in Riga against another Latvian, Communist party worker Uldis Martinsons.
42. Author's interview with Berklāvs, March 1990.
43. Author's visits to campaign centers in Riga and Jelgava as well as individual meetings with young, competent, dedicated, and exhausted election workers.
44. Author's calculations based on data of Election Center of the Popular Front of Latvia.
45. *Latvijas Padomju Socialistiskās Republikas Likums par Latvijas PSR Tautas Deputātu Vēlēšanām* (Riga: Avots, 1989).
46. *Latvijas Jaunatne*, 13 March 1990, 2.
47. U.S. Commission on Security and Cooperation in Europe, *Report on the Supreme Soviet Elections in Latvia* (Washington, D.C.: U.S. Government Printing Office, 2 April 1990), 11.
48. *Latvijas Jaunatne*, 15 March 1990.
49. Information from staff members of the Supreme Council of Latvia.
50. Table 5.2 and Dzintra Bungs, "Poll Shows Majority in Latvia Endorses Independence," *Report on the USSR*, 15 March 1991, 22.
51. *New York Times*, 5 March 1991.
52. Author's calculations; see also Table 5.2. This estimate is based on the assumption that 90 percent of Latvians went to the polls and that 95 percent of them voted "yes" on independence. If one were to assume that these two percentages were lower, or higher, the estimate for non-Latvian voting would change, but not radically so. Thus, assuming that 90 percent of registered Latvian voters voted and that of these between 100 and 90 percent voted "yes," then between 43.5 percent and 55 percent of non-Latvians voted "yes."
53. *Latvijas Jaunatne*, 14-15 February 1991: 1.
54. Bungs, "Poll Shows Majority Endorses Independence," 24.
55. See Table 5.2 and Dzintra Bungs, "Voting Patterns in the Latvian Independence Poll," *Report on the USSR*, 22 March 1991, tables 1 and 2.
56. See *Komsomol'skaia pravda*, 13 February 1991; *Literaturnaia gazeta*, 6 March 1991, 3; U.S. Commission on Security and Cooperation in Europe, *Referendum on the Soviet Union* (Washington, D.C.: U.S. Government Printing Office, April 1991); Ann

Sheehy, "The All-Union and RSFSR Referendums of March 17," *Report on the USSR*, 29 March 1991, 19–23.

57.   *TASS* text from Riga, *FBIS-SOV*, 8 March 1991, p. 64; also *Pravda*, 8 March 1991, 3.
58.   *Baltiiskoe vremia* 1991, no. 7.
59.   Dzintra Bungs, "The USSR Referendum: A Nonevent in Latvia," *Report on the USSR*, 29 March 1991, 14–16.
60.   *Neatkarība*, 1991, no. 11: 2.
61.   U.S. Commission on Security and Cooperation in Europe, *Referendum on the Soviet Union*, 20.
62.   *Atmoda*, 8 May 1990.
63.   Compare pages 92–94 and n77 for numbers of participants at rallies organized by the Popular Front and other groups.
64.   *Agence France-Presse*, 9 May 1990, as quoted in *FBIS-SOV-90-091*, 10 May 1990, p. 73.
65.   Ibid.
66.   Western wire services and *Izvestiia*, 16 May 1990, 2.
67.   *Atmoda*, 22 January 1991, cited less than ten thousand, and *Latvijas Jaunatne*, 15–19 January 1991, referred to "a few thousand."
68.   Moscow Domestic Service in Russian, *FBIS-Sov*, 18 January 1991.
69.   *Pravda*, 21 January 1991, p. 2, as cited in the *Current Digest of the Soviet Press* 43, no. 3 (1991): 18.
70.   Ibid.
71.   *Izvestiia*, 5 May 1991, 1.
72.   *New York Times*, 9 January 1991.
73.   The independent-minded procuracy of Russia handed the document over to Latvian authorities and it was published in *Neatkarīgā Cīņa*, 17 January 1992, 2.
74.   Ibid.
75.   Ibid.
76.   Eglitis, *Liberation of Latvia*, 30–31.
77.   One report stated that seven hundred thousand people had attended (*Atmoda*, 22 January 1991, 2); Eglitis mentions more than five hundred thousand. Eglitis, *Liberation of Latvia*, 33.
78.   Eglitis, *Liberation of Latvia*, 33.
79.   For one organized effort to bring in people from Talsi, see *Atmoda*, 15 January 1991; participants from other towns interviewed in *Atmoda*, 22 January 1991.
80.   The reference is to Gvido Zvaigzne and Andris Slapiņš, who worked with the world-famous filmmaker Juris Podnieks.
81.   Yeltsin issued the "Appeal to Russian Soldiers," which asked them not to participate in the crackdown. Afterward it was reported that some Soviet military units refused orders to move to Riga. Eglitis, *Liberation of Latvia*, 34.
82.   Francis X. Clines, "Stalemate in the Baltics," *New York Times*, 24 January 1991, A10. See also *New York Times*, 13 January to 21 January 1991.
83.   *Latvijas Jaunatne*, 23–26 January 1991, 4.
84.   Ibid., 27–30 January 1991, 2.
85.   *Baltiiskoe vremia*, no. 6, 28 January 1991, 1.
86.   Ibid., no. 8, 1991, 1.
87.   Rasma Karklins, "The Dissent/Coercion Nexus in the USSR," *Studies in Comparative Communism* 20 (Autumn 1987): 321–41; A. Dallin and G. W. Breslauer, *Political Terror in Communist Systems* (Stanford: Stanford University Press, 1970).
88.   Robert Dahl has made a similar argument in his Introduction to Robert A. Dahl, ed., *Regimes and Oppositions* (New Haven: Yale University Press, 1973), 18.
89.   Ted Robert Gurr, "War, Revolution, and the Growth of the Coercive State," *Comparative Political Studies* 21, no. 1 (1988): 45–65.
90.   Jon Elster, "When Communism Dissolves," *London Review of Books*, 25 January 1990, pp. 3–6; Karklins and Petersen, "Calculus of Protesters," 602–3.
91.   Alexeyeva, *Soviet Dissent*.
92.   John Armstrong, "Soviet Nations," *Problems of Communism* (July–August 1990): 82.

93. Quoted in the *New York Times*, 29 March 1991.
94. "Resistance to Soviet Takeover Grows as Defiant Crowds Rally for Yeltsin," *New York Times*, 21 August 1991, 1.
95. Gurr, "Coercive State," 49.
96. Mancur Olson, "The Logic of Collective Action in Soviet-type Societies," *Journal of Soviet Nationalities* 1 (1990): 8–27.
97. Amy Knight, "The Coup that Never Was: Gorbachev and the Forces of Reaction," *Problems of Communism* (October 1991): 36–43; Stephen M. Meyer, "How the Threat (and the Coup) Collapsed," *International Security* 16 (Winter 1991–92): 5–38.
98. Nelson Kasfir, "Explaining Ethnic Political Participation," *World Politics* 31 (April 1979): 366.
99. Tarrow, *Struggle, Politics, and Reform*, 16–17.
100. Latvia was a parliamentary democracy until May 1934 when Prime Minister Kārlis Ulmanis staged a coup d'état and established a comparatively mild authoritarian regime. See V. Stanley Vardys, "Democracy in the Baltic States, 1918–1934: The Stage and the Actors," *Journal of Baltic Studies* 10, no. 4 (1979): 320–36; Georg Von Rauch, *The Baltic States: The Years of Independence, 1917–1940*, trans. Gerald Onn (Berkeley: University of California Press, 1974); V. Stanley Vardys and Romuald J. Misiunas, eds., *The Baltic States in Peace and War 1917–1945* (University Park: Pennsylvania State University Press, 1978).
101. Samuel P. Huntington, "Will More Countries Become Democratic?" *Political Science Quarterly* 99, no. 2 (Summer 1984): 193–218; Linz, "Transitions," 144.

6

———>·◇·<———

Latvia: Client State, Settler State, or Self-Determining Nation?

Politics and ethnopolitics in the Baltic states cannot be understood without reference to international relations. Domestic politics is never divorced from international politics; this is all the more true in the Baltics. Soviet rule and numerous foreign settlers came to the Baltic states from the outside, and the problems of transition to national self-rule, democracy, and equitable ethnic politics must be viewed through the prism of this legacy. Since 1986, grass-roots initiatives and elite reforms have led to the collapse of the Soviet Union and its Communist regime and to the development of more democratic self-ruling states. Yet by 1993 the democratic transitions in Latvia and Russia were still incomplete. They faced the same complicated problems as post-Communist Eastern Europe, and in addition had to deal with the legacy of the Soviet Union's foreign policy. For Russia this challenge has included the search for a democratic approach to foreign relations and, especially, the question of how to deal with the aftereffects of Soviet expansionism and the hugely overextended military sector. Russia's decisions on these issues affect the entire international community, but particularly adjacent states such as Latvia.

The foreign and domestic policies of Latvia have always been deeply intertwined with those of the USSR and Russia, and this linkage continues in the early 1990s. What happens in Latvia depends not just on Latvia, but also on the policies of its giant neighbor to the East. Formally, their relations acquired international status when the RSFSR and the USSR recognized Latvia's independence in late August and September 1991.[1] Informally, however, many Soviet and Russian politicians continued to act as if Latvia was an extension of Russia's domestic sphere. The military forces of the former USSR have remained in Latvia without any legal basis,[2] and Russian politicians have felt it their right to interfere in Latvia's internal affairs. Many of the interventions involve the Russian postwar settler population. Russia's position about the status of these people has been highly ambivalent. Sometimes Russian authorities have argued that these are citizens of Russia and that Latvia has no jurisdiction over them, as in the case of former Soviet black berets police who were indicted for criminal offenses in Latvia.[3] Yet on other occasions Russia has argued that all postwar settlers are unconditionally entitled to Latvian citizenship without having to apply for it.[4]

For Latvia the core issue is whether it has regained full sovereignty, or whether its sovereignty remains limited and, if so, for how long. In 1993 the answer to this question remained uncertain. Latvia formally declared the restoration of its independent statehood on 21 August 1991, and the presumption of many analysts has been that the Latvian government is in charge of its affairs. It is more accurate to think of Latvia as a state undergoing a transition with an uncertain outcome, since numerous criteria of de facto independence have been met only partially. In 1993 Soviet military forces remained in Latvia despite repeated requests by Latvia and international bodies that these forces be removed immediately.[5] Until May 1992 Russia controlled Latvia's currency as well as a large part of its economy. Although some top-level administrators had been changed, much of the Russian-dominated bureaucracy of the Soviet era remained in place. Much of the Soviet legal and judicial system persisted as well. Many postwar settlers were monolingual speakers of Russian who perceived Latvia as an extension of Russia and felt that attempts to make Latvian the state language were discriminatory. Most politicians of Russia espoused the same views and pressured Latvia to change its policies.[6] In sum, we have to ask what Latvia is: Is it a dependent client state of Russia, a settler state where primary decisions are made by settlers, or a self-determining nation?

The answer is that even though Latvia's dependence has decreased over time, the period of transition to self-rule continues in the early 1990s. The political reality in Latvia is dualistic: on the one hand it is an independent self-governing state, but on the other hand it continues to be affected by the interventions of Russia and by the legacy of having been subject to Soviet rule. This dualistic reality is crucial to understanding the issues at hand. Many analysts discussing the transition of post-Communist regimes to democracy tend to apply the criteria of an ideal-type Western democracy without adjusting it to take account of the different context. Problems linked to the legacy of the old regime are pernicious, and Latvia must search for innovative ways of overcoming them. Otherwise, many people in Latvia will continue to share the views expressed by Artūrs Snips, a social commentator, in late 1991: "Where are we? Seemingly [we are] in independent Latvia and seemingly in the Soviet Union, although it supposedly doesn't exist any more . . ."[7] Snips goes on to note the continuing influence of the old system and the need to remove the military and political remnants of the occupation forces from Latvia. He also points out that old political and social inequities have persisted because the leading cadre of the old regime are best able to take advantage of new opportunities. Other residents, such as children of deportees, have to start their lives from nothing due to limited access to higher education and social mobility.

So far this study has argued that ethnopolitics in the former USSR cannot be analyzed without relating it to regime change, grass-roots democratization, shifts in political culture, and the dynamic alignment of multiple identities. Now I add international political history as a defining context. The ethnopolitical situation in Latvia is not "ethnic" in the traditional sense;[8] rather, it involves the occupation and colonization of a small state by its giant neighbor. Latvia as a state, and the nation of Latvia as a people, were victims of Soviet aggression under the Hitler-Stalin pact and were the victims of repressive and domineering central Soviet power throughout the postwar period. Latvians were a small minority within the USSR, and they were increasingly minoritized within Latvia itself, not only politically, economically, and culturally but also demographically. This political history shapes contemporary problems.

This chapter examines this legacy in regard to the quality of state-to-state relations between Latvia and Russia, the continuing Soviet/Russian military presence, the political and economic power of the settler community, demographic and linguistic imbalances, and the direction of possible international solutions. The next chapter discusses domestic Latvian policy options in dealing with this legacy.

The International Dimension of Ethnopolitics in Latvia

THE CONSEQUENCES OF FORCIBLE INCORPORATION

Latvia was an independent state and a member of the League of Nations until it was incorporated into the USSR in 1940, and afterward it continued to exist in international law, because most democracies of the world refused to accept the Soviet annexation as legal. Embassies of the Republic of Latvia continued to exist in the United States and elsewhere, and Latvian citizens in exile could travel with passports issued by these embassies.[9] De jure recognition made it possible in August 1991 for Latvia to restore its de facto statehood rather than create a new state; the same applied to Estonia and Lithuania. In this the Baltic states differ fundamentally from the new states emerging out of the former USSR. Although the governments of the Baltic states have emphasized their special status in international law and history, the governments of the USSR and Russia have equivocated in accepting the need to reckon with it. The broader issue is whether dealing with a non-democratic past is an integral part of democratization.

I propose that a transition from communism to democracy can be success-ful only if it deals with the past and instigates a foreign policy reform. Indeed, "new thinking" in foreign policy was a core component of Gor-bachev's reforms. Soviet interests were tied to a decrease of international tensions and a focus on trade and economic development—in this context the Baltic states could become a bridge to the West. The Baltics became a test case for a new foreign policy of the USSR/Russia based on international law and a repudiation of the Stalinist past. In December 1989 the Soviets took the first step by admitting the existence of the secret protocols of the Hitler-Stalin pact and by declaring them invalid in the Congress of People's Deputies.[10] The logical next step would have been to declare invalid the forced incorporation of the Baltic states into the USSR in 1940, yet this step has so far been taken only by the Supreme Soviets of Estonia (22 November 1989), Lithuania (7 February 1990), and Latvia (15 February 1990).

During 1990 central officials became more reluctant to discuss the need to rectify the Stalinist crimes against the Baltic states. In March 1990, *Pravda* refused to publish a historical essay on the events of 1940 in Latvia written by prominent Latvian reform Communists.[11] Despite official ambivalence, Russian democrats increasingly linked reform to telling the truth about the Baltics. In mid-1990, two officials in the Soviet Foreign Ministry's History and Diplomacy Department argued in *Moscow News* against using "white lies" about 1940 to justify the Soviet Baltic policy. One of the interviewed historians noted that his views had changed in early 1990:

> "While recognizing Lithuania's right to independence and understanding that their movement carries a tremendous democratic energy which has helped the entire coun-try's renewal, I feared that this change might be too great for *perestroika* to bear. But now that a number of Republics, and primarily the Ukraine and Russia, have declared their sovereignty, I have no more doubts."[12]

In a similar vein a commentator for *Radio Moscow* on 5 August 1990 linked the Kremlin's failure to rectify historical injustices in the Baltics with the accelerating independence drive. A win-win approach to Baltic indepen-dence was exemplified by the historian Yurii Afanasyev, who urged Russians to see Baltic independence in a positive light, as the acquisition of future allied states on a civilized basis. "It is necessary that people perceive this process not as the breakdown of power, not as the ruin of the USSR, but as a positive process, which is irreversible, which is not to be stopped by any means."[13]

It takes time for both leaders and masses to make the psychological adjustment to a new international position and historical revelations. While many people in the former Soviet Union found the revelations of the reform era liberating, others have not. Individuals whose own life situations are linked to consequences of history, such as the presence of the Soviet forces in the Baltic states, have had an especially difficult time. In October 1990 a survey conducted in Latvia tried to measure this difficulty. When asked, "Do you agree with the statement that, in 1940, the USSR occupied and annexed the Baltic states, incorporating them into the USSR forcibly?" 91 percent of Latvians and 41 percent of non-Latvians responded in the affirmative, 2 percent of Latvians and 27 percent of others disagreed, and 7 percent of Latvians and 32 percent of non-Latvians had difficulty answering the question.[14] We thus again find a split in the political views among non-Latvians. While one segment acknowledged the historical fate of the Republic of Latvia, another segment of non-Latvians clung to the orthodox Soviet perspective.

Throughout the transition era Baltic politicians have argued that the events of 1940 were relevant for the restoration of the statehood of Estonia, Latvia, and Lithuania as well as for the unconditional removal of Soviet troops. In a typical initiative, in November 1990 the presidents of the Baltic states issued a statement in preparation for a meeting of the Conference on Security and Cooperation in Europe (CSCE). The statement reminded the CSCE that Latvia, Lithuania, and Estonia were never legally part of the USSR and asked that CSCE countries reaffirm this point of international law when discussing issues relating to Soviet armed forces stationed in the Baltics. The Baltic presidents noted that their request was in accordance with the principles of respect for the integrity of states, self-determination, and the right to resist forcible annexation expressed by the CSCE.[15] Baltic politicians have also argued that the demilitarization of the Baltic region would contribute to the security of all concerned. The question remained unresolved in 1993.

LATVIA AS A MILITARILY OCCUPIED STATE

The incorporation of Latvia into the USSR began with ultimatums forcing the establishment of military bases in late 1939. Although the treaties limited the number of Soviet troops and specified under what conditions they would be stationed, further ultimatums in June 1940 forced the uncondi-

120

tional opening of Latvia's borders. With the Soviet occupation of 17 June 1940, Latvia lost sovereignty over its territory. The political consequences were immediate: by 21 July 1940 Latvia had a Communist government asking to become part of the USSR.[16]

Since 1940 most Balts have considered the Soviet military to be an occupation force, despite the latter's objections.[17] Whatever terms one uses, the Soviet troops have no legal basis for being on the territory of Latvia,[18] and accordingly the Latvian government has urged that the issue be resolved with the help of the international community. Since Latvia regained independence on 21 August 1991, the withdrawal of the Soviet troops has been discussed in various bilateral and multilateral negotiations, with limited success.[19] By early 1992 the government of Russia mostly used the lack of housing and other problems to defend the slow pace of withdrawal.[20] Latvian legislators have noted that they cannot accept this as an argument because social problems on the territory of the former USSR may continue forever.[21] In 1992 Latvia's prime minister Ivars Godmanis has argued that talk about difficulties is mostly a pretext, because Russia has ignored proposals by Latvia and Western countries to help build housing for the withdrawing forces.[22]

In addition, Latvia too has social problems and the situation is aggravated by the presence of ex-Soviet troops. To mention just a few examples, between 1986 and 1990 a total of 10,700 flats were built for military personnel, amounting to 23 percent of the entire housing stock built in Latvia in that period. Yet as of 1 July 1990, 170,400 civilian families in Latvia were on the waiting list for apartments, and some 34,000 families had been waiting for more than ten years.[23] As for education, in early 1992 ten of fifteen schools in the city of Liepāja used Russian as the language of instruction; among the pupils were 1,650 children of army personnel (18.1 percent of the pupils in Russian-language schools). The army paid nothing for this service, schools being funded by the city.[24] In the economic sphere, the Soviets have enjoyed their own military factories and repair shops in Latvia, managed by officers and controlled by Moscow authorities. As of autumn 1992, the fate of these military factories was uncertain. There was discussion of transforming them into civilian factories and "retaining the work-force in Latvia,"[25] the latter proposal being controversial because it suggested that more Russians would become permanent residents of Latvia.

Yet the government of Latvia has been concerned most of all about the political interference of the Soviet/Russian forces in Latvia's domestic affairs. The Baltic Military District command supported the coup attempts of January and August 1991, and on other occasions the Soviet military supported antigovernment forces by, for example, dropping Interfront leaflets from military helicopters. The linkage of troop withdrawal to Latvia's laws on citizenship and language has also been disconcerting. Latvian legislators have argued before the Council of Europe that relations between population groups in Latvia have been aggravated by the one-sided support of Russians by the huge Russian military force.[26] Yet Russia's policy of linking the military withdrawal to the position of postwar settlers in Latvia only escalated in the latter part of 1992. An initial high point was reached on 29 October 1992, when President Yeltsin issued a decree suspending the withdrawal of Russian troops due to "profound concern over numerous infringements of rights of the Russian-speaking population in the Baltic countries."[27] Similar statements had been made in previous months and the foreign minister of Russia even threatened armed intervention.[28]

Russia's policy of linking its withdrawal of troops from Latvia to demands regarding the settler population has highlighted the international nature of the issue. Russia's rhetoric became more aggressive during 1993, apparently expecting that this would promote its foreign policy interests. An official of Russia's foreign ministry has gone on record saying that

> I think that it would be altogether wrong if Russian diplomacy were not to accent human rights problems in the Baltic states. That is so both in regard to the entire Russian-speaking population and specifically the military personnel. The question of human rights is a very strong weapon. The West is highly sensitive to this issue, in contrast to us. As a result of our dipolmatic activities the reputation of the three Baltic countries can be undermined more and more and this will destroy their false image of victimization and will also serve the interests of our citizens, including military personnel.[29]

Although most Russian politicians have joined in the acusations against the Balts, this issue has been pressed most decidedly by opponents of President Yeltsin.[30] Clearly, the balance between domestic forces in Russia affects the way issues regarding Soviet-era settlers and ex-Soviet troops in Latvia will be approached from the Russian side. Yet these questions are also dominant themes in the domestic politics of Latvia.

In addition to the general link between the Soviet/Russian military presence in Latvia and ethnic problems, the issue of the settlement of retired Soviet officers and other ex-Soviet military personnel in Latvia is especially problematic. As the archives of the Communist party become available to researchers, more data on past policies of settling retired Soviet officers in Latvia are reported in the press. It was revealed that in 1960 alone, 1,736 retired Soviet officers moved to Riga, many of them obtaining government apartments ahead of local families who had waited in line for years. In 1960, the officers were assigned 18.6 percent of available apartment space in Riga.[31] Although the social equity issues involved in such policies were only beginning to be raised in late 1992, links to the demographic minoritization of Latvians have been pointed out. The representatives of Latvia at the fourth session of the European Parliament in May 1992 compared Latvia's situation with that of Cyprus. Noting that an entire plenary session was devoted to Turkey's military presence in Cyprus and to the demographic consequences connected to it, the Baltic delegations requested a similar session to examine their problems.[32] The situation is especially grave in Latvia, in part because Latvia has been the strategic heart of the Soviet Baltic Military District.

DEMOGRAPHIC MINORITIZATION OF AN INDIGENOUS NATION

In a process that has few parallels anywhere in the world, Latvians have been brought to the brink of becoming a minority in their own country. Latvians constituted 77 percent of the population of Latvia in 1935, but by 1989 this percentage had decreased to 52 percent. Moreover, Latvians had become a minority in all urban centers, including in the capital city of Riga, where they constituted just 36.5 percent (see Table 6.1). Although Russians and other eastern Slavs had become the majority in cities, most small towns and rural areas remained predominantly Latvian, with the important exception of the southeastern region. In the Daugavpils district Latvians made up only 35.9 percent of the population in 1989.[33]

Russians comprised 8.8 percent of the population of Latvia in 1935 and 34 percent in 1989 (see Table A.5 in the Appendix). Other minorities constituted 14.2 percent of Latvia's population in 1935, and although this percentage was very similar in 1989, the composition had changed dramatically. In 1935 Germans and Jews were the largest "other" minorities, but both had nearly disappeared by 1989. The German minority that had lived in Latvia for some seven hundred years was resettled to Germany in 1939–40 under the provisions of the Hitler-Stalin pact.[34] Many of Latvia's Jews were killed during the period of German occupation between 1941 and 1944, and another substantial segment emigrated to Israel or elsewhere after 1970.[35] Sizable Ukrainian and Belorussian minorities have settled in Latvia in their stead. The two historical minorities of Latvia that have experienced little demographic change are the Poles and Lithuanians.

The main reason for the demographic shift in the position of Latvians in Latvia is the immigration of Russians, Belorussians, and Ukrainians during the Soviet period. As the data in Table 6.1, Table A.5, and Figure 6.1 illustrate, the increase of eastern Slavs has been dramatic from one census to the next. The intensity of immigration to Latvia is unprecedented in Europe. Proportionally, Latvia has experienced the highest rate of immigration among all the states of Europe and the republics of the USSR.[36] An all-Soviet comparison of population increase due to migration also shows Latvia to be far ahead of all republics of the USSR.[37]

Table 6.1
Distribution of the Population of Latvia in 1989, by Ethnicity
(in thousands)

	Latvians		Russians		Others	
	n	percent	n	percent	n	percent
Latvia	1,387.7	52	905.5	34	373.3	14
Cities:						
Riga	331.9	36.5	430.5	47	147.9	16.5
Daugavpils	16.4	13	72.7	58.3	35.9	28.7
Jelgava	36.8	49.7	25.7	34.6	11.6	15.6
Jūrmala	26.8	44.2	25.5	42.1	8.3	13.7
Leipāja	44.4	38.8	49.3	43	20.7	18.1
Rēzekne	15.8	37.3	23.3	55	3.3	7.6
Ventspils	21.8	43	19.9	39.3	8.9	17.6
Towns and rural areas:	894.0	69.4	258.3	20	136.6	10.6

Source: Author's calculations based on 1989 census; see LPSR Valsts Statistikas Komiteja, *1989, gada tautas skaitīšanas rezultāti, LPSR* (Riga: Statistiska biļetēns, I. Daļa, 1989) 127. n = number.

This unprecedented immigration was closely tied to Soviet policies such as facilitating the settlement of retired Soviet officers and their families by preferential access to state housing and by other regulations. Similarly, many high state and party officials were brought in to oversee political life, especially after 1959 when numerous Latvian Communists were purged for alleged "bourgeois nationalism."[38] Most important, Soviet economic policies sponsored huge enterprises that could not be staffed locally and led to the importation of managers as well as workers.[39] Many vacation areas along the coast of Latvia were taken over by Soviet ministries and labor unions who also brought in their own staffs. Central ministries even created their own Russian-speaking educational institutions without considering the ethnic consequences. Apart from military academies, the most telling example is that of the Riga Aviation Institute, which brought thousands of Russian-speakers to Latvia, where they remained in 1992 (see Table A.7 in the Appendix). One consequence of these policies was that Russian became the dominant language in public life, a topic discussed further in the next chapter.

Uncontrolled immigration has practically rendered Latvians a minority in their own country, but an even more traumatic development for the Latvian people has been their decimation in absolute terms. Figure 6.1 and Table

FIGURE 6.1. Population of Latvia by ethnicity.

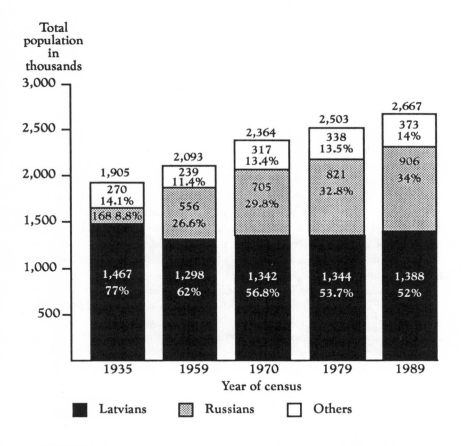

Source: See Table A.5 in the Appendix.

A.5 illustrate that in absolute numbers there were more Latvians in Latvia in 1935 than at any time since. Again, no other nation in Europe has undergone a similar fate. Most Latvians perceive that this is due to the genocidal policies and activities of the Soviet Union, especially the mass deportations in June 1941 and March 1949 when whole families were brutally transported to Siberia where many perished. It is difficult to determine the exact number of victims, but calculations put the number of 1941 and 1949 deportees at between 58,312 and 85,081 people.[40] An unspecified number survived Siberia and returned to Latvia in the late 1950s and 1960s. Many other lives were shattered or lost through the terrorism of the Soviet secret police. The total number of Latvia's inhabitants killed or arrested in 1940–41 and 1944–53 is around 180,000.[41]

The experience of terror during the initial year of Soviet occupation in 1940–41 also was the main cause for large-scale flight from Latvia when the Soviets came back in 1944. Some 120,000 Latvians fled to an uncertain fate in the West, fearing that otherwise they too would become victims of the Stalinist terror. Some Latvians ended up as refugees due to German policies of military and labor conscription and evacuation in the face of an advancing Soviet army. Other Latvians were killed in German concentration camps together with most of Latvia's Jews and Gypsies, and many others were killed while fighting in the ranks of the German-organized Latvian Legion against the Soviet army.[42] Latvians never recovered from the losses inflicted under the rules of Stalin and Hitler. Even after the decrease of physical terror that followed Stalin's death, Latvians as a people show limited demographic growth.[43] At least in part, this too can be blamed on Soviet policies. Demographic studies show that birth rates decrease in times of war and other political trauma such as foreign rule.[44] In addition, birth rates were negatively affected by policies limiting access to housing and social services for young families.

The demographic minoritization of Latvians in the urban centers of Latvia has had numerous consequences, including on the demography itself. The data of the 1989 Soviet census show that most children from mixed Latvian-Russian marriages in Riga assimilated to the Russian side of the family.[45] The process was reversed in rural areas, which also experienced fewer mixed marriages.[46] The trend in Riga marked an ominous reversal of trends in the 1960s, when the Latvian side of mixed families had stronger assimilative powers.[47] As illustrated in Figure A.2 (see Appendix), the ratio of non-Latvians in the population is especially strong for the ages twenty to forty-four, whereas the Latvian population share is strongest in the age group over seventy.

Past policies have contemporary consequences. Since the 1980s Latvians have feared cultural and political extinction. It has been argued that Soviet policies amount to demographic genocide.[48] The combination of deliberate deportation of indigenous inhabitants and the state-sponsored settlement of large numbers of eastern Slavs is seen as especially invidious. Many Latvians appeal to the Genocide Convention of the United Nations,[49] which recognizes that a collective entity has rights as a corporate body, specifically the right not to be destroyed, in whole or in part, as a national, ethnic, racial, or religious group.[50] Other international conventions recognize the rights of peoples to self-determination and the preservation of cultural identity.[51] In recent years Latvian politicians have cited numerous specific international laws, for example UN Resolution 2189 passed in December 1967 repudiating policies of colonial power "that, in contravening of the rights of the indigenous nation, systematically promote the influx of immigrants from foreign lands as well as the dislocation and deportation of the indigenous inhabitants."[52]

Worldwide, ethnic groups that are numerically overwhelmed by larger neighbors or immigrants typically start feeling anxiety about extinction.[53] Artificial "minoritization" through uncontrolled immigration is one of the recurrent themes in claims for secession. Government-sponsored colonization schemes that bring ethnic strangers into the region are uniformly regarded as plots to overwhelm the existing majority in the region by the weight of numbers.[54] In such situations, the democratic response is to safeguard the rights of the smaller nation to its homeland.

The Soviet government's policy of promoting intrarepublic migration of Russians and others was aimed at an "internationalization" of its population, yet just the opposite happened. As theorists have pointed out, collective identities are activated by the presence of strangers and competitors within the state,[55] and this dynamic seems to have been at work in the Baltic states. By the mid-1980s ethnic relations in the region were becoming more tense. Commenting on a survey in Estonia showing that 69 percent of Estonians and 43 percent of others stated that ethnic relations had worsened between 1986 and 1988, a prominent Russian ethnosociologist adduced three explanations. First, he noted that the indigenous inhabitants see the influx of migrants as an ecological threat to the region, since they constitute most of the persons working in industrial concerns. Second, he noted the intense pressure on the social infrastructure, expressed especially in a shortage of living space. And third, he noted that the "social functions of the Estonian language inevitably are diminished" as more foreigners move to Estonia.[56] To these three points one could add the resentment of political dominance.

POLITICAL CONTROL BY SOVIETS

For more than forty years Latvia was a dependent territory of the USSR: armed power belonged to the Soviet military and it was this power that sustained the local political authorities. Latvia's government, judicial system, police, state administration, and Communist party were little more than extensions of the central Soviet government in Moscow. As outlined in chapters 1 and 2, the gradual emancipation from this dominance of Latvia and other republics was a crucial part of the democratization and breakup of the Soviet Union. The struggle for devolution took place on two levels—the level of interaction between republics and central authorities, and the level of political confrontations within the republics. Here we focus on the intra-republic level in the case of Latvia, but it is crucial to remember the close links to the larger Soviet and international theater. Even as we focus on the internal politics of Latvia in the transition period, we find that major players such as local branches of central Soviet authorities and their supporters defined their identity in direct opposition to the separate state identity of Latvia.

Before analyzing the position of subsidiary Soviet groupings in Latvia, one needs to clarify the position of central Soviet authorities and institutions. The struggle for political devolution in Latvia began before 4 May 1990, but it reached a new stage on that date. On 4 May 1990 the newly elected Supreme Soviet of Latvia declared its intent to restore the independent statehood of the Republic of Latvia after a transitional period. A few days later, Soviet President Gorbachev and the first secretary of the Communist Party of Latvia (CPSU platform) labeled this declaration as unconstitutional.[57] As noted in chapter 5, several hundred Soviet servicemen and other anti-independence forces took this declaration by Gorbachev as a green light for direct action against the legislature and on 15 May tried to force their way into the Parliament Building. Other Soviet institutions made more formal attempts to retain Soviet rule in Latvia, most importantly the Soviet Ministry of Internal Affairs and the procuracy of the USSR. Both had been crucial institutions representing central Soviet power in Latvia and both tried to preserve their role and the supremacy of their decisions. The Prosecutor of the USSR instructed its offices in the Baltic "to pay special attention to strict supervision over the observance of the USSR Constitution and Union laws in the republics."[58] The response of the new government of Latvia was to create alternative structures loyal to itself, but the situation was more complicated in the case of the KGB. In July 1990 the chairman of Latvia's Supreme Council's Defense and Internal Affairs Committee noted that the new government had no means to control the activities of the Soviet KGB in Latvia.[59]

After Latvia established an independent procuracy in 1990, the Latvian branch of the procuracy of the USSR refused to disband and remained in existence as a parallel structure. Each of the two procuracies claimed to be the sole legal body empowered to oversee the judicial process, but as time passed Latvia's procuracy gained the upper hand, especially after 288 of 340 officials of the Soviet procuracy moved over to it in September 1990.[60] Nevertheless, the split over loyalty to Latvia or the Soviet Union was also reflected in the police forces. Among the militia some supported the laws of the government of Latvia and others union laws. "Approximately two-thirds of Riga Militia personnel—and some 40 percent of the republic's militia is concentrated here—are backing union legislative acts."[61] In addition, the notorious black beret special police force of the Soviet Ministry of Interior remained loyal to the union, as demonstrated in the January 1991 crackdown.

As previously noted, the democratization process in the former USSR was strongly promoted by the emergence of the independent-minded Russian Republic and its institutions. These institutions were natural allies of the independent institutions of Latvia. Thus, in May 1991, the procuracy of the RSFSR signed an agreement of recognition with the independent procuracies of Latvia and Lithuania; in response "workers of the procuracy of the Latvian SSR" adopted a resolution of protest and vowed that they would remain loyal to the procuracy of the USSR.[62] This and other power structures of the USSR continued to exist in Latvia until the demise of the USSR itself, with some even prolonging their presence after that, most notably the renamed Soviet military forces. Furthermore, most of the personnel of these institutions remained in Latvia after the declaration of full independence on 21 August 1991. These people constituted the hard core of the "Soviets without the Soviet Union" with which the new state of Latvia has had to reckon.

Antigovernmental Activities of Soviet Loyalists

The split between pro-Soviet and independent political forces in Latvia was reflected in other groupings, as well. The larger part of the Communist Party of Latvia remained loyal to Moscow when the party formally split on 7 April 1990. The political split coincided with a rift along ethnic lines, since most reformist party members were Latvian, whereas the old-style CPL consisted mostly of Russians, except for a few high-level apparatchiki led by First Secretary Alfrēds Rubiks. In late May 1990 the Communist Party of Latvia (CPSU platform), Interfront, and members of the armed forces serving in Latvia forged an alliance of pro-Soviet forces, the Committee for the Defense of the USSR Constitution and the Citizens of the Latvian SSR.[63] Other pro-Soviet Communist political forces consisted of factions in local councils and the Parliament of Latvia,[64] and of an array of self-appointed bodies calling themselves National Salvation Committees and the like. The difficulty posed by these groups to the government of Latvia was that they went far beyond expressing differing opinions; they wanted to revert to the old-time Communist and all-Soviet regime. In order to reach this goal they forged alliances with like-minded groupings in Moscow, activities that reached their zenith in the hard-line coup attempts of January and August 1991.[65]

During the weeks before the January 1991 coup attempt in Latvia the pro-Moscow National Salvation Committees increasingly claimed that the lives of Soviet military personnel and local Russians were threatened and that Soviet authorities had to intervene to save them from a terrible fate.[66] In December 1990, orthodox Communist newspapers such as *Cīņa*, *Sovetskaia Latviia*, and *Novosti Rigi* demanded that power be taken over by the National Salvation Committee.[67] In addition, the black beret, Otriady Militsii Osobogo Naznacheniia (OMON) force became increasingly threatening. On 9 November 1990, black berets brutally beat several city employees in Jūrmala who tried to evict the local Communist party group from offices that it was no longer entitled to rent.[68] Shortly afterward Latvia's minister of the interior stated that even though the OMON troops were formally subordinate to the Soviet Army of the Interior, "in reality the OMON is under the command of the Central Committee of the Republic's Communist Party."[69]

The pro-Moscow CPL complained that its appeals to Moscow were disregarded,[70] but it did have supporters among Communist hard-liners. *Pravda* published articles in support of Interfront,[71] and statements issued by the National Salvation Committee were broadcast on central Soviet radio and other media. These media broadcast in January 1991 that the National Salvation Committee was taking power and dissolving the legislature and government of Latvia, that it wanted Latvia to be "within the body of a renewed USSR," that the laws of the Latvian SSR and USSR had to be followed, and that the committee would "cooperate with all sociopolitical forces which favor the socialist road of social development."[72] The government-controlled evening television show *Vremia* broadcast reports contending that the Russian minorities in the Baltics were being so abused as to require drastic protection.[73]

A pro-Soviet All-Latvian People's Assembly appealed to Gorbachev to take all necessary measures "up to and including the imposition of presidential rule" to strengthen "law and order in the Soviet Baltic republics." At the same time it fiercely denounced Yeltsin for his "anti-people, provocative activities, which benefit extremists and separatists," referring to his signing of a document of mutual support with the leaders of Estonia, Latvia, and Lithuania on 13 January 1991.[74] After this coup attempt was aborted similar activities were repeated in August 1991. This time the focus of the hard-line coup was in Moscow and Leningrad, but parallel activities occurred in the Baltic States. The themes raised were similar to those of the January events.

Thus on 20 August 1991, the politburo of the CPL issued a statement in support of the putchists, emphasizing that "the Latvian Soviet Socialist Republic . . . is an integral part of the USSR."[75]

The groups supporting the August coup attempt were the same as well: in addition to the Communist party, the Baltic Military District also declared its support for the National Salvation Committee,[76] and army helicopters distributed its appeal all over Latvia.[77] The appeal was signed by the *Ravnopravie* faction of deputies, the International Workers' Front of the Latvia SSR, the United Council of Workers' Collectives, the Council of the Veterans of Work and War, the Central Committee of the CPL, and the Central Committee of the Communist Youth Organization. They referred to the Soviet law on state of emergency and called on all citizens to follow the instructions of the National Salvation Committee "for the sake of saving our Latvia and our Soviet Homeland."[78] In addition, the leadership of the Communist party sent out instructions to its sections throughout Latvia asking them to support the coup.[79] These seditious acts triggered the outlawing of the CPL after the collapse of the coup. As for the role of the *Ravnopravie* faction in the legislature, the Parliamentary Committee of Investigation found that fifteen deputies were implicated in the coup attempt and annulled their mandates in July 1992.[80]

After the breakup of the Soviet Union, many of the people linked to the coup attempts continued to work for a reversal of recent history. For example, the leader of the Interfront in Latvia, Igor Lopatin, had become active in regional political movements working for a rebuilding of the USSR. One such failed attempt was the convening of the USSR's Supreme Soviet Deputy Congress on 17 March 1992 in Moscow.[81]

Latvia: A Settler State?

Discussions of ethnic politics rarely include an international political context. Yet clearly, numerous minority situations owe their existence to international processes such as conquest and war, the redrawing of borders, and migration and colonization. The case of Latvia highlights the international dimension of ethnopolitics, yet precise conceptualization remains difficult. Former Soviet rule and contemporary Russian influence in Latvia can be denoted by concepts such as incorporation, occupation, or the notion of a dependent client state. Yet these parameters capture only the state-to-state relationship and ignore the importance of the postwar settlers. Some analysts have applied the concept of a colony, but the concept of a settler state is closer to the mark because it denotes more pervasive political and economic controls, as well as the intensive settlement of people from abroad. Ronald Weitzer refers to Rhodesia, South Africa, Liberia, Northern Ireland, Israel, and Taiwan as settler states, his main criterion being that "settler societies are founded by migrant groups who assume a superordinate position vis-á-vis native inhabitants and build self-sustaining states that are *de jure* or *de facto* independent from the mother country."[82] Latvia differs in that the settlers have been closely tied to the Soviet/Russian motherland rather than representing their own state, yet this could change depending on the return of political events in Russia. In our context the heuristic usefulness of the concept is that it pinpoints the superordinate position of a settler population. This has been the crux of the political reality of Latvia under Soviet rule, with change beginning only slowly since 1990.

In a Communist system, one measure of political dominance is the distribution of power within the party. The CPSU did not publish data on its ethnic composition within specific republics, but in 1989 an official of the Communist Party of Latvia stated that Latvians made up 39 percent of the membership,[83] a number very close to existing estimates showing their underrepresentation.[84] In early 1990 Latvians were reported to constitute 26.8 percent of the members of the Jūrmala city party organization.[85] The Soviet system of nomenklatura appointments—that is, the assignment of leading positions in all spheres only with the approval of the Communist party—led to significant bias in favor of party loyalists, frequently Russians and/or demobilized soviet officers.[86] As Table 6.2 illustrates, Russians as a group dominated the governmental and party bureaucracies. As late as January 1992, Latvians comprised just 15 percent of the police and other employees of the Ministry of Interior in Riga, and 35 percent in all of Latvia.[87]

It is difficult to measure the economic power of non-Latvian settlers in Latvia, but it appears to be considerable. It has been suggested that about 80 percent of privately held business in Latvia is in the hands of non-Latvians.[88] Another large segment of the nonindigenous population is employed by the industries formerly controlled by central Soviet ministries. Although privileged in the past by the command economy, many of these enterprises will be unable to make the transition to a market economy. The resulting industrial unemployment is likely to take on an ethnic dimension in the mid-1990s.

In this chapter we noted the demographic dominance of non-Latvians in urban centers, and the next chapter will provide details about Russian linguistic predominance. The dominance of Russians and Russian-speakers in the urban industrial sector of Latvia, as contrasted to the dominance of Latvians in rural society, agriculture, and arts and culture,[89] reflects the marginalization of an indigenous population typical of settler societies. Many Latvian citizens such as the lawyer and parliamentary deputy Ruta Marjaša perceive this subordinate position as the discrimination of an indigenous people in its homeland.[90] One might note that historically, too,

Table 6.2
Employment, by Nationality, in 1989

	Total Number	Latvians (percent)	Others (percent)
Total employed	1,458,554	49.4	50.6
Industry[1]	448,038	40.6	59.4
Agriculture	229,215	71.5	28.5
Transport	99,078	37.2	62.8
Culture and arts	24,419	69.2	30.8
State administration and CPSU professionals	68,820	31.5	68.5

Source: LPSR Valsts statistikas komiteja, 1989. *Gada tautas skaitīšanas rezultāti*, LPSR (Riga: Statistiska biļetēns, II. Daļa, 1989), 46, 55.

[1]Only those branches of the economy where the balance between ethnic groups is off by more than a few percentage points are listed.

Latvians have been subordinate to a different settler group—the German aristocracy that formed the cultural, economic, and political elite until World War I.

Analysts of settler dominance over an indigenous people emphasize that the power resides in control over the political and security sectors. Limiting this control has been one aspect of democratization in Latvia. Another ethnopolitical issue is how to deal with a large settler community that includes many people who do not speak the local language and reject the sovereignty of the state in which they reside. As for the future, it is worthwhile to remember a statement by Donald Horowitz that the outcome of political conflicts is determined not only by relative numbers and power, but also by the impact of unevenly distributed legitimacy, and "by far the most common claim to legitimacy is predicated on indigenousness."[91]

Conclusion

Some ethnic conflicts are internationalized;[92] in Latvia an international conflict has been "ethnicized." Decades of illegal Soviet rule in Latvia have created an unprecedented ethnopolitical situation where the indigenous nation is weak, yet Soviet-era settlers claim that their rights are infringed upon. As Latvia struggles to undo the legacy of Soviet policies, much depends on the extent to which cooperative solutions can be found with Russia and the international community.

Despite the formal restoration of independence in August 1991, in 1993 Latvia is still struggling to emancipate itself from the position of an internationally and militarily subject state of the USSR/Russia. Innumerable problems between Russia and Latvia remain unsolved, including the role of the Soviet-era settler community in Latvia. In 1993 it remains unclear whether Latvia is a self-determining nation, a settler state, or a client state of Russia.

The status of a client state is indicated by the fact that Latvia's massive neighbor to the East continues to exert direct power through its huge unauthorized military presence. It also continues to exert power indirectly by taking on the role of protector of Russians in Latvia, though remaining contradictory as to whether it views them as its own citizens or citizens of Latvia. In addition, Russia seems ambivalent about its position toward the legacy of the Soviet Union as it concerns the Latvian state and nation. Until the demise of the USSR, the Yeltsin forces denounced the Soviet legacy of international lawbreaking and the use of the military to compel Latvia to do its will. Beginning in the spring of 1992, however, Russia's policies became more threatening and contradictory. Moscow has tried to use the troop withdrawal for political leverage. Russia has also claimed ownership of former Soviet facilities in Latvia, such as military factories and the building of the former Soviet embassy in Riga, yet it has disclaimed responsibility for all destructive policies of the Soviet period, denying, for example, payment of pensions to Latvian citizens deported to the GULAG. Rhetorically, the statements by Russian politicians about Latvia became more hard-line and accusatory during 1992. Latvian politicians have reacted with concern toward what they see as Russia's Orwellian logic of painting itself as the victim in relation to its small neighbor.

The government of Latvia has been successful in winning the support of the United Nations and other international organizations for unconditional withdrawal of the former Soviet troops. The role of the international community in regard to other issues remains unclear. Some political forces have argued that because Latvia has been an illegally occupied state, and former Soviet forces remain on its territory in contravention of international law, solutions to Latvia's problems can only be found with international support. From this perspective the formal restoration of Latvia's independence is seen as less preferable than assuming the status of a country that needs de-occupation and decolonization under United Nations auspices. In early 1991 the Council of the Popular Front of Latvia appealed to the Supreme Council of Latvia to clarify that Latvia has the status of an occupied and colonized country as defined in Resolution 103 of the United Nations' thirty-sixth session. It also asked that UN observers be brought to Latvia to gather information showing this relationship.[93] The Citizens' Congress has similarly asked that international organizations be made responsible for the internal affairs of Latvia.[94]

Besides questions about Russia's continuing military presence, there is the issue of the status of the postwar settler community. The military, police, and bureaucracy are power bases of the state, and Latvia has to contend with the legacy that an ethnically non-Latvian cadre has dominated these areas. The issue is compounded by problems of political loyalty. As highlighted before, a considerable segment of the postwar settler community has supported Latvia's independence and democracy, yet there also exists the opposite group that has been the backbone of Soviet and communist rule. As the coup attempts of January and August 1991 show, there are people who wish to restore the old regime and thus pose a threat to the integrity of the Latvian state. This group consists of retired Soviet officers, former Soviet state administrators, state procurators, KGB and other police personnel, and professional cadres of the CPSU. Latvia's policies toward these people have been very liberal. As of mid-1993 the only legal or political restriction imposed on them has been the provision in the draft citizenship law that some categories of people linked to Soviet rule may not be eligible for naturalization. If they continue to reside in Latvia, one can expect their continued calls for Moscow's intervention in Latvia.[95]

In sum, we must examine the broad political context to make sense of issues in Latvian ethnopolitics. This context is one of international relations with the USSR/Russia as well as intragroup relations within Latvia. During the transition to democracy and full independence much is determined by preexisting conditions. In 1993 Latvia is still making the transition from a dependent territory to a self-determining nation. Transition means that many old structures and relationships persist while new ones are beginning to emerge. The more optimistic view sees transition as a continuum where change means a consistent movement away from authoritarianism and toward democracy. The alternate view conceptualizes transition as a period with a dualistic system of power and as a complex struggle between conflicting powers for the upper hand. This chapter follows the thrust of the other chapters—that the latter model is more applicable to the case of the former Soviet Union than to that of Latvia.

NOTES

1. The RSFSR officially recognized the independence of Latvia on 23 August 1991, and the USSR followed suit on 6 September 1991. For the RSFSR this was the second time that it had recognized Latvia's independence in this century. The first time was in August 1920, when it signed a peace treaty with Latvia stating that "Russia unreservedly recognizes the independence, self-subsistency and sovereignty of the Latvian State and voluntarily and forever renounces all sovereign rights over the Latvian people and territory." *Latvian-Russian Relations*, Documents, 2d printing, comp. Alfred Bilmanis (Washington, D.C.: The Latvian Legation, 1978), 70.

2. Dzintra Bungs, "Soviet Troops in Latvia," *RFE/RL Research Report*, 28 August 1992, 18–27.

3. One of the police officers accused of the January 1991 killings in Riga, Sergei Parfjonov, acquired citizenship of the Russian Federation on 27 April 1992. See photocopy of original document in *Diena*, 9 May 1992, 1. Apparently this was intended to suggest that Latvia has no jurisdiction over Parfjonov. When Latvia's criminal police went to Russia and arrested him and other black beret troops accused of crimes during the coup attempts of January and August 1991, *Pravda* on 22 October 1991 denounced this as the violation of a Soviet law stating that USSR citizens could not be extradited to a foreign state. After Parfjonov was convicted in Latvia Russia demanded that he "be returned to his native country" to serve out his sentence (*Nezavisimaia gazeta*, 17 April 1993). Parfjonov was turned over to Russia in early August 1993 and was welcomed home at the Moscow train station by enthusiastic communists playing the old Soviet anthem (*Diena*, 7 August 1993).

4. During troop withdrawal negotiations with Latvia, Russia has demanded that Latvia guarantee citizenship to all its residents, including those military persons wishing to remain in Latvia. *Diena*, 5 May 1992.

5. Following similar resolutions by other international bodies, the United Nations General Assembly in late November 1992 passed a resolution calling for a complete withdrawal of Russian troops from the Baltic states. *Baltic Observer*, 1992, no. 41: 1.

6. See, for example, *Rossiskaia gazeta*, 23 June 1992.

7. Artūrs Snips, "It kā," *Kultūras fonda avīze*, November 1991.

8. Walker Connor suggests a typology of states based on different configurations of ethnic groupings. He differentiates among nation-states, multinational states, immigrant states, and mestizo states. Although he acknowledges that recent global migratory movements may change this typology, in any case his typology cannot accommodate Latvia. Walker Connor, "Ethnonationalism," in Myron Weiner and Samuel P. Huntington, eds., *Understanding Political Development* (Boston: Little, Brown, 1987), 212.

9. William J. H. Hough III, "The Annexation of the Baltic States and Its Effect on the Development of Law Prohibiting Forcible Seizure of Territory," *New York Law School Journal of International and Comparative Law* 6 (Winter 1985), passim; see also Boris Meissner, *Die Sowjetunion, die Baltischen Staaten und das Völkerrecht* (Cologne: Politik und Wirtschaft, 1956).

10. See *Osteuropa* 1990, no. 10: A623-N25; Thomas Sherlock, "New Thinking on the Nazi-Soviet Pact," *Report on the USSR*, 28 July 1989, 12–15. For a time the Soviets argued that they could not find their copies of the relevant documents. On 29 October 1992 an aide to President Yeltsin showed on television the Soviet originals of the secret protocols to the Hitler-Stalin pact. *New York Times*, 29 October 1992, 7. All along, the documents had been in the archive of the Central Committee. See Bernd Bonwetsch and Marc Junge, "Die Vertuschung der deutsch-sowjetischen Geheimabkommen von 1939—eine unendliche Geschichte," *Osteuropa* 43, no. 2 (February 1993): 132–38.

11. *Latvijas Jaunatne*, 20 March 1990, 4.

12. "The Baltics: That Very Difficult Year," *Moscow News* 1990, no. 32: 15.

13. *Lithuanian Review*, 13 April 1990.

14. *Sovetskaia molodezh*, 24 November 1990, as cited in *FBIS-SOV-90-246*, 21 December 1990; the survey was conducted by the Center for Sociological Research and was based on a sample of one thousand residents.

15. Official communiqué, Vilnius, 9 November 1990, as printed in *Neatkarīgā Cīņa*, 13 November 1990, p. 1.

16. See texts of the various documents in Bilmanis, *Latvian-Russian Relations*: also Meissner, *Die Sowjetunion*, entire; U.S. Congress, House, *Baltic States Investigation: Hearings before the Select Committee to Investigate the Incorporation of the Baltic States into the U.S.S.R.*, on H.R. 346, 83d Cong., 1st sess., 1953. See also George Ginsburgs, "Nationality and State Succession in Soviet Theory and Practice—The Experience of the Baltic Republics," in Adolfs Sprudzs and Armin Rusis, eds., *Res Baltica: A Collection of Essays in Honor of the Memory of Dr. Alfred Bilmanis* (Leyden: A. W. Sijthoff, 1988), 160–90. Latvia was forced to yield to the Soviet ultimatiums of 1939–40 due to the agreement between Hitler and

Stalin that allowed Hitler to attack Poland in September 1939—thus starting World War II—and as a reward for Stalin's promise of neutrality put the Baltic states and Finland in the Soviet "sphere of interest." Whereas the Baltic states felt unable to defend themselves, Finland did not yield and was attacked by the Soviets, leading to the Winter War of 1939–40 and the USSR's expulsion from the League of Nations.

17. *Pravda* (8 March 1989) and other Soviet newspapers have rejected the epithets "migrant" and "occupant" as provocative.

18. The Baltic governments have had no authority over the Baltic Military District, e.g., "The Baltic Military District covers the territory of the three Baltic republics plus Kaliningrad (previously Königsberg) province (*oblast*) of the RSFSR, but all military matters are administered by Moscow, and are not subject to interference by the local administration." Teresa Rakowska-Harmstone, "Baltic Nationalism and the Soviet Armed Forces," *Journal of Baltic Studies* 17 (Fall 1986): 180.

19. Dzintra Bungs, "Soviet Troops in Latvia," *RFE/RL Research Report*, 28 August 1992, 18–27, and Dzintra Bungs, "Progress on Withdrawal from the Baltic States," *RFE/RL Research Report*, 18 June 1993, 50–59.

20. Social problems were mentioned by Russia at the Group of Seven meeting in Munich, July 1992. *Washington Post*, 8 July 1992. Soviet officers in the Baltics have convened meetings to discuss concerns about the effects of withdrawal on their social welfare and to put pressure on Moscow authorities. Riina Kionka, "Officers in the Baltic Take the Initiative," *Report on the USSR*, 15 November 1991, pp. 27–29.

21. *Latvijas Jaunatne*, 4 February 1992.

22. *Diena*, 26 November 1992, p. 8.

23. Data compiled from official sources by the Commission on Human and National Rights Questions, Supreme Council of the Republic of Latvia, 14 April 1992.

24. *Diena*, 13 February 1992.

25. *Neatkarīgā Cīņa*, 13 February 1992, 2.

26. *Diena*, 13 February 1992.

27. *New York Times*, 30 October 1992, 7. Yeltsin made a similar statement on 4 April 1993 at the end of the Vancouver Summit (live television broadcast).

28. *ITAR-TASS*, 1 April 1992; *FBIS*, Central Eurasia, 1 April 1992, p. 18; *Izvestiia*, 2 April 1992, 5.

29. V. N. Trofimov, "Rossiia—Pribaltika: Kak zhit' dal'she?" *Diplomaticheskii vestnik*, 15–31 July 1992, nos. 13–14: 76–80; 79.

30. Statement by Russia's foreign minister in *New York Times*, 3 July 1992; see also Stephen Foye, "Russian Politics Complicates Baltic Troop Withdrawal," *RFE/RL Research Report*, 20 November 1992, 30–35, and an article in *Izvestiia* saying that "there is no doubt that the campaign under way in Russia in defense of the Russian-speaking population in the Baltics is being used by all kinds of political forces to further their own interests," *Izvestiia*, 18 March 1993, 3, as translated in *The Current Digest of the Post-Soviet Press*, 11 (1993), 18.

31. *Neatkarīgā Cīņa*, 1 December 1992, 2.

32. *Diena*, 12 May 1992, 1.

33. LPSR Valsts statistikas komiteja, 1989. *Gada tautas skaitīšanas rezultāti*, LPSR (Riga: Statistisks Biļetēns, I. Daļa, 1989), 128. The Daugavpils region is exceptional in that historically it has had many Russian and Polish inhabitants, many of whom have been loyal citizens of the Republic of Latvia.

34. See Dietrich A. Loeber, *Diktierte Option: Die Umsiedlung der Deutsch-Balten aus Estland und Lettland 1939–1941* (Neumunster: K. Wachholz, 1972); David Crowe, "Germany and the Baltic Question in Latvia 1939–1940," *East European Quarterly* 26 (September 1992): 371–89; Joseph B. Schechtman, *Postwar Population Transfers in Europe, 1945–55* (Philadelphia: University of Pennsylvania Press, 1963).

35. See Table A.3 in the Appendix, and Juris Dreifelds, "Demographic Trends in Latvia," *Nationalities Papers* 12, no. 1 (1984): 51–54.

36. P. Zvidriņš and P. Eglīte, "Demogrāfiskā situācija un demogrāfiskā politika Latvijā," *Latvijas PSR Zinātņu Akadēmijas Vēstis* 1990, no. 5: 72.

37. L. L. Rybakovskii and I. V. Tarasova, "Migratsionnye protsessy v SSSR: Novye iavleniia," *Sotsiologicheskie issledovaniia* 1990, no. 7: 35.

38. Michael Jean Widmer, "Nationalism and Communism in Latvia: The Latvian Communist Party under Soviet Rule," Ph.D. diss., Harvard University, 1969.

39. See Tönu Parming, "Population Processes and the Nationality Issue in the Soviet Bloc," *Soviet Studies* 32 (July 1980): 398–414; Gundar J. King, *Economic Policies in Occupied Latvia: A Manpower Management Study* (Tacoma, Wash.: Pacific Lutheran University Press, 1965), passim. See also Ellu Saar and Mikk Titma, *Migrationsströme im sowjetischen Baltikum und ihre Nachwirkung auf die baltischen Staaten nach Wiederherstellung der Selbstständigkeit* (Cologne: Berichte des Bundesinstituts für ostwissenschaftliche und internationale Studien no. 9, 1991), 18.

40. The head of the KGB in Latvia has stated that 43,231 people were deported on 25 March 1949 (*Cīņa*, 4 March 1988); it is calculated that at least 15,081 persons were deported on 14 June 1941 (Ādolfs Šilde, "Neskaidrā skaitļu valoda," *Laiks*, 15 June 1988). According to testimony collected by the Latvian Red Cross, Šilde puts the number of 1949 deportees at 70,000 (Šilde, "Neskaidrā").

41. This is the minimum given by Šilde, "Neskaidrā."

42. Dreifelds, "Demographic Trends"; Parming, "Population Processes." For a recent discussion of the Jewish Holocaust in Latvia, see *Diena*, 16 October 1992 and 1 December 1992.

43. See Table A.3 in the Appendix; it should be noted that part of the number for Latvians in 1959 reflects postwar immigrants from the Soviet Union, mostly reliable Communist cadres.

44. Various demographic studies summarized in Stanley Lieberson, *Making It Count: The Improvement of Social Research and Theory* (Berkeley: University of California Press, 1985), 51–52.

45. P. Eglīte, "Iedzīvotāju ataudzes etniskie aspekti Latvijā," *Latvijas PSR Zinātņu Akadēmijas Vēstis* 1991, no. 2: 30.

46. Ibid., 29–30. Assimilation is measured by choice of passport nationality at age sixteen.

47. See Rasma Karklins, *Ethnic Relations in the USSR: The Perspective from Below* (Boston and London: Allen and Unwin, 1986), 36–41.

48. See sources cited in Juris Dreifelds, "Immigration and Ethnicity in Latvia," *Journal of Soviet Nationalities* 1 (Winter 1990–91): 42–81.

49. See for example, *Atmoda*, 25 February 1992, 13.

50. See Vernon Van Dyke, *Human Rights, Ethnicity, and Discrimination* (Westport, Conn.: Greenwood Press, 1985), 81. The charge of genocide was raised by the Fourth Congress of the Popular Front of Latvia in November 1991. It cited the murder of Latvian citizens by Soviet occupying forces after 1940, the large-scale deportations of civilians to Siberia, the deliberate flooding of Latvia with Russian-speaking settlers who were given privileges in access to scarce housing and key jobs, and the introduction of Russian as the dominant language in public interaction. Popular Front of Latvia, Fourth Congress, Resolution Regarding the Occupying Forces' Policy of Genocide of the Latvian Nation and the People of Latvia," Riga, 17 November 1991.

51. Van Dyke, *Human Rights*, passim.

52. Quoted by Visvaldis Lācis in *Atmoda*, 23 May 1991, 4.

53. Donald L. Horowitz, *Ethnic Groups in Conflict* (Berkeley: University of California Press, 1985), 177.

54. Ibid., 263.

55. Milton J. Esman, "Political and Psychological Factors in Ethnic Conflict," in Joseph V. Montville, ed., *Conflict and Peacemaking in Multiethnic Societies* (Lexington, Mass.: Lexington Books, 1990), 53.

56. A. A. Susokolov, "Etnosy pered vyborom," *Sotsiologicheskie issledovaniia* 1988, no. 6, 32–40.

57. *Izvestiia*, 7 May 1990, 2. Similar statements were repeated throughout the transition period until Latvia's declaration of full independence on 21 August 1991. See, for example, *TASS Statement*, 9 June 1990, as quoted in *FBIS-SOV-90-113*, 12 June 1990, 89.

58. *Izvestiia*, 18 May 1990.

59. *Radio Riga,* 7 July 1990; "staff-members of the Latvian Soviet Socialist Republic's KGB" supported Gorbachev's decree as early as 16 May 1990. *Leta-TASS* International Service, as quoted in *FBIS-SOV-90-096,* 17 May 1990, 54.

60. See *Sovetskaia Latviia,* 29 May 1990; *Pravda,* 27 December 1990; *Atmoda,* 16 October 1990, 14, and 4 July 1991, 8–9.

61. TASS International Service, 26 January 1991, quoted in *FBIS-SOV,* 28 January 1991.

62. *Jūrmalas Rīts,* 22 July 1991, 2.

63. Nils Muiznieks, "The Pro-Soviet Movement in Latvia," *Report on the USSR,* 24 August 1990, 24.

64. The "Soiuz" (union) association of Latvia, consisting of 370 people elected to soviets and councils of different levels, was formed on 22 April 1990, TASS, 22 April 1990.

65. Russians such as Gavriil Popov, the democratic mayor of Moscow, realized that the political force behind the Baltic crackdown in January 1991 was the old apparatus of the CPSU, the KGB, the army, and the military-industrial complex. Gavriil Popov, "Kogda ishchut vragov," *Komsomol'skaia pravda,* 26 March 1991, 3, as cited in Victor Zaslavsky, "The Evolution of Separatism in Soviet Society under Gorbachev," in Gail W. Lapidus, Victor Zaslavsky, with Philip Goldman, eds., *From Union to Commonwealth: Nationalism and Separatism in the Soviet Republics* (Cambridge: Cambridge University Press, 1992), 75.

66. Francis X. Clines, *New York Times,* 16 January 1991, 1.

67. See newspapers themselves and summary of articles in *Atmoda,* 20 December 1990, 2.

68. Ibid., 15.

69. Ibid., 3.

70. For example, *Jūrmalas Rīts,* 22 July 1991.

71. *Pravda,* 6 October 1990, 2.

72. *Moscow Domestic Service in Russian,* 19 January 1991, as cited in *FBIS,* January 1991, 76.

73. Francis X. Clines, *New York Times,* 16 January 1991, 4.

74. *FBIS-SOV,* 20 January 1991.

75. *Moscow All-Union Radio,* cited in *FBIS-SOV,* 21 August 1991.

76. *Sovetskaia Latviia,* 23 August 1991, 2. The commander of the Baltic Military District threatened the chairman of Latvia's Parliament with arrest. On 19 August 1991 Soviet tanks and armored vehicles set up checkpoints at strategically important points, organized patrols, and claimed to be in charge. In the early hours of 20 August Soviet troops together with the Soviet black beret troops occupied the buildings of the Ministry of Internal Affairs, the telephone and telegraph building, and the premises of television, radio, and other media. They dealt roughly with scores of people and killed three. Dzintra Bungs, "Latvia Reaffirms Its Independence," *Report on the USSR,* 6 September 1991, 54–62.

77. *Daugavpils Vēstnesis,* 24 August 1991; also *Diena,* 27 August 1991.

78. Leaflet reprinted in *Daugavpils Vēstnesis,* 24 August 1991, 2.

79. *Diena,* 28 August 1991.

80. *Diena,* 10 July 1992.

81. Interview with Lopatin, *Diena,* 7 March 1992.

82. Ronald Weitzer, *Transforming Settler States: Communal Conflict and Internal Security in Northern Ireland and Zimbabwe* (Berkeley: University of California Press, 1990), 25.

83. *Cīņa,* 7 September 1989, 2.

84. Rasma Karklins, "The Analysis of National Cadre Politics," *Journal of Baltic Studies* 18 (Summer-Fall 1987): 165–73.

85. *Jūrmalas Rīts,* organ of the CPL city organization of Jurmala, 1990, no. 18.

86. This statement is based on my work in party archives and the interview with historian Ilga Apine in *Rīgas Balss,* 8 May 1992, 5.

87. Data given by the minister of interior, *Diena,* 8 January 1992.

88. "Anywhere from 75 to 82 percent of the republic's private capital is held by the so-called Russian-speaking people," Vladimir Yemelyanenko, "Will a Colonialist Become a Citizen?" *Moscow News* 1992, no. 40: 4.For similar estimates see *Neatkarīgā Cīņa,* 5 Novem-

ber 1991. There have been no scholarly studies of ethnic stratification in Latvia. According to Latvian and Russian public opinion "Russian-speakers" control much of urban economic life and profit from close economic contacts to Russia. On the latter point, see *Literaturnaia gazeta*, 8 April 1992, 12.

89.   See Table 6.2.

90.   *Diena*, 14 May 1992, 2.

91.   Horowitz, *Ethnic Conflict*, 202, see also 139.

92.   See Astri Suhrke and Lela Garner Noble, eds., *Ethnic Conflict in International Relations* (New York: Praeger, 1977), 2.

93.   *Atmoda*, 5 February 1991, 2.

94.   O. Dzenītis, *Neatkarīgā Cīņa*, 1 October 1992, 2.

95.   The history of decolonization shows that European settlers in the colonies were among the most vociferous opponents of the transfer of power to indigenous majorities. They fought hard to retain influence over local state administration and military power, and tried to influence the metropolis to intervene in their favor. Miles Kahler, *Decolonization in Britain and France: The Domestic Consequences of International Relations* (Princeton, N.J.: Princeton University Press, 1984), especially 16 and 321.

7

———⟫•◇•⟪———

Dealing with the Legacy:
What Ethnic Policy?

T his study has followed the logic that one must diagnose a problem
       before discussing possible cures.[1] Ethnic issues in the Soviet Union
       and its successor states have been complicated by a strong linkage to
regime structures and political culture. For democratic ethnopolitics to
emerge, democratic regimes have had to emerge, and this is a complex
process. The historical trend toward democracy in the region has provided a
basis for change, yet the legacy of Soviet rule has continued to pose numerous problems. As noted in the previous chapter, in Latvia many of the
remaining issues in 1993 were of an international nature. The presence of ex-
Soviet troops and political personnel required that Russia adopt a forthcom-
ing position and that the international community offer assistance. The
same applied to problems posed by the huge Soviet-era settler population.
How could one deal with them equitably, without infringing on the rights of
individual settlers or the Latvian nation?

As argued in chapter 1, ethnopolitics is about the distribution of power,
status, and goods in society. As such it involves all groupings in a state, not
just certain "ethnics." In the case of Latvia this means that ethnic policy
involves the position of Latvians as well as non-Latvians. Furthermore,
ethnic policy revolves around institutional arrangements as well as around
political culture and attitudes. Ethnic relations are interactive; their quality
depends on how two or more groupings, rather than only one, approach an
issue. All sides must participate in conflict resolution for satisfactory results.

141

As Latvia continues the transition to democracy, it must also search for the most democratic ethnic policy. The example of Western democracies offers certain principles that can be followed, yet the basis for comparison has to be valid, and this qualification is difficult because all post-Soviet states face special problems—and Latvia even more so. Historically the ethnic diversity of Latvia has always called for accommodation, but the rate of recent Slavic immigration is unprecedented in any comparative terms. Special care must be given to clarifying the base point for analysis; it has to be rooted in empirical assessment. As will be noted in this chapter, for example, Latvia's language policy must be assessed in light of the consequences of Soviet language policy, namely the preeminence of the Russian language in Latvia in the early 1990s. Few outside commentators have realized the weak position of the Latvian language in Latvia. As noted by one scholar immersed in these issues, it would be absurd to speak of the rights of the French in France, but it is a dire necessity to speak of the rights of Latvians in Latvia.[2]

Democratic ethnopolitics is based on a political culture that welcomes diversity and accommodates the underprivileged. But this statement begs the questions about the meaning of diversity in a specific context and about who is underprivileged. Since titular nations typically infringe on the rights of other ethnic groups, the analytical assumption is in favor of nontitular groups. In the Latvia of 1993 this view is misleading, because the shift in state boundaries did not signify a comprehensive shift in power relations. Many of the Soviet-era privileges bestowed on the settler community have persisted, and in the opinion of many Latvians, "Latvians were the most discriminated-against people in Latvia."[3] For them, the core ethnopolitical goal was to emancipate the Latvian people and their culture. Equalizing the position of Latvians as an ethnic as well as a political nation was seen as the precondition for the stability of any present and future political community. In order to normalize the situation, special steps had to be taken. Opinions differed about the content of such policies—some are more integrative than others—yet there was broad consensus that the perpetuation of Soviet-era dominance and privileges was intolerable. This view also entailed the implementation of policies to redress the neglect experienced by the smaller historical minorities of Latvia such as Poles, Jews, and Gypsies. Moreover, ways had to be found to revitalize the traditional Russian community of Latvia, which was also suppressed under Soviet rule because it included old believers, an independent Orthodox church, and numerous distinct cultural and political identities.[4]

From this perspective an equitable ethnic policy meant differentiating among subgroups of the non-Latvian population. It provided new opportunities for ethnic communal development where that had been suppressed and renewed the rights of all who had been part of the political nation of Latvia. Soviet-era settlers were perceived as a separate category, because they came to Latvia as representatives of alien rule. Opinions differed about the extent to which this group could be integrated politically. As for ethnic communal provisions, it was accepted that settlers had the rights of a cultural minority, but that their former privileges could not be perpetuated.

Russian leaders in Latvia and in Russia have taken a different perspective, however, especially since mid-1992 when they began to focus on "numerous violations of the rights of ethnic Russians" in the Baltic states.[5] Few concrete examples have been mentioned except for broad references to citizenship and language laws. Nevertheless, in 1992 Russia asked that a special commission of the United Nations go to Latvia to investigate charges of human rights violations. This commission issued a report in October 1992 stating that it did not find any systematic violations by Latvian policymakers. It also noted that it cannot be said that Latvia is in breach of international law by the way it determines the criteria for granting citizenship and that "it should be emphasized that no instances of violence, no mass dismissals from employment, exclusion from educational establishments, evictions from apartments, or expulsions"[6] were reported. Despite such reports from fact-finding missions, some Russians in Latvia remained aggrieved and were supported by politicians in Russia. These groups denied that the legacy of the Soviet period had to be addressed, arguing instead that one had to start by looking at contemporary "realities."[7] In practice, they were seeking to perpetuate the status quo ante that existed at the time of the collapse of the USSR in 1991. More likely than not this would have been impossible even if Latvian policymakers had desired it, but time was needed for people to recognize available options.

Three Policy Models

The range of ethnic policy choices in Latvia has consisted of three ideal-types that I characterize as nominally integrative, partly integrative, and nonintegrative. Integration refers to the extent that the identity and interests of various population groups are balanced and reconciled. Theoretically, there could be a fully integrative option as well, but in light of Latvia's recent political history and the distribution of power in the early 1990s this option was unrealistic.

To assess the integration of identity and interests, this chapter focuses on citizenship as a representative political issue, and on language policy as a core cultural issue and a means by which governments attempt to manage ethnic conflict.[8] Both issues have been crucial in the ethnopolitical debate in Latvia since the late 1980s. Moreover, both relate to public life rather than personal or social relations.

Of the three options outlined here, the nominally integrative approach to ethnic policy had the appearance of best preserving social peace because it would have perpetuated the ethnic relations of the late 1980s. Thus citizenship would have been given unconditionally to every resident and no attempt would have been made to promote the use of the Latvian language in public life. At face value, this policy appeared to avoid conflict because it would have left things as they were, but in practice it was unacceptable to many Latvians because the status quo favored the settler community. In the language sphere, leaving things as they were meant the de facto predominance of the Russian language. (Language predominance is defined as the ability of a monolingual person to function fully in a multilingual environment.) As for citizenship, the suggestion that it could be granted regardless of a person's length of residence, loyalty to the state, and familiarity with the history and culture of the state would have alienated too many people to be called truly integrative. The nature of citizen status is that it not only grants rights but also involves duties, such as loyalty to the state and the constitution. How can citizenship be granted to people who oppose the existence of the state? Citizenship is defined as membership in a political community,[9] and extending it formally without regard to the identity of the applicants and the nature of the community creates new conflicts.

Dankwart A. Rustow argues that national unity is a crucial precondition for the transition to democracy, and defines this unity as a condition where "the vast majority of citizens in a democracy-to-be must have no doubt or mental reservations as to which political community they belong to."[10] The problem faced by Latvia has been that a subgroup of inhabitants, most of them Soviet-era settlers and would-be citizens, have had just such doubts and reservations. A small minority has remained openly hostile, working for the rebirth of the Soviet state and regime.[11] Although it is possible for communities to coexist in the same state if they have different ethnic cultures, it is highly problematic if they have different political cultures. Finding a solution entails working toward stronger consensus about a common political identity and providing alternative options for citizenship and residence.

The partially integrative approach to ethnopolitics in Latvia is based on the recognition that not all interests can be accommodated in full, and focuses on restoring the rights of the Latvian nation—defined both politically and ethnically—and on integrating those postwar settlers who respect these rights and wish to be part of the community of citizens. This approach also recognizes that another group of settlers is neither able nor willing to be integrated and therefore searches for other options, such as various forms of resident status and voluntary resettlement eastward or westward. The simultaneous pursuit of three goals—restoring the rights of the Latvian people, extending generosity toward settlers wishing to integrate, and finding democratic alternatives for nonintegrative settlers—is a difficult task. Neverthe-less, it is not impossible, as evident from some policy initiatives advanced during the last few years.

The third approach to ethnic policy in Latvia is nonintegrative and exclu-sionary, and has several faces. The variant found among some Latvian groups is based on the belief that the Soviet past has been so destructive to the Latvian nation that it cannot afford any compromise. Thus the Citizens' Committees emphasize that postwar settlers came to Latvia illegally and as representatives of an occupying power. Consequently they have no legal standing, and offering citizenship to them conditionally or unconditionally would be politically suicidal to Latvians. As noted by the chairman of the Citizens' Committee, "We cannot accept as part of the nation of Latvia citizens of the USSR who have entered Latvia in the course of a deliberate colonial policy to subjugate this territory."[12] In ethnic terms, too, the Lat-vian nation has been brought to the brink of extinction, according to the third approach. Demographic and cultural genocide has proceeded so far that only a drastic change of policy bears any hope. Because most Russians represent an oppressing colonial group, the Latvian state has no responsibil-ity toward them. Russia and other successor states of the USSR should accept them as their citizens and coethnics and take care of their needs. It is hoped that international organizations will join in rectifying the genocidal effects of Soviet policy in Latvia.[13]

The Russian variant of the nonintegrative approach partly agrees with the last point in that Russia is perceived to have a duty to intervene on behalf of the Russian-speaking population of Latvia. Yet the nature of this responsibil-ity is interpreted differently—not as Russia's duty to provide these people with the rights to citizenship,[14] residence, social services, and education in their native language, but rather as Latvia's responsibility to do so. Latvia must do without any stipulations of its own, however, such as requiring public employees to know the Latvian language. In effect, the Latvian state is called on to safeguard a segregated Russian community that is self-contained and relies on ties with Russia.

These three ideal-type approaches are outlined as a tool to sharpen analy-sis. None of these approaches has been consistently followed in Latvia since the late 1980s. There have been few clear policy initiatives, with actual policy consisting of a laissez-faire attitude and a patchwork of individual decisions.

Citizenship and Migration Policy

The issue of how to deal with Soviet-era settlers, the large majority of whom are Russians, involves conditions for acquiring citizenship, the status of noncitizen residents, and resettlement policy.

Dealing with the Legacy: What Ethnic Policy?

Citizenship is linked to statehood, which raises the underlying issue of whether the Latvian state is the legal heir of the Republic of Latvia as it was incorporated into the USSR in July 1940. It is the position of the government of Latvia that, according to international law, the Western policy of nonrecognition of the incorporation, and the will of its people, legal succession applies. Accordingly, Latvia's legislature passed a decree on 15 October 1991 recognizing that people who were citizens of the Republic of Latvia before 17 June 1940, and their descendants, had retained their citizenship throughout the years of occupation. The decree also noted that the status of other residents and the conditions for acquiring citizenship would have to be determined by separate laws.[15] A law on the conditions for naturalization had not been passed by mid-1993 due to strong public opinion that such a law should be passed only by a legislature elected in an independent Latvia by its citizens.[16] As noted in chapter 5, the elections of March 1990 were held under Soviet law, and with the participation of all residents, including Soviet army personnel. Elections solely for citizens were held in June 1993 and a new parliament convened one month later. It held a preliminary vote on a new citizenship law on November 26, 1993. The draft law foresees that people who have resided in Latvia for ten years, know Latvian to some extent, and are familiar with the Constitution and are ready to swear loyalty to it would be eligible for naturalization. It also foresees that the Cabinet of Ministers will set quotas for the number of people who can become new citizens. Preference is to be given to spouses of citizens and to some other groups. Several categories of people are ineligible for naturalization, for example, individuals who have used anti-constitutional means against Latvia's independence.[17]

The 1991 recognition of citizenship derived from succession to the Latvian state as it existed in 1940 meant that about 70 percent of Latvia's inhabitants were recognized as citizens. The exact percentage was difficult to determine due to five decades of demographic upheaval including deportations, emigration, immigration, and high intermarriage rates. A process of registering all inhabitants of Latvia was set up in 1991, one of the goals being to establish who was already a citizen and who might wish to become one. The estimate of preexisting citizenship for about 70 percent of Latvia's inhabitants emerged from this registration process. Since Latvians make up only 53.5 percent of the population, one may estimate that about 31 percent of non-Latvians were registered as citizens in June 1993. This included most, but not all, ethnic Latvians, a segment of Latvia's Russian population, and members of smaller minority groups.[18]

The parliamentary faction representing postwar settlers denounced the October 1991 citizenship decree as discriminatory and suggested that it would aggravate ethnic relations in Latvia.[19] This faction as well as the government of Russia proposed the so-called zero option whereby "every person who lived on the territory of the Republic of Latvia at the time of the declaration of independence has the right to opt for citizenship."[20] In contrast to the legal position of the Latvian government, supporters of the zero option have argued that the Republic of Latvia is the successor of the Latvian Soviet Socialist Republic rather than of the interwar state.[21]

Russia and representatives of the postwar settlers argue that the granting of an unconditional citizenship option was crucial for preserving ethnic concord. Most Latvian politicians argued the opposite. In their view, political integration in a state is the precondition for citizenship, rather than vice versa. Successful integration of potential new citizens can only be achieved if they have lived there for some time, know the local language, and feel loyalty toward the state and its constitution. Citizenship involves certain duties, such as defending the laws of the land and the land itself if need be. As noted in the October 1991 debate on these issues in the legislature of Latvia, the *Ravnopravie* faction voted against Latvia's independence in May 1990, supported the coup attempts of January and August 1991, yet demanded unconditional rights of citizenship in a state whose right to exist it had consistently challenged.[22] Moreover, even if the zero option had been made law, it would not have been integrative in that it would have provoked protests on the part of the indigenous population and citizens. The majority of people in Latvia supported a policy that set certain conditions for naturalization. This implies that one segment of the postwar settler community would be integrated into Latvia's political community and another segment would not.

As the March 1991 referenda and various survey data have shown, the split between loyal and nonloyal groups among settlers is approximately fifty-fifty.[23] The rate of individuals desiring Latvian citizenship has increased since the collapse of the USSR, yet as Table 7.1 illustrates, many still prefer the citizenship of other countries, or are unsure as to what they want. Survey data have also shown that a subgroup of Latvia's residents has been considering emigration.[24] This is not surprising since most of the eastern Slavs who came to Latvia in the postwar period left again within a few years. Between 1961 and 1990, 1.67 million migrants came to Latvia and 1.3 million departed, leaving a net inflow of 371,900 persons.[25] For most of the immigrants Latvia was merely a waystation to other destinations within the Soviet Union. As depicted in Figure 7.1, this migratory movement changed by the late 1980s in that more people were emigrating from Latvia than immigrating; by 1992 the net emigration had reached 47,000 people and the trend continued in 1993.[26]

The increased emigration from Latvia during 1992 was partly the result of policies that encouraged voluntary resettlement. On 10 January 1992, the Council of Ministers of Latvia decreed that persons emigrating from Latvia were to be provided with funds for their expenses and for the state-owned

Table 7.1
Citizenship Preference of Non-Latvians, 1991–92

	September 1991 (percent)	October 1992 (percent)
Respondent plans to get or keep citizenship of:		
Latvia	44	64
USSR	18	—
Russia	—	4.8
Other former Soviet republic	—	3.2
A foreign country	—	1.6
Difficult to say	27	20.8
No answer or other	11	5.6

Source: Surveys conducted by the Social Research Center of Latvia. Very similar results were reported by another survey organization, the Baltic Studies Center, in early 1993 (*Diena*, 12 February 1993). — = data not available or applicable.

housing they vacated. By March several dozen such cases from Riga involved payments between 27,000 and 91,000 rubles,[27] and similar instances were reported from other parts of the country. The implementation of this plan was hampered by the poor financial situation of most local governments. In addition, some Latvians resented these payments, either in principle or because Russian occupation forces had forcibly taken over furnished apartments from local families in 1940 and later.[28]

Another group of Russians emigrating from Latvia solved their housing problems by direct exchange of apartments with Latvians residing in Russia who wished to return to Latvia. In addition, Latvian governmental commissions discussed resettlement possibilities with local authorities of nearby regions in Russia that had been depopulated during the last decades.[29] Yet many of the Russians interested in moving away from Latvia were content to live only in St. Petersburg or Moscow, and the city governments there did not welcome them.[30] This may change if funding for financial incentives can be found. The chairman of the parliamentary Commission on National and Human Rights Questions, Andrējs Pantelējevs, has expressed the hope that the international community would assist in such endeavors. He argues for a differentiated approach to Latvia's settler community according to which one segment would be given incentives to emigrate and another segment would be given the opportunity to integrate in Latvia.[31]

FIGURE 7.1. Migration to and from Latvia, 1961–92.

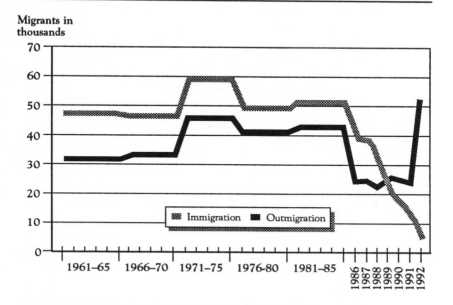

Source: Juris Dreifelds, "Immigration and Ethnicity in Latvia," *Journal of Soviet Nationalities* 1 (Winter 1990–91): 52. Data beginning with 1986 are from *Diena*, 28 November 1992, p. 1, and 24 February 1993. Between 1961 and 1985 only five-year totals are available, therefore "average per year" is used for these intervals.

Such a policy may work to the extent that the postwar settlers represent economic migrants. Comparative studies show that migrants who move for individual or family benefits differ significantly from territorially based minority communities in a state. Typically, economic migrants focus on their economic rights rather than on group rights involving culture or political representation; consequently they assimilate more quickly. In this situation the migrants are less a source of ethnic tension than are the titular nationals who fear ethnic contamination by foreigners.[32]

In Latvia this fear of contamination is represented by more nationalist groups, who argue that in light of its weak demographic and cultural position the Latvian people cannot afford to try to integrate a large mass of foreign settlers. Groups such as the Citizens' Committees also emphasize the illegality of colonization under Soviet rule. They point to documents such as the Geneva Convention of 1949, which specifies that an occupying power does not have the right to settle its own people in an occupied territory. Other tenets of international law are cited to justify denying postwar settlers electoral and citizenship rights, such as the precedent of the UN-sponsored vote in Western Sahara when voting rights were given only to those who had lived there before occupation and not to Moroccans who had been settled there.[33] Other precedents set by the United Nations are the rejection of a French referendum in New Caledonia and of the British proposal to hold a plebiscite in Gibraltar. In the latter case the United Nations argued that the indigenous Spanish inhabitants had been ejected from the area.[34]

Above all, arguments about the international legal position of Latvia and its citizens invoke the right of self-determination.[35] It is also emphasized that Latvia is the only territory where the Latvian people have a historical home-land, in contrast to Russian or Ukrainian settlers. Consequently, leaders of the Citizens' Movement have been advocating the "civilized repatriation of the citizens of the USSR and the rebirth of Latvia as a national state."[36]

Although most proponents of strict limits on naturalization used legal and political arguments, pleas regarding demography and ethnic equity were used as well. Because of the uncontrolled immigration of non-Latvians dur-ing the Soviet era, the zero option for citizenship would have meant that about half of Latvia's citizens would be non-Latvians. Since a state cannot deny its citizens full rights, such as unification with family members living abroad, this could lead to many more eastern Slavs immigrating in the following decades, transforming Latvians into a demographic minority in all of Latvia. If so, what could prevent the Slavic majority from democratically voting for unification with Russia?[37] This scenario becomes more unlikely as increasing numbers of non-Latvians identify with Latvia, but as noted, a subgroup of postwar settlers clearly does not do so. This ethnopolitical dilemma is likely to remain unsolved for some time to come. ·

The ethnic equity argument against the zero option was that such a plan would have perpetuated past injustices against ethnic Latvians and against people who stood up for an independent and democratic Latvia during Soviet rule. Such people were sent to prison and they and their families were discriminated against socially and economically. In practice, "point zero" would perpetuate this injustice because persecuted individuals and those favored by the Soviet establishment have unequal levels of education, pro-fessional experience, and social and economic goods.[38] Access to state-owned housing is an especially sensitive issue. Under glasnost even *Izvestiia* noted that "indigenous inhabitants—not only Latvians—are offended, for example, by the fact that for many years they are forced to live in communal housing, with no hope of getting a new apartment. However, people who have come to Latvia quite recently are able to hold house-warmings in a comparatively short time."[39] It is difficult to erase such past privileges retro-actively, and few people propose that this be attempted, but past injustice explains why the citizenship issue is so sensitive. Citizenship involves more than concrete rights and duties; it is also a national symbol. As a symbol, it cannot be dealt with lightly, or it loses its meaning. Moreover, if it is used to bestow legitimacy upon past injustice, it creates new injustice.

Language Use in Public Life and Education

In a multilingual environment it is crucial to ask what language or languages the government uses to conduct its affairs, deal with the public, and educate the young. Since 1989 Latvian has been the state official language of Latvia, yet the actual predominance of the Russian language in public life and education has been eroding only slowly. In 1993 Latvia was moving toward a system of bilingualism based on the personality principle. As noted by Milton Esman,[40] such a system is characterized by two (or more) sets of public educational institutions and the requirement that officials and public servants be able to function in two (or more) languages. I analyze the situa-tion with respect to the legacy of Soviet language policy, the policies of the independence forces, and the position of monolingual Russian-speakers.

SOVIET POLITICS OF LANGUAGE

The nominally integrative approach to language policy implies returning to the status quo as it existed until the early 1990s. We therefore have to ask about Soviet language policy. In practice, if not always in theory, it was a policy of one-sided bilingualism, meaning that non-Russians were to be fluent in Russian, but Russian-speakers were not expected to learn or use non-Russian languages.[41] Soviet census data illustrate the resulting linguistic imbalance: as Table 7.2 shows, 68 percent of Latvians knew Russian fluently in 1989, but only 21 percent of Russians knew Latvian. The trend toward the increasing predominance of Russian was clear: in the nineteen years between the censuses of 1970 and 1989, knowledge of Russian among Lat-vians increased from 47 percent to 68 percent, whereas the rate of Latvian language fluency among Russian residents was stagnant.

Because of Russian monolingualism and the huge influx of non-Latvians, Russian increasingly became the dominant language of public communica-tion in Latvia, especially in urban centers. Many official documents and meetings used Russian only[42] and it dominated informal public interaction. One survey shows that in 1989 only 17 percent of Latvians used Latvian in opening a conversation with strangers in Riga, as did only 4 percent of Russians.[43]

During the last decades of Soviet rule the Communist party attacked as a manifestation of nationalism any attempts to promote the use of non-

Table 7.2
Knowledge of Languages, by Nationality[1]

	Latvians Knowing Russian (percent)	Russians Knowing Latvian (percent)
1970	47	18
1979	61	20
1989	68	21

Sources: Official census data; LPSR Valsts Statistikas Komiteja, *1989. gada tautas skaitīšanas rezultāti, LPSR* (Riga: Statistisks biļetēns, I. Daļa, 1989), 127; *Itogi vsesoiuznoi perepisi naseleniia SSSR 1970 goda* (Moscow: Statistika, 1973), 152–320; *Vestnik statitiski* 1980, no. 7–8.

[1] "Knowledge" is defined as self-proclaimed fluency.

Russian languages and lauded the increased use of Russian as an expression of internationalism. After 1987 reformers began to criticize this policy.[44] Professor V. Vsevolodova of Moscow State University called for "parity bilingualism," noting that typically in the union republics "only one type of bilingualism exists and is being developed—bilingualism in one's national language plus Russian." She added that for years officials had not discussed the question of the study of the indigenous nationality's language by members of other population groups, and she suggested that intensive language courses be developed to overcome this problem. If all residents knew the languages of the titular nations of the union republics there would be no difficulty in making them state languages.[45]

Significantly, this Russian scholar suggested improving language relations through reciprocal bilingualism rather than through the official dominance of an indigenous language in specified territories, as practiced in multilingual democracies such as Switzerland, Belgium, and Canada.[46] If the USSR had followed their model, this would have meant making Latvian the dominant language in the public life of the Latvian SSR. The safeguarding of minority languages is a hallmark of democratic ethnopolitics. During the Gorbachev reform era the central government's language policy remained far from this ideal, no matter whether practiced in the form of indigenous language dominance or language parity.

The predominance of the Russian language until the early 1990s was also evident in education, from kindergarten to the university level. Parents complained about the insufficient provision for Latvian-language kindergartens, and as Table A.6 (in the Appendix) illustrates, a disproportionate number of children were enrolled in groups using the Russian language, or both Russian and Latvian. A similar situation existed in primary and secondary schools, with the underenrollment of Latvians in Latvian-language schools being especially dramatic in urban centers (see Table 7.3). Theoretically, parents could choose where to enroll their children, but they were pushed toward Russian-language schools because Russian carried greater career prestige and Russian schools were more prevalent in the cities. Latvian schools were more accessible in rural areas, with the exception of the Latgallia region where Latvian children often have had no choice but to attend Russian-language preschools and schools, because nothing else has been available.[47]

As for higher education, Soviet language policy meant that in Latvia universities held parallel courses in Russian and Latvian. As Table A.7 (in the Appendix) illustrates, the parallel availability of higher education in both languages continued during the 1991–92 academic year. In the past, the Russian language has been predominant in that Russian students could easily finish their university training without knowing Latvian, whereas it was impossible for Latvian students to obtain higher education without fluency in Russian.[48]

INDEPENDENCE AND LANGUAGE POLICY

When the legislatures of the non-Russian republics of the USSR started to act independently from the central government in the late 1980s, laws on

Table 7.3
Language in Schools in Latvia, 1989–90

	Latvian (percent)	Russian (percent)	Other (percent)
Student enrollment by language of instruction			
All of Latvia	52.5	47.5	
Urban centers	30.7	69.3	
Nationality of school-age children			
All of Latvia	53.3	36.5	10.2
Urban centers	45.6	43.6	10.8

Source: Author's calculations, based on *Obshcheobrazovatel'nye shkoly vsekh vidov, vysshie i srednie spetsial'nye uchebnye zavedeniia na nachalo 1989/90 uchebnogo goda* (Riga: Gosudarstvennyi komitet statistiki Latviiskoi SSR, 1990), 26; LPSR Valsts Statistikas Komiteja, *1989. gada tautas skaitīšanas rezultāti, LPSR* (Riga: Statistisks biļetēns, II. Daļa, 1989), 32–34. Because of census categories school-age children are defined as those five to nineteen years old.

language were among the first to be passed. Usually they aimed at linguistic reciprocity in the public sphere.[49] Thus the Law on Languages of the Latvian Soviet Socialist Republic passed on 5 May 1989 was intended to allow people to use their language of choice in interaction with public officials. Since this is only possible if public officials know the language they are addressed in, the new language laws asked that public officials know both Latvian and Russian "on the level necessary for the execution of their professional responsibilities."[50] The decree specifying the implementation of the new law stipulated a three-year transition period during which state employees lacking Latvian language facility could acquire it.[51] Huge numbers of language learning materials were published in this period (see Figure A.3 in the Appendix).

Latvia's law on languages and the administrative decrees connected with it were revised in 1992, mostly because little had changed in the actual language situation since 1989. Even in late 1992, a survey showed that more Latvians than Russians still could not use the language of their choice when interacting with public officials (see Table A.8 in the Appendix). Compared with the 1989 law on languages, the 1992 revisions put a stronger emphasis on Latvian as the state language.[52] More significant, however, was the creation of a mechanism to implement the law in the form of the State Language Inspectorate and the requirement that public employees pass a Latvian language exam appropriate to their professional duties. Language attestation was required at three levels of stringency: an elementary knowledge of Latvian for low-level positions, such as guards of public buildings; an intermediary level applying to postal employees, nurses, and so on; and the highest level of Latvian language competency required of officials in responsible positions such as heads of administrative offices, judges, and doctors in the state medical service.[53] During 1992 many state employees passed the language exams and those who failed were given time to improve their language facility and retake the exam.[54]

The language attestation exams have forced Russian monolinguals to take the Latvian language requirement seriously. Since knowing the state language to the degree necessary for the performance of professional duties was made a job requirement, the logical consequence was that state employees who do not qualify may be fired.[55] Whether this step is taken depends on the employing institution. By early 1993 there were few indications that people were being fired. Thus a doctor in a Riga hospital noted that most of the nurses did not speak Latvian, but he needed them to do the work.[56] It was not the intent of the language requirement to penalize people, but to provide incentives to learn Latvian. Some legislators have suggested that officials with inadequate language facility be given lower salaries due to insufficient job qualifications.[57] Monetary sanctions were supposed to discourage other instances of noncompliance with the language law—for example avoidance of Latvian on product labels—with fines ranging from one thousand to ten thousand rubles.[58]

In the educational sphere the state has attempted to increase the use of Latvian while protecting the right to education in other native languages. In contrast to the Soviet approach the biggest change has been the promotion of education in the languages of smaller minorities. In 1989 a Hebrew school opened in Riga and since 1991 classes using Polish and Ukrainian were offered in Daugavpils. Some of the teachers came from abroad, for example fifteen from Poland, two from Israel, and one from Ukraine. Most of the textbooks also came from abroad, including a primer in the Romani language used in special classes for Gypsies in Ventspils.[59] The Ministry of Education has aimed at resurrecting multilingual education as it existed during the parliamentary period of interwar Latvia when general education was available in eight languages: Latvian, German, Russian, Yiddish (as well as Hebrew), Polish, Belorussian, Estonian, and Lithuanian. In 1919 Latvia passed a law on education mandating that the language of instruction in general schools coincide with each student's native language. Ethnic minorities had their own primary, secondary, and sometimes higher schools. Each ethnic group set up its own educational council to determine autonomously the types of schools and the kind of instruction provided, and other educational matters. The expense was covered by a proportional amount allotted to each minority from the national budget.[60] In practice, most students did in fact attend educational institutions in their native languages.[61]

Although the position of non-Russian minority languages improved after 1989, little changed in regard to the availability of education in Russian. Forty-six percent of Latvia's schoolchildren were enrolled in Russian-language schools in 1991–92.[62] As a comparison with the census data in Table 7.3 indicates, this meant that practically all Russian children attended Russian-language schools, as did most other non-Latvians. Educational officials have repudiated misleading rumors about alleged plans to close Russian-language primary and secondary schools.[63] Plans have been developed to switch to Latvian as the language of instruction in publicly financed specialized and higher educational institutions, beginning with the second year of studies. To facilitate this, intensive Latvian language courses will be available to students needing them.[64] Yet any such change will take years to complete, because in 1993 many textbooks were still available only in Russian, and many instructors, especially in technical fields, could communicate only in Russian.[65]

The situation regarding kindergartens was mixed. Among families eager to integrate in Latvian society a trend emerged to send one's children to Latvian kindergartens. Yet fewer preschool facilities were available due to the intensifying economic crisis, and in some areas the effect has been most detrimental on Latvian-language institutions.[66]

How is one to assess the ethnopolitical nature of recent language policy? It appears that it can be characterized best as a mixed policy that has combined an increased use of Latvian and minority languages with an acceptance of the continuing strong position of Russian. The latter was due in part to a decade-long predominance of Russian that could not be changed in a few months or years, but it also reflected governmental policy of recognizing Russian as a minority language.

The emancipatory emphasis on the Latvian language has appeared crucial for the following reasons:

1. As the data in Table 7.2 show, in the past most Russians in Latvia have not learned Latvian, and some Latvians did not know Russian (especially children and the elderly). This meant that some people could not communicate at all with each other and if there was a common language, it was usually Russian. The language law aimed at making it possible for Latvians to use Latvian in public interactions. This was especially crucial for those individuals who did not know Russian, or knew it badly, as they are otherwise denied full access to public services. The consequences can be dire, as in the case of patients seeking medical help and confronted by monolingual Russian doctors.[67] In addition, the predominance of the Russian language in public interactions has weakened Latvian culture and identity.

2. As noted by Donald Horowitz, "The status of the language is a symbol of newfound group dignity"[68] and is often used as an expression of status and power. Language can be a symbol of domination and it is typical for colonial groups to claim that their languages are more advanced than those used locally. If such denigration occurs, the minority tends to become more insistent on the use of its own language, because added status and symbolic value are attached to it.[69] In addition, the predominance of one or the other language has consequences for socioeconomic advancement, since those people who speak the dominant language best have a competitive advantage.[70] The predominance of Russian has been an expression of the politically inferior status of Latvia, and this contradicts independence. By mid-1992 the emancipation of the Latvian language in Latvia was given a significant sociopolitical and psychological role in strengthening perceptions of self-worth and identity.

3. Most of the Russian-speakers in Latvia are recent settlers, rather than members of a historical minority. Although many countries recognize language rights of indigenous minorities, "immigrant communities, in particular, have no claims at all to official status for their languages."[71] Worldwide, the burden of using a language other than the mother tongue is placed on those who come into the region from the outside. As Vernon Van Dyke

notes, "The common attitude is that people who choose to migrate into an area where the language is foreign to them have no right to special consideration; they should either learn the new language or accept the consequences. The case for this is especially strong when their migration threatens to expand the territory of one language community at the expense of another."[72] The latter case is what happened in Latvia during the Soviet period, as the Russian language expanded from Russia into Latvia. Russian is not just any language, it is the language of Latvia's giant neighbor. Latvian sensitivities about this linguistic expansion were heightened by associations of the Russian language with political incorporation into the USSR.

4. Russian monolingualism has hindered the integration of the non-Latvian population in Latvia's society, economy, and politics. This has been recognized by that part of the non-Latvian population that has always had a welcoming attitude toward the Latvian language or has developed such an attitude in the course of the transition from communism. As soon as the first stirrings of civil society began in 1987, people who did not know Latvian started to study it at an accelerated rate, as indicated by the high demand for various Latvian language instruction materials.[73] Since the late 1980s numerous new materials have been printed and special language courses held.[74] No new census data are available to measure the results, but sociological surveys suggest that although fluent Latvian-speakers are still the minority among non-Latvians, many now claim to have at least some knowledge of it.[75]

THE NONINTEGRATIVE APPROACH TO LANGUAGE POLICY

The nonintegrative approach to language policy in Latvia has been taken primarily by a segment of the Russian-speaking population and by much of the central Soviet and Russian press. In May 1989, *Pravda* denounced Latvia's language law as discriminatory, stating that it posed difficulties for Russian monolinguals to continue work in civil service.[76] Similar accusations were repeated often, including that the language requirements for public officials were a human rights violation.[77]

It is worthwhile to reflect on such statements because they illustrate a significant ethnopolitical outlook. It means that in real terms and in terms of language psychology these people want to work and publicly interact in a purely Russian-speaking environment. Furthermore, they want this environment to be outside of Russia, in Latvia. Concretely, this can indicate only two things. First, it could mean that they expect to interact purely with other Russian monolinguals, implying that they live in a state of language segregation where they do not speak to Latvians at all and choose to have no exposure to Latvian-language media, culture, or discussions. Alternatively, it could mean that they do expect to interact with Latvians, but that the latter should learn and use the Russian language. Apparently this view is not seen by them as an infringement of Latvian rights, interests, or identity.

In effect, the Russian monolinguals are saying that they have a human right to be monolingual no matter where they live and work. They see Latvia as a mere extension of Russia and do not wish to integrate into a culturally and otherwise distinct country. They resent the suggestion that they might change their outlook and learn Latvian. Their view is antithetical to one of the tenets of a democratic ethnopolitical culture, that knowing and interacting with other cultures and peoples is enriching.

In addition, over the years some Russian-speakers have exhibited a racist attitude by demanding to be addressed "in a human language" on occasions when spoken to in Latvian.[78] Teachers of the Latvian language in Russian schools have complained bitterly about the enmity they have felt from their colleagues.[79] Such occurrences can hardly be explained by the issue of language learning per se; broader political attitudes and interests are involved. A subgroup of Russians in Latvia had difficulty adjusting to being a minority in an independent Latvia. This was noted in 1992 by Mark Diachkov, a professor at the Moscow Pedagogical Institute who surveyed the situation of Russians in Latvia. He argued that the media and politicians were remiss in highlighting the advantages of knowing Latvian and contrasted this to the work of a special Russian-Estonian Institute in Tallinn deliberating an integration program for Russians in Estonia.[80]

Soviet ethnosociologists have shown that more harmonious ethnic relations are correlated with knowledge of the language of the indigenous nation.[81] The same conclusion emerges from surveys undertaken in Latvia in recent years. As illustrated in Table A.9 in the Appendix, those non-Latvians who know Latvian have a more optimistic outlook on ethnic relations. Although Latvia's language policy has begun to pursue this aim, the trend toward learning Latvian may also be promoted by economic incentives, as increasingly many businesses require that their workers know both Latvian and Russian.[82]

Conclusion

As of 1993 numerous ethnic policy issues in Latvia remained unresolved. Most important, the legal, political, and cultural status of the postwar settlers had yet to be clarified. In light of the experience of the transition era, one could expect that democratic principles would continue to be used in the search for solutions. Any resolution had to take into account the position of all concerned groups, and especially those who had been dealt with unfairly in the past: the lingering Soviet legacy meant that (aside from smaller cultural minorities) this stipulation primarily indicated the Latvians.

Unless the nationhood of the Latvian people can be recovered in full, the basis for harmonious relations with non-Latvians will remain in question.

In the Latvian context the recovery of nationhood has three dimensions: the full recovery of legal sovereignty of the Republic of Latvia as a state, the political recovery of the people of Latvia as a civic nation, and the recovery of the Latvians as the core ethnocultural nation of the country. As discussed in the previous chapter, the recovery of legal sovereignty depends on recognition by Russia. Although Russia formally recognized the independent state of Latvia in August 1991, its leaders have tended to view it as a special territory where they can act without being bound by international law. This has been expressed by the continuation of Russia's unauthorized military presence and by its linkage of this presence to Latvia's citizenship law. Russia can legitimately inquire about the status of people who are its own citizens, but it cannot tell Latvia who *its* citizens are. Regulating membership in a state "is an essential attribute of sovereignty; the principle of the liberty of the state in the attribution of citizenship is firmly established in international law."[83]

Furthermore, the citizenship issue is central to Latvia's recovery as a political nation. Citizenship is more than a legal status, it is an institution through which every state constitutes itself as an association of citizens.[84] Every political community depends on "the achievement of consent based on a common sense of belonging."[85] This sense is unlikely to emerge between the people who have been subjugated for decades and the people who were the subjugators. Thus the inclusion of active Soviet (or Russian) military personnel in the political nation as happened in the elections of 1990 is not only problematical, it is anathema to the principle of political nationhood itself. The need to accept such realities in the past has led to dangerous political alienation, cynicism, and apathy among Latvia's populace,[86] characteristics that undermine democracy.

As noted, in 1993 Latvian views on the political integration of Soviet-era settlers varied. While some Latvians envisioned the possibility of naturalization for individuals who satisfied certain conditions,[87] others rejected that possibility with limited exceptions. There was broad consensus that active proponents of Soviet rule should remain ineligible for citizenship; among this group are the personnel of the former Soviet army, the KGB and other police forces, the military-industrial complex, and central Soviet administration. Since many of these individuals never thought they would end up "living abroad" and have fought against Latvia's independence, the hope is that they will return to their countries of origin. If they remain in Latvia, they will represent a destabilizing force.

Many people in Latvia have differentiated between settlers who represented Soviet rule and others who turned against it. The distinction has depended on the activities and self-identification of the people involved. As for political self-identification, the data cited throughout this volume show that during the struggle for the restoration of Latvia's independence, one-third to one-half of the non-Latvian population was supportive of this goal. Since this population includes Russians and others who have always been citizens of the Republic of Latvia, one can calculate that the rate of identification with the political community of Latvia was lower among Soviet-era settlers. At the time of the March 1991 referendum, between 50 and 70 percent of the settlers preferred another state and political community. For some this was the Soviet Union, for others it was Russia, Ukraine, or some other state. Since the restoration of independence, a subgroup of settlers has chosen the option of another state by emigrating or by remaining in Latvia with non-Latvian citizenship. Many others apparently wish to acquire citizenship in Latvia (see Table 7.1) for pragmatic reasons. This poses a problem from the perspective of state and nation building, which require a sense that membership has intrinsic value. Most governments and long-term residents emphasize the dignity and even sacredness of citizenship, whereas immigrants everywhere have a more instrumentalist approach.[88] For this and other reasons states set limits on immigration and naturalization.

Another issue concerns links between citizenship and the ethnocultural identity of a nation. Although this view often is not stated explicitly, most states expect that new citizens will become ethnocultural members of the nation before or after they are given citizenship. Thus Germany has a highly restrictive naturalization law requiring significant cultural assimilation before citizenship can be granted. France has a more liberal citizenship law due to an explicitly state-centered conception of nationhood, yet it is linked to the expectation that new citizens will be politically and culturally assimilated in a short period of time.[89] If Latvia were to adopt the German model, very few settlers would be naturalized, and though their ethnocultural distinction would be accepted in principle, few cultural provisions would be made in practice. Accepting the French model would mean extending comparatively broad citizenship rights, but other state policies would implement a strictly assimilationist program according to which all citizens would be expected to become purely "Latvian" in a relatively short time period.

As discussed in regard to language, Latvia is far from such an assimilationist policy and is in fact fighting the consequences of Soviet policy of linguistic Russification. As for the settler community, it has shown ambivalence not just in regard to its political identity, but also culturally. The settlers have to decide what identity they want to pursue. The issue is not whether they will become assimilated Latvians, but whether they remain "Russians" or "Ukrainians" who are part of the culture of their countries of origin, or become "Latvian Russians" or "Latvian Ukrainians" in the sense of distinct cultural minorities of Latvia.[90] Concretely, do they plan to remain cut off from Latvian society due to a lack of language skills, or to interact with this society? As of 1993 individual settlers were making a clear choice in one or the other direction, but for the majority the answer to this question remained unclear.

Latvian policymakers have to assess these questions as well. One concrete issue is which textbooks to use in Russian-language schools of Latvia: books written in Latvia or in Russia? To date, most textbooks are imported from Russia, including a 1992 Russian history text for the eleventh grade entitled *History of the Homeland* that takes an ambivalent position on topics such as the independence of the Baltic states in the interwar period and their incorporation into the USSR in 1940.[91] Such educational choices hardly encourage the integration of Russian youth in the political community of Latvia.

In Latvia as elsewhere in the former Soviet bloc individuals and entire polities face decisions about alternative conceptions of ethnic and political nationhood. I return to this issue in the final chapter, but it should be reiterated here that the basic model pursued by Latvia in the 1990s is one that explicitly seeks to balance a state-centered and ethnocultural conception of nationhood. In 1993 Latvia was trying to return to the best traditions of its parliamentary period. This has meant returning to the 1922 Constitution that speaks of the "people of Latvia" as a community of citizens. Thus the primary notion of citizenship was a civic one. Yet other laws and public policy practice showed that Latvia was a state where a core ethnocultural nation, the Latvians, was exercising its right to self-determination, and joined this principle with a pluralist approach to minorities. Ethnic minorities were given group rights in education and other cultural matters. In addition, political culture and practice promoted ethnically based political parties and other institutions of civil society.

NOTES

1. Donald Horowitz, *Ethnic Groups in Conflict* (Berkeley: University of California Press, 1985), 564.
2. Elmārs Vēbers, opening remarks at the Conference on Ethnopolitics and Democratization in Latvia, Riga, 19 May 1992.
3. *Jaunais Laiks*, 23 July 1991. The chairman of Latvia's Supreme Council's Commission on Human and National Rights Questions, Andrējs Panteļējevs, too, has emphasized that one has to analyze the problems of Latvians in Latvia as those of a minority. His thesis is that there is no majority in Latvia, just minorities. *Atmoda*, 15 October 1991, 4.
4. Soviet-era policies included turning Riga's Orthodox cathedral into a planetarium and destroying the Ivanov Library, the oldest Russian library in Riga. On the latter case see Temira Pachmuss, "Russian Culture in the Baltic States and Finland, 1920–1940," *Journal of Baltic Studies* 16 (Winter 1985): 383–98. On interwar Polish cultural institutions in Latvia, see E. Jēkabsons, "Poļu minoritāte Latvijā," *Latvijas Zinātņu Akadēmijas Vēstis*, no. 2 (1993): 6–10.
5. *Nezavisimaia gazeta*, 31 October 1992.

6. Ibrahima Fall, *Allegations of Discriminatory Practices against Minorities in Latvia*, Report on a Fact-Finding Mission to Riga, Latvia, 27 to 30 October 1992 (New York: United Nations, 1992), 9 and 23. *Diena*, 2 December 1992, 1. Many fact-finding commissions have been sent to Latvia. In early May a delegation of the Council of Europe also established that "there are no grounds for accusations" about mass violations of human rights in Latvia (*The Baltic Observer*, 1993 May 14–20, 3).

7. Typical statements are: "It wasn't Russia or Russians, but the ruling elite of the totalitarian union state that sent troops into the Baltics in 1939, into Hungary in 1956. . . . And it is utterly inadmissible to cite the past as 'justification' for rash anti-Russian actions, in particular the clear discrimination of the 1.5 million ethnic Russians who live in Estonia and Latvia" (Sergei Stankevich in *Nezavisimaia gazeta*, 6 November 1992, p. 2, as translated in the *Current Digest of the Soviet Press* 1992, no. 45: 11), and "However much we may now curse Stalinism, voluntarism, and the aggressive, deformed economic policy of stagnation, which led to the disproportionate influx of forces from other regions of the country, realities are realities. You have to build on them, while taking into account the full range of interethnic interests" (*Pravda*, 1 March 1989, 6, as translated in *FBIS-SOV-89-046*, 10 March 1989, 56–57).

8. Milton J. Esman, "The State and Language Policy," *International Political Science Review* 13, no. 4 (1992): 381–396.

9. Maurice Roche, "Citizenship, Social Theory, and Social Change," *Theory and Society* 16 (May 1987): 368.

10. Dankwart A. Rustow, "Transitions to Democracy: Toward a Dynamic Model," *Comparative Politics* 2 (April 1970): 350.

11. On 9 May 1992, the former Victory Day of the USSR, several hundred pro-Soviet loyalists met to mark the occasion in Riga. The speeches of Viktors Alksnis and the former leader of the Interfront, Lopatin, were notable for the statement "The Soviet Union continues to be and will be again." Live television transmission, Riga, 9 May 1992.

12. *Latvijas Jaunatne*, 19 June 1990.

13. *Diena*, 4 April 1992.

14. In fact some of Latvia's residents have acquired Russian citizenship, and in early 1992 the Association of Citizens of Russia was formed in Latvia. *SM–segodnia*, 5 June 1992.

15. Decree of the Supreme Council of the Republic of Latvia, "On the Restoration of the Rights of Citizens of the Republic of Latvia and Regulations for Naturalization," 15 October 1991.

16. This position has been expressed in numerous resolutions and individual statements; see *Diena*, 22 October 1991.

17. *Latvijas Vēstnesis*, 27 November 1993, 3. Latvia's parliament takes three votes on each law for it to become active, the second and third rounds of voting on the citizenship law are scheduled for February 1994 and a national referendum will be held afterward.

18. By June 1993, the Department of Immigration and Citizenship had registered 2,426,991 inhabitants, 1,718,274 as citizens (*Latvijas Jaunatne*, 7 June 1993). The cited percentages are based on a calculation using these data and total population data cited in Table A.5. Most Latvian Poles, Jews, and Gypsies are citizens, and so are about 25 percent of Russians. Since former citizenship is the decisive criterion, Latvians who were not citizens on 17 June 1940 also have to apply for naturalization. It is misleading to allege that Russians are denied automatic citizenship in Latvia because they are Russians, a view presented by Vladimir Yemelyanenko, "Will a Colonialist Become a Citizen?" *Moscow News* 1992, no. 40: 4.

19. *Diena*, 17 October 1991.

20. Letter by an official representative of the government of Russia to Latvia's legislature, *Diena*, 4 January 1992. This is the position of most Russian political organizations in Latvia. See also the position of the initiators of the Russian National Party, *Sovetskaia molodezh*, 20 March 1992.

21. For example the chairman of the *Ravnopravie* faction; see *Atmoda*, 20 November 1990, 3.

22. Various speakers in debate, author's on-site observation; see also Jēkabs Gailītis, "Victims of a Double Standard," *Baltic Observer*, 24–30 September 1992, 11.

23. See chapters 3 and 5, especially Table 5.2.

24. A November 1990 survey of the Social Research Center of Latvia showed that 17 percent of non-Latvian respondents were considering moving to the USSR and 10 percent to other countries.

25. Juris Dreifelds, "Immigration and Ethnicity in Latvia," *Journal of Soviet Nationalities* 1 (Winter 1990–91): 52–53. The general pattern of re-emigration of Russians from non-Russian republics over the last decades is discussed by Anatolii Vishnevskii and Zhanna Zaionchkovskaia, "Waves of Migration," as translated in *Russian Social Science Review* 34 (July–August 1993): 37–55.

26. During 1992, 4,590 people immigrated to Latvia and 51,778 emigrated, nearly all of them to the countries of the former USSR. See Latvijas Republikas Valsts statistiska komiteja, *Latvijas demogrāfijas gadagrāmata 1992* (Riga: n.p., 1993), 193. Between January and June 1993, 17,685 people migrated from Latvia: 10,155 went to Russia, 3,427 to Belorussia, 2,165 to Ukraine, 445 to Israel, 430 to Germany, 348 to the United States, and 207 to Lithuania (*Latvijas Vēstnesis*, 7 September 1993, 3).

27. *Rīgas Balss*, 12 March 1992, 7.

28. *Diena*, 10 March 1992.

29. *Atmoda*, 6 August 1991, 12.

30. *Diena*, 10 March 1992. For years, Moscow and the former Leningrad, as well as other cities in Russia, have had strict requirements for residence permits.

31. *Diena*, 3 October 1992, 2.

32. David D. Laitin, "The National Uprisings in the Soviet Union," *World Politics* 44 (October 1991): 171.

33. *Atmoda*, 25 February 1992, 13.

34. Visvaldis Lācis, "Nepieļausim, lai mūs, kapā liekot, apglabātu stāvus," *Atmoda Atpūtai*, 22 April 1992.

35. See, for example, Egīls Levits, "Pamatnāciju tiesības uz pašnoteikšanās . . . ," *Literatūra un Māksla*, 23 September 1989, 10–11.

36. Māris Grīnblats in *Atmoda*, 22 October 1991, 5; similar statement by Aigars Jirgens, *Atmoda*, 14 September 1991, 14.

37. *Diena*, 3 October 1992, 2.

38. *Jūrmala*, 22 October 1991, 1, 5.

39. *Izvestiia*, 27 January 1989, 3.

40. Esman, "The State and Language Policy," 387.

41. See Isabelle T. Kreindler, "Baltic Area Languages in the Soviet Union: A Sociolinguistic Perspective," *Journal of Baltic Studies* 19 (Spring 1988): 5–20; see also Rasma Karklins, *Ethnic Relations in the USSR: The Perspective from Below* (Boston: Allen and Unwin, 1986), 103–15.

42. Examples are cited during the debate about state language status for Latvian, for example in *Literatūra un Māksla*, 5 October 1988, 2; examples about prevalent use of Russian in administrative offices in Riga are cited in *Temīda* 1992, no. 2: 12–13; see also detailed analysis of one district of Riga in *Atmoda*, 25 September 1989, 2; on the general dominance of Russian in Latvia see I. Druviete, "Funktsionirovanie i status latyshskogo iazyka," *Kommunist Sovetskoi Latvii* 1988, no. 12: 45–52.

43. *Jūrmala*, 12 January 1989, cited in Dreifelds, "Immigration and Ethnicity," 55.

44. Michael Kirkwood, "Glasnost, 'The National Question' and Soviet Language Policy," *Soviet Studies* 43, no. 1 (1991): 61–81, especially 68 and 73.

45. *Pravda*, 6 March 1989, 3.

46. See chapters 1 and 2, and Esman, "The State and Language Policy."

47. Interview with an inspector of the Ministry of Education, *Literatūra un Māksla*, 11 May 1991.

48. Until July 1990 candidates for higher degrees (*kandidat nauk* and *doktor nauk*) were required to use Russian for dissertations. Aleksei Levin, "Organizational Changes in Soviet Science and Learning," *Report on the USSR*, 9 December 1990.

49. Interview with members of the commission preparing the language law in Latvia, *Skolotāju Avīze*, 16 November 1988, 110.

50. English translation of the law in *FBIS-SOV-89-104*, 1 June 1989, 45–47.

51. The decree on the implementation of the language law was passed by the Supreme Council on 5 May 1989.
52. Valdis Čeičs, ed., *Valsts valoda: Dokumenti, intervijas, uzziņas* (Riga: Latvijas Republikas Ministru Padome, 1992).
53. Ibid., 10–11; the language commission for the testing of Latvian language facility was created in February 1992. *Diena*, 27 February 1992.
54. Author's interview with the head of Latvia's State Language Inspectorate, December 1992.
55. Decree of the Presidium of the Supreme Council of Latvia, 20 August 1992.
56. *Diena*, November 1992, 3.
57. *Diena*, 26 September 1992.
58. The law entitled "Revision of Latvia's Code on Administrative Infringements in Regard to the State Language," 1 July 1992.
59. *Neatkarīgā Cīņa*, 1 October 1991; by the 1993–94 school year 461 students were taught in Hebrew, 256 in Polish, 72 in Ukrainian, and 40 in Estonian. *Diena*, 13 September 1993.
60. Royal Institute of International Affairs, *The Baltic States* (London: Oxford University Press, 1938), 33–35.
61. *Latvijas Kultūras Statistika 1918–1937* (Riga: Valsts statistiskā pārvalde, 1938) and T. Feigmane, "Russkoe naselenie Latvii (1920–1940): Razvitie obrazovaniia," *Latvijas Zinātņu Akadēmijas Vēstis* 10 (1992): 16–19.
62. Mežs, *Latvieši Latvijā*, 26. The situation had not changed much by the 1993–94 school year: only 55.3 percent of students were taught in Latvian, 44.4 percent in Russian, and 0.3 percent in other languages. *Diena*, 13 September 1993.
63. *Rīgas Balss*, 6 May 1992, 4. In 1992, some 8.5 million schoolchildren attended Russian language schools in the former non-Russian union republics of the USSR. All textbooks were published in Russia but paid for by the other states (*Nezavisimaia gazeta*, 17 March 1993, 1, as translated in the *The Current Digest of the Post-Soviet Press*, 11, 1993, 23). In contrast to the availability of Russian language schools outside Russia, there were no native language schools for Latvian or Ukrainian children living in Russia.
64. *Diena*, 6 June 1991.
65. In May 1993, the rector of Riga Technical University stated that many lecturers do not speak Latvian (*Jūrmala*, 27 May 1993, 2). In 1991 the Russian Community in Latvia sponsored the establishment of a private college geared mostly toward teaching business and technical subjects. It foresees that students will first get a bachelor's degree and continue studies at universities in Russia or the West. Interview with the chairman of the association, *Rīgas Balss*, 4 September 1991. The interview also noted that the association is purely cultural and has more than a thousand members.
66. A 1992 report about the Kurzeme sector of the city of Riga noted that it had a total of forty-four day-care centers, seven of them with Latvian as a language of activities. Twenty-two of these were under the authority of the former Soviet army or large Soviet enterprises and had Russian as the language of activities. Of the twenty-two city-operated day-care centers, fourteen were Russian, one was mixed, and seven were Latvian. In light of financial constraints the local council determined to "equally " close three Latvian and three Russian facilities, leaving four Latvian-language kindergartens and eleven Russian. A worker in one of the Latvian-speaking kindergartens sees this policy as a sign of continuing cultural genocide against the Latvian nation. *Atmoda Atpūtai*, 29 April 1992, 11.
67. *Literatūra un Māksla*, 5 October 1988, 2, mentions instances of elderly Latvians not being able to communicate with their doctor, as well as similar situations.
68. Horowitz, *Ethnic Groups*, 222.
69. Ibid., 219–21; see also Howard Giles, *Language, Ethnicity, and Intergroup Relations* (London: Academic Press, 1977).
70. Horowitz, *Ethnic Groups*, 221; Karklins, *Ethnic Relations*.
71. Esman, "The State and Language Policy," 392.

72. Vernon Van Dyke, *Human Rights, Ethnicity, and Discrimination* (Westport, Conn.: Greenwood Press, 1985), 49, see also 28.
73. *Padomju Jaunatne*, 8 December 1987.
74. See Figure A.3 in the Appendix; *Diena*, 6 March 1992 and 16 May 1992; *Rīgas Balss*, 5 May 1992, 4.
75. A September 1990 survey by the Social Research Center of Latvia found that 22 percent of non-Latvians said that they knew Latvian fluently, 17 percent had a "fair" knowledge, 46 percent knew "a little," and 13 percent knew none. A survey undertaken in April 1993 found that 58.4 percent of Russian respondents said that they knew Latvian. The survey question did not differentiate levels of language knowledge (Elmārs Vēbers et al., *Comparative Study of Ethnic Groups in Latvia*, unpublished research report to the Research Support Scheme of the Central European University, Riga, 1993, 43).
76. *Pravda*, 8 May 1989.
77. For example, *Diena*, 4 April 1992 and 12 May 1992, 4; other interviewees in the same article stated that it is normal to speak the language of the country one lives in.
78. Letters to the newspaper *Literatūra un Māksla*, 5 October 1988, 2; see also Rein Taagepera, "Ethnic Relations in Estonia, 1991,"*Journal of Baltic Studies* 23 (Summer 1992): 124.
79. *Jēkabpils Vēstnesis*, 4 September 1991, 1.
80. *Diena*, 22 April 1992, 5.
81. Iu. V. Arutiunian, "Sotsial'no-kul'turnoe razvitie i natsional'noe samosoznanie," *Sotsiologicheskie issledovaniia* 1990, no. 7: 46; L. D. Gudkov, "Attitudes toward Russians in the Union Republics," unpublished study by the All-Union Public Opinion Research Center, translated in *Russian Social Science Review* 34 (January–February 1993): 61.
82. *Neatkarīgā Cīņa*, 24 January 1992.
83. Rogers Brubaker, *Citizenship and Nationhood in France and Germany* (Cambridge, Mass.: Harvard University Press, 1992), 180.
84. Ibid., xi.
85. Esman, "The State and Language Policy," 383; see also similar definitions cited in chapter 3.
86. These qualities are evident from sociological surveys conducted between 1991 and 1993. For example, nearly half of respondents surveyed in January 1993 by the Social Research Center of Latvia were uncertain whether there was any point in participating in the June 1993 elections.
87. The leader of the Social-Democratic Party of Latvia, the poet Uldis Bērziņš, has been especially clear in emphasizing that the crucial criterion for citizenship is willingness to be a constructive part of Latvia's "political nation." *Diena*, 8 January 1993.
88. Brubaker, *Citizenship and Nationhood*, 148.
89. Ibid., 3, 183, and passim; see also the Conclusion.
90. Some people already identify as such. As noted by one prominent journalist "we are not Russians, Poles, or Jews, but rather Latvia's Russians, Latvia's Poles, Latvia's Jews, etc. We represent the Latvian subculture of our peoples" (Ābrams Kļockins, "Vai mēs spējam runāt par būtību?" *Diena*, 23 October 1992).
91. The publishers in Moscow stated that this book would be exported to schools in Latvia. *Diena*, 29 August 1992.

Conclusion

=>·◈·<=

The collapse of the Soviet Union meant the emergence of new regimes, states, and nations. I have argued that this threefold transition was part and parcel of a single process, and that it was impossible to have one without the others. The transition to democracy was unavoidably linked to the quest for self-rule by the constituent state units of the USSR and to their emancipation as new political and ethnocultural nations. Yet while the logic of this linkage can be shown rather clearly for the period of the collapse of the old system, many observers worry about the feasibility of the transition to a peaceful and democratic new system. In particular, observers fear that the Pax Sovietica will be replaced by violent conflicts within—and between—the new states and nations. My response to such fears is that although such conflicts are possible, so are peaceful solutions. One key to the latter option lies in creative application of the principles of pluralist democracy.

As argued in chapters 1 and 2, a political system that is decentralized and welcomes pluralism in many forms allows for ethnocultural and other forms of communal diversity to express themselves autonomously and harmoniously. In a state such as the United States, where religious groups are autonomous and rely entirely on their members, as do a variety of ethnic cultural and social self-help groups, ethnicity has a way of expressing itself without destructively entering the arena of political competition.[1] In other words, a strong civil society, defined as a realm of social pluralism, implicitly safeguards some forms of ethnic pluralism. Although many analysts of transition to democracy have pinpointed the emergence of civil society as a crucial requirement for its general success, I argue that it is also a crucial step in the development of ethnic democracy.

In Latvia and elsewhere in the ex-Soviet bloc, communal ethnic identity was one of the bases of the nascent civil society that challenged Communist dictatorships. Ethnic, regional, and other particularist identities formed building blocks of social solidarity and political action. More often than not, larger movements were built on this basis, with the popular fronts being prime examples. This unity built on diversity worked especially well as long as there was a common enemy in the old regime. Once the old regime and the Soviet empire collapsed, the position of diverse groupings had to be redefined in the context of new regimes and new states.

166

In this study I have argued that a pluralist form of democracy holds the most promise for dealing with the heterogeneity of nations and ethnic groups in the former Soviet region. Pluralist democracy accommodates ethnic groupings indirectly by its general acceptance of group autonomy. Yet more explicit accommodation is required if a state consists of several territorial nations or includes historical minorities eager for autonomy and retaining their distinct identity. These situations require explicit political power sharing and arrangements to safeguard the viability of minority cultures. Beyond structural arrangements, the successful building of a multiethnic political community requires a political culture of mutual respect and valuation. At least this is the conclusion emerging from the experience of consociational democracies such as Switzerland and Belgium. As also concluded from our discussion of these ethnopluralist precedents, this model is most useful in principle rather than in detail.

The key principle is that safeguards have to be found for minority nations and historical groups to feel secure against encroachments by larger nations and groups. The many ethnocultural nations and groups of Eastern Europe and the former USSR reject cultural assimilation and political control by others. In other words, the new states and democracies must be crafted in a way that allows ethnocultural nations and minorities to retain their distinct identity, yet also act as real partners in the formation of political nations. Extensive federalism and power sharing in common institutions is a key principle if the political nation involves two or more ethnocultural nations. Yet as is shown by the recent example of the former Czechoslovakia, both ethnocultural nations, and especially the smaller one, have to believe that political unity is to their advantage. Since public beliefs change over time, and are influenced by the interpretation of charismatic leaders, the attitudinal basis of multiethnic states is the most fragile part of such arrangements.

Recent experience in Eastern Europe and the former USSR shows that in the 1990s ethnocultural nations in the region strive to develop into independent political nations. This striving is seen as a way of breaking with the past that has involved too much centralized rule and cultural homogenization. Self-rule in independent states and the renascence of distinct identities are core values seeking expression. If this striving expresses itself in a constructive democratic nationalism, it need not lead to inter- or intrastate national strife. As the postwar experience of Western Europe has shown—and the western part of Europe is the ultimate model for the eastern part of it— independent democratic states can live peacefully side by side and gradually work toward integration based on a reconciliation of mutual interests. The question of intrastate national peace is more complex in Eastern Europe, of course, due to cultural and political geography and history.

The central ethnogeographic fact is that although distinct ethnocultural nations form the basic multinational mosaic of the region, there is also an intermixture of smaller groups and individual minority members dispersed across it. Therefore, no matter how state lines are drawn, most states in the region will include minorities, as has been the historical pattern. The danger occurs when xenophobic nationalists try to change this pattern by force. One peaceful alternative is voluntary resettlement. Although it is beyond the scope of this study to explore such a topic, it should be noted that resettlement from the former USSR and various East European states—especially of Germans, Jews, and Poles—has been occurring throughout the postwar period.[2]

In regard to those minority members who will always remain in the region there are two alternatives: cultural assimilation or pluralism. I suggest that pluralism is both more democratic and more viable, especially in East Central Europe where a ethnopluralist model has been developed in the past and is reemerging today.

As discussed in chapter 1, the Central European model of ethnopluralism was first outlined by the Austrian socialists Otto Bauer and Karl Renner. It involves cultural self-rule and some political guarantees for nonterritorial historic minorities. In the interwar period the model was implemented most thoroughly in Estonia, closely followed by Latvia. It is based on a non-assimilationist cultural conception of nationhood, joined with an integrationist political conception of the civic nation. In this it is similar to consociationalism, except that it focuses on smaller and dispersed minorities rather than fully developed ethnocultural nations.

The theoretical and practical relevance of this model is that it provides a pluralist answer to the primary issue of nationhood in the post-Communist world. Traditional nationalists argue that the only way to safeguard nationhood is to form states and political communities that are congruent with cultural historical nations. In contrast, liberals and Marxists argue that the only option is to focus on "supranational" entities. Yet though modern history has seen many challenges to the nation-state, it remains the basis of the contemporary international system. The last decades have also shown the persistence of ethnicity all over the world. This means that ways must be found to reconcile communalism and ethnocultural nationhood with the principles of civic democracy. Pluralist arrangements make this possible.

Yet the crux of the matter is that ethnic federalism and other ethnoplural democratic arrangements[3] will work only if the politicians crafting the new states and regimes are successful in balancing the two types of nationhood they have to deal with: the political nation defined as a civic community, and one or several ethnic communal entities. Proposed solutions cannot rely on simplistic general rules but must be grounded in an empirical assessment of the situation in each state. As outlined in the case of Latvia, there are instances when the ethnocultural and political position of a titular nation is much weaker than one might expect, and it is unclear who is the minority. What's more, the harmonious accommodation of ethnic diversity in Latvia is aggravated by the consequences of the political, demographic, and linguistic expansion of a giant neighbor. Thus all the players, both small and large, face the task of recovering their domestic and international nationhood in meaningful ways.

The new Russia, too, is faced with the task of defining its political and ethnocultural nationhood. In addition, the Russian case illustrates how the emerging redefinitions of national identity in the region are interrelated. The question of the nationhood of Russia is linked to the nationhood of Russia's neighbors in that the latter depend for their own unhindered development on the emergence of a nonimperial democratic Russian national identity. If the imperial strains in Russian nationalism should take the upper hand, this will endanger democracy and state building not just for Russia, but also for its smaller neighbors. In other words, much depends on whether Russia accepts the principles of sovereignty and self-rule for all the nations in the region of the former USSR, or reverts to an imperial mentality.

The perestroika-era rejection of the Soviet identity by many Russians meant the acceptance of self-rule for all nations. In the words of Mark Beissinger, "The construction of a modern Russian identity could occur only on the basis of the deconstruction of the symbiosis between Russian and Soviet imperial identities."[4] Yet by mid-1992 the hardships of the post-Communist transition presented fertile soil for a resurgence of more expansionist forces and neo-imperialist pressures on the Russian leadership have been growing.[5] The reassessment of Russia's relationship to its imperial legacy began to focus on the Russian diasporas now living abroad. As these new minorities lost their former privileges as representatives of central Soviet rule, Russian politicians began to intervene on their behalf. In 1993 it is unclear whether this impulse to intervene abroad will persist, or whether Russia will turn inward.

The search for Russia's national identity involves first of all a conception about what constitutes the core of the Russian nation and what its relationship is to the ethnic minorities of the Russian Federation. If the latter is defined as the basis of a civic nation, is Russia going to make ethnopluralist arrangements for its territorial and nonterritorial minorities, or is it going to pursue a basically assimilationist policy? And, returning to the question of ethnic diasporas, since Russians in neighboring states enjoy numerous cultural provisions, will Russia make reciprocal provisions for Latvians or Ukrainians living in Russia?[6] In sum, the nature of Russian nationalism will shape Russia's own identity as well as that of other states—but that is the topic of another book.

NOTES

1. America's history of focusing on the indirect accommodation of ethnic pluralism may explain the controversy surrounding initiatives toward its more formal recognition in regard to ethnic quotas, electoral districting, or public school programs promoting multiculturalism.
2. Hundreds of thousands of Germans and Jews have been emigrating from the former USSR and Eastern Europe since the early 1970s, and in the 1950s many Poles were resettled to Poland from the territories annexed by the USSR in 1939. See Joseph B. Schechtman, *Postwar Population Transfers in Europe, 1945–1955* (Philadelphia: University of Pennsylvania Press, 1963), and numerous articles on Jewish and German emigration.
3. On the role of a careful design of electoral systems and the encouragement of multiethnic political organizations, see Donald L. Horowitz, "Ethnic Conflict Management for Policymakers," in Joseph V. Montville, ed., *Conflict and Peacemaking in Multiethnic Societies* (Lexington, Mass.: Lexington Books, 1990), 115–39, and Donald L. Horowitz, "Making Moderation Pay: The Comparative Politics of Ethnic Conflict Management," in ibid., 451–75.
4. Mark B. Beissinger, "Elites and Ethnic Identities in Soviet and Post-Soviet Politics," in Alexander J. Motyl, ed., *The Post-Soviet Nations: Perspectives on the Demise of the USSR* (New York: Columbia University Press, 1992), 150. The construction of a Russian nation-state that is not at the same time an empire is unprecedented in history, yet it is crucial if Russia hopes to build a democracy and get away from an imperial mind-set in relations with its neighbors. See also Sergei Maksudov and William Taubman, "Russian-Soviet Nationality Policy and Foreign Policy: A Historical Overview of the Linkage between Them," in Michael Mandelbaum, ed., *The Rise of Nations in the Soviet Union* (New York: Council on Foreign Relations, 1991), 15–43.
5. Vera Tolz, "The Burden of the Imperial Legacy," *RFE/RL Research Report*, 14 May 1993, 41–46.
6. Until 1993 such provisions were practically nonexistent, causing increasing concern; see, for example, *Atmoda*, 25 February 1992, 13.

Appendix

━━▷◆◁━━

Methodological Note on Survey Data

This study uses surveys undertaken by various sociological institutions in Latvia and the former Soviet Union. Especially intensive use is made of original data sets of the Social Research Center of Latvia. Other results were available only from published sources and it was impossible to determine how meticulous the researchers had been in sampling and other technical aspects of survey research.[1] Nevertheless, the results are cited here as illustrations of broad social trends, without the claim of total accuracy.

Most of the survey data on Latvia come from the Social Research Center of Latvia, directed by sociologist Brigita Zepa. She and her colleagues have also conducted surveys as the Social Research Center of the Sociological Association of Latvia. This staff has undertaken numerous surveys and has established a reliable network of more than a hundred interviewers throughout Latvia. Most of the research conducted by the Social Research Center of Latvia is based on a national sample (1,000 to 1,200 respondents) which is representative of the adult population of Latvia. The center uses stratified random sampling in conducting monthly public opinion polls.

The stratified random sampling method is used to obtain a sample where the proportions of the most important geographic and social groupings are close to those in the general population. To determine these proportions, the center uses 1989 census data and statistical data updated yearly by the State Statistical Committee. These are the stratification indicators in use in the late 1980s and early 1990s:

A.	Geographic Area	Riga	(City)	34%
		Kurzeme	(West)	16%
		Vidzeme	(Center and North)	22%
		Zemgale	(South)	10%
		Latgale	(East)	18%
B.	Size of Populated Point	Cities (> 100,000)		43%
		Towns		28%
		Countryside		29%
C.	Gender	Male		46%
		Female		54%

171

D.	Age	15–24	18%
		25–34	19%
		35–44	16%
		45–54	17%
		55–64	15%
		65 and older	15%
E.	Education	Lower than middle school	39%
		Middle school	47%
		Higher than middle school	14%
F.	Nationality	Latvian	52%
		Non-Latvian	48%

The center reaches these proportions in the sample by the regional distribution of questionnaires and through instructions given to the interviewers. Across Latvia there are thirteen supervisors who oversee more than one hundred interviewers in thirty-five sample points. Each interviewer receives detailed instructions about how to choose respondents (in most cases, the supervisor chooses a random first address, then the interviewer follows the procedure described in the instructions). The center gives the supervisors and the interviewers rough proportions for each category and not a definite number of respondents. If at the final stage, there are some oversampled or undersampled subgroups in the sample, then the center introduces weighing or randomly withdraws sample questionnaires from the oversampled group.

NOTES

1. Methodological problems confronted with survey research conducted in the region are analyzed by Michael Swafford, "Sociological Aspects of Survey Research in the Commonwealth of Independent States," *International Journal of Public Opinion Research* 4, no. 4 (1992): 346–57; Richard B. Dobson and Steven A. Grant, "Public Opinion and the Transformation of the Soviet Union," *International Journal of Public Opinion Research* 4, no. 4 (1992): 302–20. See also Albert Motivans, guest ed., "A Special Issue: Public Opinion in the Baltic States," *Journal of Baltic Studies* 24, no. 2 (Summer 1993).

Table A.1
Preferred Status for Latvia among Non-Latvians, by
Support for Popular Front

Preference for Latvia	Support Popular Front		
	Yes (n = 180) (percent)	Don't Know (n = 75) (percent)	No (n = 170) (percent)
Independence	50	9	8
Independent state within USSR as confederation	38	56	52
Part of USSR	3	14	34
Don't know	9	21	6

Source: Social Research Center of Latvia, September 1990. n = number.

Table A.2
Preferred Status for Latvia among Non-Latvians, by
Support for Interfront

Preference for Latvia	Support Interfront		
	Yes (n = 116) (percent)	Difficult to Say (n = 123) (percent)	No (n = 206) (percent)
Independence	3	10	47
Independent state within USSR as confederation	61	53	36
Part of USSR	31	20	8
Don't know	5	17	9

Source: Social Research Center of Latvia, September 1990. n = number.

Table A.3
Evaluation of Social Movements, by Nationality

	Latvians (percent)	Others (percent)
Informal groups		
Help solve problems	51	20
Engage in extremism	32	63
Gained information from informal group meetings		
Very much	12	4
A little	36	20
Not at all	45	65

Source: Original data from "Forum" survey (Social Research Center of Latvia), November 1988. Missing percentages refer to "no answer" and "difficult to say" responses.

Table A.4
Electoral Candidates by Nationality

Nationality	All		Popular Front		Other	
	%	n	%	n	%	n
Latvian	65.4	251	82.3	154	39.6	78
Russian	24.4	94	8.6	16	49.3	97
Ukrainian	3.4	13	0.5	1	6.1	12
Belorussian	2.1	8	1.1	2	3.0	6
Polish	1.3	5	2.7	5	0.0	
Jewish	1.3	5	2.7	5	0.0	
Other	2.1	8	2.1	4	2.0	4
Total	100	384	100	187	100	197

Source: Data for two hundred election districts as of 16 March 1990; raw data from Election Center of the Popular Front of Latvia, author's calculations. n = number.

Table A.5
Population of Latvia by Ethnicity: 1935–93 (in thousands)

Ethnicity	1935 n	1935 %	1959 n	1959 %	1970 n	1970 %	1979 n	1979 %	1989 n	1989 %	1993 n	1993 %
Total	1,905.9	100.0	2,093.5	100.0	2,364.1	100.0	2,502.8	100.0	2,606.1	100.0	2,606.1	100.0
Latvians	1,467.0	77.0	1,297.9	62.0	1,341.8	56.8	1,344.1	53.7	1,387.8	52.0	1,395.5	53.5
Russians	168.3	8.8	556.4	26.6	704.6	29.8	821.5	32.8	905.5	34.0	872.4	33.5
Belorussians	26.8	1.4	61.6	2.3	94.7	4.0	111.5	4.5	119.7	4.5	109.8	4.2
Ukrainians	1.8	0.1	29.4	1.4	53.5	2.3	66.7	2.7	92.1	3.4	82.1	3.2
Poles	48.6	2.6	59.8	2.9	63.0	2.7	62.7	2.5	60.4	2.3	58.4	2.2
Lithuanians	22.8	1.6	32.4	1.5	40.6	1.7	37.8	1.5	34.6	1.3	33.6	1.3
Jews	93.4	4.9	36.6	1.7	36.7	1.6	28.3	1.1	22.9	0.9	14.8	0.6
Germans	62.1	3.3	1.6	0.1	5.4	0.2	3.3	0.1	3.8	0.1	2.6	0.1
Others	7.7	0.4	13.2	0.7	19.3	0.8	23.2	1.0	36.5	1.4	37.0	1.4

Sources: Latvijas Republikas Valsts statistikas komiteja, *Latvijas demogrāfijas gadagrāmata* (Riga: n.p., 1993), 46, LPSR Valsts statistikas komiteja, *1989, gada tautas skaitīšanas rezultāti*, LPSR (Riga: Statistisks biļetēns, I. Daļa, 1989), and Statistics Committee of the Republic of Latvia and Institute of Philosophy and Sociology, Latvian Academy of Sciences, *The Ethnic Situation in Latvia Today: Facts and Commentary* (Riga: Conference on Democracy and Ethnopolitics, May 1992), 4. n = number.

Table A.6
Language in Kindergartens in Latvia, 1989

	Latvian (percent)	Russian (percent)	Mixed (percent)	Other (percent)
Enrollment of children in language groups	36.5	41.9	21.6	
Nationality of children age 0 to 9*	54.3	36.8		8.9

Source: Author's calculations based on unpublished statistics of the Ministry of Education of Latvia and on data from the 1989 census, LPSR Valsts statistikas komiteja, *1989. Gada tautas skaitīšanas rezultāti, LPSR* (Riga: Statistisks biļetēns, II. Daļa, 1989), 34.
*The census puts children in the age groups 0 to 4 and 5 to 9.

Table A.7
Language of Instruction in Higher Educational
Institutions (at the start of the 1991–92 academic year)

	Total Students	Latvian (percent)	Russian (percent)	Latvian and Russian (percent)
		Receive their education in:		
University of Latvia	13,368	62.5	37.5	
Riga Technical University	10,278	36.2	47.1	16.7
Latvian Academy of Agriculture	5,772	94.1	5.9	
Latvian Academy of Medicine	2,641	62.0	38.0	
Daugavpils Pedagogical Institute	2,736	34.6	65.4	
Liepāja Pedagogical Institute	2,530	74.2	25.8	
Latvian Academy of Music	803	96.5	3.5	
Latvian Academy of Art	574	100		
Latvian Academy of Physical Education	1,106	64.9	35.1	
Riga Aviation Institute	3,948		100	
Latvian Institute of Rail Transport Engineers	1,010		100	
Latvian Academy of Culture	63	100		
Riga Higher School of Aeronavigation	105		100	
Latvian Police Academy	698	15.8		84.2
Riga Branch of Kaliningrad Technical School of Fisheries and the Kaliningrad Higher Nautical School	647		100	
Training and Re-training Center for Grownups	93	66.7	33.3	

Source: Statistics Committee of the Republic of Latvia and Institute of Philosophy and Sociology, Latvian Academy of Sciences. *The Ethnic Situation in Latvia Today: Facts and Commentary* (Riga: Conference on Democracy and Ethnopolitics, May 1992), 18–19.

Table A.8
Responses to the Question "Do Public Officials Observe the Language Law and Interact with You in the Language of Your Choice?"

	Yes (percent)	Sometimes (percent)	No (percent)
Nationality of Respondent			
Latvian	32	57	11
Russian	58	37	5

Source: *Diena*, 12 November 1992, p. 3, citing a survey conducted by the Baltic Studies Center in Riga.

Table A.9
Responses to the Question "How Likely Are Interethnic Conflicts in Latvia?" (September 1991)

	Latvians (n = 448) (percent)	Russians and Others (n = 384) (percent)
Very likely	1	4
Likely	17	21
Unlikely	62	48
Nearly none	7	9
Difficult to say	12	19

	Among Russians and Others	
	Speak Latvian (n = 174) (percent)	Do Not Speak Latvian (n = 205) (percent)
Very likely	3	4
Likely	18	23
Unlikely	56	42
Nearly none	9	9
Difficult to say	14	22

Source: Social Research Center of Latvia. n = number.

FIGURE A.1. Russian support for Latvia's independence, by age.

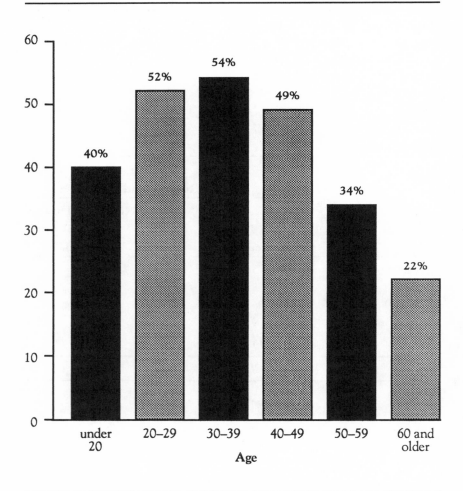

Source: Survey conducted by the sociological section at the Supreme Council of Latvia in December 1990, random sample of 1,675 people throughout Latvia. Cited in *Latvijas Jaunatne,* 29 December 1990, 2.

FIGURE A.2.   Age groups by nationality.

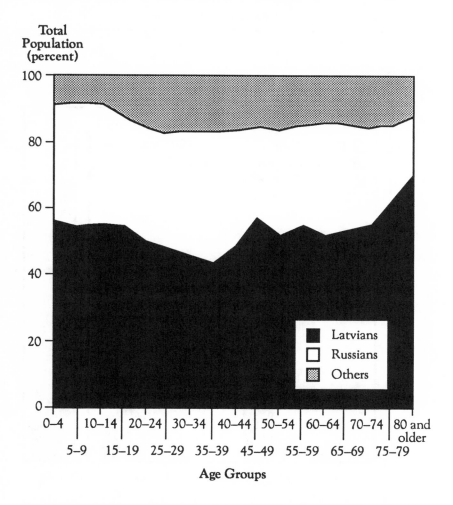

Source: LPSR Valsts statistikas komiteja, *1989. Gada tautas skaitīšanas rezultāti, LPSR* (Riga: Statistiks biļetēns, II. Daļa, 1989), 31.

FIGURE A.3. Number of Latvian language instruction
manuals (for adults) and dictionaries
published, 1945–92.

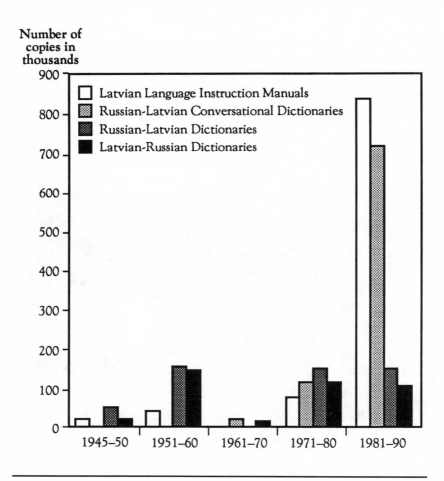

Source: State Language Inspectorate of Latvia. In 1991 and 1992 more Latvian-language
instruction manuals (55,000) and Russian-Latvian conversational dictionaries (85,000) were
published.

Selected Bibliography

<hr>

Newspapers and Periodicals

A. In Latvian

Atmoda, Popular Front of Latvia, Riga, 1989–93.

Auseklis, underground periodical, 1988.

Avīzīte, Association of Politically Repressed People, Riga, 1991–92.

Balvu Atmoda, Popular Front of Latvia, Balvi, 1991.

Cīņa, Communist Party of Latvia, Riga, 1988–91.

Daugavpils Vēstnesis, Daugavpils, 1991.

Diena, daily newspaper, Riga, 1990–93.

Elpa, Ecological Education Publishers of Latvia, Riga, 1990–93.

Informācija, Aktualitātes, Diskusijas, Citizens' Committees of the Republic of Latvia, 1989.

Informācijas Lapa, National Independence Movement of Latvia, 1989.

Izglītība, For the Renewal of Education in Latvia, Riga, 1990–93.

Jaunais Laiks, Youth Association of Latvia, Liepāja, 1990–91.

Jēkabpils Vēstnesis, independent newspaper, Jēkabpils, 1991.

Jelgavas Ziņotājs, Jelgava, 1989–92.

Jelgavnieks, National Independence Movement of Latvia in Jelgava, 1991.

Junda, Rebirth Party of Latvia, Riga, 1989–91.

Jūrmala, city newspaper, Jūrmala, 1992–93.

Jūrmalas Rīts, Communist Party of Latvia, Jūrmala city section, Riga, 1991.

Kultūras Fonda Avīze, Cultural Fund of Latvia, Riga, 1989–92.

LatNIA, Press Bulletin of the Independent Information Agency of Latvia, Riga, 1989.

Latvijas Jaunatne, previously *Padomju Jaunatne*, newspaper of Latvia's Komsomol, later—daily newspaper, Riga, 1988–93.

Latvijas Jurists, Association of Lawyers of Latvia, Riga, 1990–91.

Lauku Avīze, weekly newspaper, Riga, 1989–93.

Liepājas Vārds, Popular Front of Latvia, Liepāja, 1990–91.

Literatūra un Māksla, Creative Unions of Lativa, Riga, 1988–93.

Neatkarība, National Independence Movement of Latvia, Riga, 1989–92.

Neatkarīgā Cīņa, daily newspaper, Riga, 1991–93.

Opozīcija, independent political periodical, Riga, 1990.

Padomju Jaunatne, see *Latvijas Jaunatne.*

Pilsonis, Citizens' Congress of the Republic of Latvia, Riga, 1990–92.

Rīgas Balss, daily newspaper, Riga, 1990–93.

Skolotāju Avīze, Riga, 1988–90.

Sociāldemokrāts, Social-Democratic Party of Latvia, Riga, 1989.

Staburags, Journal of the Environmental Protection Club, 1988.

Temīda, Ministry of Justice, Riga, 1991–92.

B. In Russian

Baltiiskoe vremia, Popular Front of Latvia, Riga, 1990–91.

Edinstvo, International Front of Workers of the Latvian SSR, Riga, 1989–91.

Men'shevik, Latvian Social-Democratic Party, Riga, 1990.

Mir mnenii i mneniia o mire, Public Opinion Research Service VP, Moscow, 1991.

Nezavisimaia baltiiskaia gazeta, Riga, 1991–92.

Nezavisimaia gazeta, Moscow, 1991.

Novosti Rigi, Communist Party Organization of Riga, 1990.

SM–segodnia, Riga, 1992.

Soglasie, Lithuanian Movement for Perestroika, 1989–90.

Sovetskaia Latviia, Riga, 1988–91.

Sovetskaia molodezh, Riga, 1988–90.

Vremia, Riga, 1990.

C. In English

Baltic Observer, weekly newspaper, Riga, 1992–93.

Current Digest of the Post-Soviet Press, 1992–93.

Current Digest of the Soviet Press, 1949–91.

Foreign Broadcast Information Service (FBIS), Washington, D.C.

Moscow News, Moscow, 1989–93.

Report on the USSR, Munich, 1989–91.

RFE/RL Research Report, Munich, 1992–93.

Social Review, Social Research Center of Latvia, Riga, 1991.

Books and Articles

Alexeyeva, Ludmilla. *Soviet Dissent: Contemporary Movements for National, Religious, and Human Rights.* Middletown, Conn.: Wesleyan University Press, 1985.

Almond, Gabriel A., and Sidney Verba. *The Civic Culture.* Boston: Little, Brown, 1965.

Anderson, Benedict. *Imagined Communities: Reflections on the Origin and Spread of Nationalism.* London: Verso, 1983.

Armstrong, John. "Assessing the Soviet Nationalities Movements: A Critical Review." *Nationalities Papers* 19 (Spring 1991): 1–18.

———. "The Ethnic Scene in the Soviet Union: The View of the Dictatorship." In Erich Goldhagen, ed., *Ethnic Minorities in the Soviet Union,* 3–49. New York: Praeger, 1968.

Arutiunian, Iu. V. "Sotsial'no-kul'turnoe razvitie i natsional'noe samosoznanie." *Sotsiologicheskie issledovaniia* 1990, no. 7: 42–49.

Azrael, Jeremy R., ed. *Soviet Nationality Policies and Practices.* New York: Praeger, 1978.

Barth, Frederick, ed. *Ethnic Groups and Boundaries: The Social Organization of Culture Differences.* London: Allen and Unwin, 1969.

Beissinger, Mark R. "The Deconstruction of the USSR and the Search for a Post-Soviet Community." *Problems of Communism* (November–December 1991): 27–35.

———. "John Armstrong's Functionalism and Beyond: Approaches to the Study of Soviet Nationalities Politics." *Journal of Soviet Nationalities* 1 (Spring 1990): 91–100.

Bilmanis, Alfred. *A History of Latvia.* Princeton: Princeton University Press, 1947.

Birch, Anthony H. "Minority Nationalist Movements and Theories of Political Integration," *World Politics* 30 (April 1978): 325–44.

Blalock, Hubert, Jr. *Toward a Theory of Minority-Group Relations.* New York: Wiley, 1967.

Bremmer, Ian, and Ray Taras, eds. *Nations and Politics in the Soviet Successor States.* Cambridge: Cambridge University Press, 1993.

Brovkin, Vladimir. "Revolution from Below: Informal Political Associations in Russia 1988–1989." *Soviet Studies* 42 (April 1990): 233–57.

Brown, Archie, ed. *Political Culture and Communist Studies.* Armonk, N.Y.: Sharpe, 1985.

Brubaker, Rogers. *Citizenship and Nationhood in France and Germany.* Cambridge, Mass.: Harvard University Press, 1992.

————, ed. *Immigration and the Politics of Citizenship in Europe and North America*. Lanham, Md.: University Press of America, 1989.

Butterfield, Jim, and Marcia Weigle. "Unofficial Social Groups and Regime Response in the Soviet Union." In Judith B. Sedaitis and Jim Butterfield, eds., *Perestroika from Below: Social Movements in the Soviet Union*, 175–95. Boulder, Colo.: Westview Press, 1991.

Čeičs, Valdis, ed. *Valsts valoda: Dokumenti, intervijas, uzziņas*. Riga: Latvijas Republikas Ministru Padome, 1992.

Coakley, John. "The Resolution of Ethnic Conflict: Towards a Typology." *International Political Science Review* 13, no. 4 (1992): 343–58.

Cobban, Alfred. *The Nation-State and National Self-Determination*. New York: Crowell, 1970.

Connor, Walker. "Ethnonationalism." In Myron Weiner and Samuel P. Huntington, eds., *Understanding Political Development*, 196–219. Boston: Little, Brown, 1987.

————. *The National Question in Marxist-Leninist Theory and Strategy*. Princeton: Princeton University Press, 1984.

————. "Self-Determination: The New Phase." *World Politics* 20 (October 1967): 30–53.

Connor, Walter D. "Class, Social Structure, Nationality." In Alexander J. Motyl, ed., *The Post-Soviet Nations: Perspectives on the Demise of the USSR*, 272–301. New York: Columbia University Press, 1992.

Dahl, Robert A., ed. *Regimes and Oppositions*. New Haven: Yale University Press, 1973.

Dallin, A., and G. W. Breslauer. *Political Terror in Communist Systems*. Stanford: Stanford University Press, 1970.

Deutsch, Karl W. *Nationalism and Social Communication*. 2d ed. Cambridge, Mass.: MIT Press, 1966.

Di Palma, Giuseppe. "Legitimation from the Top to Civil Society: Politico-Cultural Change in Eastern Europe." *World Politics* 44 (October 1991): 49–80.

Dišlers, K. *Latvijas valsts varas orgāni un viņu funkcijas*. Riga: Tieslietu Ministrija, 1925.

Dreifelds, Juris. "Demographic Trends in Latvia." *Nationalities Papers* (Charleston, Ill.) 12, no. 1 (1984): 49–84.

———. "Immigration and Ethnicity in Latvia." *Journal of Soviet Nationalities* 1 (Winter 1990–91): 42–81.

———. "Latvian National Rebirth." *Problems of Communism* (July–August 1989): 77–95.

Drobizheva, Leokida. "Perestroika and the Ethnic Consciousness of Russians." In Gail W. Lapidus and Victor Zaslavsky, with Philip Goldman, eds., *From Union to Commonwealth: Nationalism and Separatism in the Soviet Republics*, 98–113. Cambridge: Cambridge University Press, 1992.

Druviete, I. "Funktsionirovanie i status latyshskogo iazyka." *Kommunist Sovetskoi Latvii*, 1988, no. 12: 45–52.

Dutter, Lee E. "Theoretical Perspectives on Ethnic Political Behavior in the Soviet Union." *Journal of Conflict Resolution* 34 (June 1990): 311–34.

Dzyuba, Ivan. *Internationalism or Russification? A Study in the Soviet Nationalities Problem.* London: Weidenfeld and Nicolson, 1968.

Eglīte, P. "Iedzīvotāju ataudzes etniskie aspekti Latvijā." *Latvijas PSR Zinātņu Akadēmijas Vēstis* 1991, no. 2: 23–32.

Eglitis, Olgerts. *Nonviolent Action in the Liberation of Latvia.* Monograph series no. 5. Cambridge, Mass.: The Albert Einstein Institution, 1993.

Ekmanis, Rolf. *Latvian Literature under the Soviets 1940–1975.* Belmont, Mass.: Nordland, 1978.

Emerson, Rupert. *From Empire to Nation: The Rise to Self-Assertion of Asian and African Peoples.* Cambridge, Mass.: Harvard University Press, 1960.

Enloe, Cynthia H. *Ethnic Conflict and Political Development.* Boston: Little, Brown, 1973.

Esman, Milton J. "Political and Psychological Factors in Ethnic Conflict." In Joseph V. Montville, ed., *Conflict and Peacemaking in Multiethnic Societies*, 53–64. Lexington, Mass.: Lexington Books, 1990.

———. "The State and Language Policy." *International Political Science Review* 13, no. 4 (1992): 381–96.

Evans, Peter B., Dietrich Rueschemeyer, and Theda Skocpol, eds. *Bringing the State Back In.* Cambridge: Cambridge University Press, 1985.

Finifter, Ada W., and Ellen Mickiewicz. "Redefining the Political System of the USSR: Mass Support for Political Change." *American Political Science Review* 86 (December 1992): 857–74.

Furtado, Charles F., Jr., and Andrea Chandler, eds. *Perestroika in the Soviet Republics: Documents on the National Question.* Boulder, Colo.: Westview Press, 1992.

Garleff, Michael. "Ethnic Minorities in the Estonian and Latvian Parliaments: The Politics of Coalition." In V. Stanley Vardys and Romuald Misiunas, eds., *The Baltic States in Peace and War 1917–1945*, 81–94. University Park: Pennsylvania State University Press, 1978.

Ginsburgs, George. "Nationality and State Succession in Soviet Theory and Practice—The Experience of the Baltic Republics." In Adolfs Sprudz and Armins Rusis, eds., *Res Baltica: A Collection of Essays in Honor of the Memory of Dr. Alfred Bilmanis*, 160–90. Leyden: A. W. Sijthoff, 1968.

Glaser, Daniel. "Dynamics of Ethnic Identification." *American Sociological Review* 23 (February 1958): 31–40.

Glazer, Nathan, and Daniel P. Moynihan, eds. *Ethnicity: Theory and Experience.* Cambridge, Mass.: Harvard University Press, 1975.

Glubotskii, Aleksei. *Strany Baltii: Politicheskie partii i organizatsii.* Moscow: Panorama, 1992.

Goble, Paul. "Central Asians Form Political Bloc." *Report on the USSR*, 13 July 1990, pp. 18–20.

————. "Soviet Citizens Blame System for Ethnic Problems." *Report on the USSR*, 29 June 1990, p. 5.

Graham, Malbone W. *New Governments of Eastern Europe.* New York: Henry Holt, 1927.

Greenfeld, Liah. *Nationalism: Five Roads to Modernity.* Cambridge, Mass.: Harvard University Press, 1992.

Gross, Jan T. "Poland: From Civil Society to Political Nation." In Ivo Banac, ed., *Eastern Europe in Revolution*, Ithaca: Cornell University Press, 1992.

Gudkov, L. D., "Attitudes toward Russians in the Union Republics." Unpublished study by the All-Union Public Opinion Research Center. Translated in *Russian Social Science Review* 34, no. 1 (January–February 1993): 52–69.

Halbach, Uwe. "Nationalitätenfrage und Föderation." *Osteuropa* 11 (November 1990): 1011–24.

Havel, Václav, et al. *The Power of the Powerless.* Armonk, N.Y.: Sharpe, 1985.

Heisler, Martin O. "Ethnicity and Ethnic Relations in the Modern West." In Joseph V. Montville, ed., *Conflict and Peacemaking in Multiethnic Societies*, 21–52. Lexington, Mass.: Lexington Books, 1990.

Horowitz, Donald L. *Ethnic Groups in Conflict*. Berkeley: University of California Press, 1985.

———. "Ethnic Identity." In Nathan Glazer and Daniel P. Moynihan, eds., *Ethnicity: Theory and Experience*, 111–40. Cambridge, Mass.: Harvard University Press, 1975.

———. "How to Begin Thinking Comparatively about Soviet Ethnic Problems." In Alexander J. Motyl, ed., *Thinking Theoretically about Soviet Nationalities*, 9–22. New York: Columbia University Press, 1992.

Hough, William J. H. III. "The Annexation of the Baltic States and Its Effect on the Development of Law Prohibiting Forcible Seizure of Territory." *New York Law School Journal of International and Comparative Law* 6 (Winter 1985): entire.

Huntington, Samuel P. *The Third Wave: Democratization in the Late Twentieth Century*. Norman: University of Oklahoma Press, 1991.

———"Will More Countries Become Democratic?" *Political Science Quarterly* 99, no. 2 (Summer 1984): 193–218.

Johnston, Hank. "The Comparative Study of Nationalism: Six Pivotal Themes from the Baltic States." *Journal of Baltic Studies* 23 (Summer 1992): 85–104.

Karklins, Rasma. "The Dissent/Coercion Nexus in the USSR." *Studies in Comparative Communism* 20 (Autumn 1987): 321–41.

———. *Ethnic Relations in the USSR: The Perspective from Below*. London and Boston: Allen and Unwin, 1986.

———. "Soviet Elections Revisited: The Significance of Voter Abstention in Non-Competitive Voting." *American Political Science Review* 80 (June 1986): 449–69.

———, and Roger Petersen. "The Calculus of Protesters and Regimes: Eastern Europe 1989." *Journal of Politics* 55 (August 1993): 588–614.

Kasfir, Nelson. "Explaining Ethnic Political Participation." *World Politics* 31 (April 1979): 365–88.

King, Gundar J. *Economic Policies in Occupied Latvia: A Manpower Management Study*. Tacoma, Wash.: Pacific Lutheran University Press, 1965.

Kirkwood, Michael. "*Glasnost'*, 'The National Question' and Soviet Language Policy." *Soviet Studies* 43, no. 1 (1991): 61–81.

Kornhauser, William. *The Politics of Mass Society*. Glencoe, Ill.: Free Press, 1959.

Kreindler, Isabelle T. "Baltic Area Languages in the Soviet Union: A Socio-linguistic Perspective." *Journal of Baltic Studies* 19 (Spring 1988): 5–20.

Kux, Stephan. "Soviet Federalism." *Problems of Communism* (March–April 1990): 1–28.

Laitin, David D. "The National Uprisings in the Soviet Union." *World Politics* 44 (October 1991): 139–77.

Lapidus, Gail W., and Victor Zaslavsky, with Philip Goldman, eds. *From Union to Commonwealth: Nationalism and Separatism in the Soviet Republics.* Cambridge: Cambridge University Press, 1992.

Laserson, Max M. "The Jewish Minorities in the Baltic Countries." *Jewish Social Studies* 3 (1941): 273–93.

Levine, Daniel H. "Paradigm Lost: Dependence to Democracy." *World Politics* 40 (April 1988): 337–94.

Levits, Egil. "The Development of Legal Relations between the Communist Party of Latvia and the Communist Party of the Soviet Union." In Dietrich A. Loeber et al., *Ruling Communist Parties and their Status under Law*, 57–74. Dordrecht, Boston, Lancaster: Martinus Nijhoff, 1986.

———. "Lettland unter sowjetischer Herrschaft, Die politische Entwicklung 1940–1989." In Boris Meissner, ed., *Die Baltischen Nationen: Estland, Lettland, Litauen*, 131–70. Cologne: Markus, 1990.

Lieberson, Stanley. *Language Diversity and Language Contact.* Stanford: Stanford University Press, 1981.

Lijphart, Arend. *Democracies: Patterns of Majoritarian and Consensus Government in Twenty-One Countries.* New Haven: Yale University Press, 1984.

———. *Democracy in Plural Society.* New Haven: Yale University Press, 1977.

———. "Political Theories and the Explanation of Ethnic Conflict in the Western World: Falsified Predictions and Plausible Postdictions." In Milton J. Esman, ed., *Ethnic Conflict in the Western World*, 61–62. Ithaca: Cornell University Press, 1977.

———. "The Power-Sharing Approach." In Joseph V. Montville, ed., *Conflict and Peacemaking in Multiethnic Societies*, 491–510. Lexington, Mass.: Lexington Books, 1990.

Linz, Juan. "From Primordialism to Nationalism." In Edward A. Tiryakian and Ronald Rogowski, eds., *New Nationalisms of the Developed West: Toward Explanation*, 203–53. Boston: Allen and Unwin, 1985.

———. "Transitions to Democracy." *Washington Quarterly* (Summer 1990): 143–164.

Lustick, Ian. "Stability in Deeply Divided Societies: Consociationalism versus Control." *World Politics* 31 (April 1979): 325–44.

McAuley, Mary. "Political Participation under Review." *Studies in Comparative Communism* 17 (Fall-Winter 1984–85): 241–51.

McHale, Vincent E. "The Party Systems of the Baltic States: A Comparative European Perspective." *Journal of Baltic Studies* 17 (Winter 1986): 295–312.

McRae, Kenneth, ed. *Consociational Democracy: Political Accommodation in Segmented Societies.* Toronto: McClelland and Stewart, 1974.

———. "Theories of Power-Sharing and Conflict Management." In Joseph V. Montville, ed., *Conflict and Peacemaking in Multiethnic Societies,* 93–106. Lexington, Mass.: Lexington Books, 1990.

Meissner, Boris. *Die Sowjetunion, die Baltischen Staaten und das Völkerrecht.* Cologne: Politik und Wirtschaft, 1956.

Melson, Robert, and Howard Wolpe. "Modernization and the Politics of Communalism: A Theoretical Perspective." *American Political Science Review* 64 (December 1970): 1112–30.

Meyer, Stephen M. "How the Threat (and the Coup) Collapsed." *International Security* 16 (Winter 1991–92): 5–38.

Mežs, Ilmārs. *Latvieši Latvijā.* Kalamazoo, Mich.: Latvian Studies Center, 1992.

Mickiewicz, Ellen. "Ethnicity and Support: Findings from a Soviet-American Public Opinion Poll." *Journal of Soviet Nationalities* 1 (Spring 1990): 140–47.

Misiunas, Romuald J., and Rein Taagepera. *The Baltic States: Years of Dependence, 1940–1980.* Berkeley: University of California Press, 1983.

———. "The Baltic States: Years of Dependence, 1980–1986." *Journal of Baltic States* 20 (Spring 1989): 65–88.

Montville, Joseph V., ed. *Conflict and Peacemaking in Multiethnic Societies.* Lexington, Mass.: Lexington Books, 1990.

Moore, Barrington Jr. *Social Origins of Dictatorship and Democracy.* Boston: Beacon Press, 1986.

Morris, Raymond N., and C. Michael Lanphier. *Three Scales of Inequality: Perspectives on French-English Relations.* Don Mills, Ont.: Longman Canada, 1977.

Motyl, Alexander J. "'Sovietology in One Country' or Comparative Nationality Studies?" *Slavic Review* 48 (Spring 1989): 83–88.

———, ed. *Thinking Theoretically about Soviet Nationalities.* New York: Columbia University Press, 1992.

Nichol, Jim. *Stalin's Crimes against the Non-Russian Nations: The 1987–1990 Revelations and Debate.* The Carl Beck Papers in Russian and East European Studies, no. 906. Pittsburgh, Penn.: University of Pittsburgh Center for Russian and East European Studies, 1991.

Olcott, Martha Brill. "The Soviet (Dis)union." *Foreign Policy* 82 (Spring 1991): 118–37.

Olson, Mancur. *The Logic of Collective Action.* Cambridge, Mass.: Harvard University Press, 1965.

———. "The Logic of Collective Action in Soviet-type Societies." *Journal of Soviet Nationalities* 1 (1990): 8–27.

Olzak, Susan. "Analysis of Events in the Study of Collective Action." *Annual Review of Sociology* 1989, no. 15: 119–41.

Pachmuss, Temira. "Russian Culture in the Baltic States and Finland, 1920–1940." *Journal of Baltic Studies* 16 (Winter 1985): 383–98.

Page, Stanley W. *The Formation of the Baltic States.* Cambridge, Mass.: Harvard University Press, 1959.

Pain, E. A., and A. A. Popov. "Mezhnatsional'nye konflikty v SSSR (nekotorye podkhody k izucheniiu i prakticheskomu resheniiu)." *Sovetskaia etnografiia* no. 1 (January–February 1990): 3–15.

Parming, Tönu. "Population Processes and the Nationality Issue in the Soviet Bloc." *Soviet Studies* 32 (July 1980): 398–414.

Pateman, Carole. "Political Culture, Political Structure and Political Change." *British Journal of Political Science* 1 (July 1971): 291–305.

Peled, Yoav. "Ethnic Democracy and the Legal Construction of Citizenship: Arab Citizens of the Jewish State." *American Political Science Review* 86 (June 1992): 432–43.

Penrose, Jan, and Joe May. "Herder's Concept of Nation and Its Relevance to Contemporary Ethnic Nationalism." *Canadian Review of Studies in Nationalism* 18, no. 1–2 (1991): 165–78.

Pinard, Maurice. "Ethnic Movements and the Competition Model: Some Missing Links." *American Sociological Review* 56 (August 1991): 446–57.

————, and Richard Hamilton. "Motivational Dimensions in the Quebec Independence Movement: A Test of a New Model." In Kurt Lang and Gladys Engel Lang, eds., *Research in Social Movements, Conflicts and Change*, vol. 9, 225–80. Greenwich, Conn.: JAI Press, 1978–93.

Pipes, Richard. *The Formation of the Soviet Union: Communism and Nationalism 1917–1923*. Cambridge, Mass.: Harvard University Press, 1970.

Plakans, Andrejs. "The Latvians." In Edward C. Thaden, ed., *Russification in the Baltic Provinces and Finland, 1855–1914*, 207–86. Princeton: Princeton University Press, 1981.

Przeworski, Adam. *Democracy and the Market: Political and Economic Reforms in Eastern Europe and Latin America*. Cambridge: Cambridge University Press, 1991.

Przeworski, Adam, and Henry Teune. *The Logic of Comparative Social Inquiry*. New York: Wiley, 1970.

Pye, Lucian W., and Sidney Verba. *Political Culture and Political Development*. Princeton: Princeton University Press, 1965.

Ra'anan, Uri. "The Nation-State Fallacy." In Joseph V. Montville, ed., *Conflict and Peacemaking in Multiethnic Societies*, 5–20. Lexington, Mass.: Lexington Books, 1990.

Rakowska-Harmstone, Teresa. "Baltic Nationalism and the Soviet Armed Forces." *Journal of Baltic Studies* 17 (Fall 1986): 179–93.

————. "The Dialectics of Nationalism in the USSR." *Problems of Communism* (May–June 1974): 1–22.

————. "The Study of Ethnic Politics in the USSR." In George W. Simmonds, ed., *Nationalism in the USSR and Eastern Europe in the Era of Brezhnev and Kosygin*, 20–36. Detroit, Mich.: University of Detroit Press, 1977.

Rauch, Georg von. *The Baltic States: The Years of Independence, 1917–1940*. Trans. Gerald Onn. Berkeley: University of California Press, 1974.

Resis, Albert. "The Baltic States in Soviet-German Relations, 1939." *Nationalities Papers* 17 (Fall 1989): 116–54.

Richmond, Anthony H. "Ethnic Nationalism: Social Science Paradigms." *International Social Science Journal* 39 (February 1987): 3–18.

Roche, Maurice. "Citizenship, Social Theory, and Social Change." *Theory and Society* 16 (May 1987): 363–99.

Rothschild, Joseph. *East Central Europe between the Two World Wars*. Seattle: University of Washington Press, 1974.

———. *Ethnopolitics: A Conceptual Framework*. New York: Columbia University Press, 1981.

Rudenshiold, Eric. "Ethnic Dimensions in Contemporary Latvian Politics: Focusing Forces for Change." *Soviet Studies* 44, no. 4 (1992): 609–39.

Rustow, Dankwart A. "Transitions to Democracy: Toward a Dynamic Model." *Comparative Politics* 2 (April 1970): 337–63.

Saar, Ellu, and Mikk Titma. *Migrationsströme im sowjetischen Baltikum und ihre Nachwirkung auf die baltischen Staaten nach Wiederherstellung der Selbstständigkeit*. Cologne: Berichte des Bundesinstituts für ostwissenschaftliche und internationale Studien no. 9, 1991.

Safran, William. "Ethnicity and Pluralism: Comparative and Theoretical Perspectives." *Canadian Review of Studies in Nationalism* 18, no. 1–2 (1991): 1–12.

Sapiets, Marite. "'Rebirth and Renewal' in the Latvian Lutheran Church." *Religion in Communist Lands* 6 (Autumn 1988): 237–49.

Schöpflin, George. "Post-communism: Constructing New Democracies in Central Europe." *International Affairs* 67, no. 2 (1991): 235–50.

Senn, Alfred Erich. "Toward Lithuanian Independence: Algirdas Brazauskas and the CPL." *Problems of Communism* (March–April 1990): 21–28.

Shils, Edward. "Primordial, Personal, Sacred, and Civil Ties." *British Journal of Sociology* 8 (1957): 130–45.

Šilde, Ādolfs. *Resistance Movement in Latvia*. Stockholm: The Latvian National Foundation, 1972.

———. "The Role of Russian-Latvians in the Sovietization of Latvia." *Journal of Baltic Studies* 18 (Summer 1987): 191–200.

Simmonds, George W., ed. *Nationalism in the USSR and Eastern Europe in the Era of Brezhnev and Kosygin*. Detroit, Mich.: University of Detroit Press, 1977.

Simon, Gerhard. *Nationalism and Policy toward the Nationalities in the Soviet Union: From Totalitarian Dictatorship to Post-Stalinist Society*. Trans. Karen Forster and Oswald Forster. Boulder, Colo.: Westview Press, 1991.

Smith, Anthony D. "Ethnic Identity and Territorial Nationalism in Comparative Perspective." In Alexander J. Motyl, ed., *Thinking Theoretically about Soviet Nationalities*, 45–66. New York: Columbia University Press, 1992.

———. *The Ethnic Revival.* Cambridge: Cambridge University Press, 1981.

Solchanyk, Roman. "Ukraine, the (Former) Center, Russia, and 'Russia.'" *Studies in Comparative Communism* 25 (March 1992): 31–45.

Starovoitova, G. V. *Etnicheskaia gruppa v sovremennom sovetskom gorode.* Leningrad: Nauka, 1987.

Starr, S. Frederick. "Voluntary Groups and Initiatives." In Anthony Jones and David E. Powell, eds., *Soviet Update, 1989–1990,* 97–116. Boulder, Colo.: Westview Press, 1991.

Stein, Michael B. "Federal Political Systems and Federal Societies." *World Politics* 20 (July 1968): 721–48.

Steiner, Jurg. "Power-Sharing: Another Swiss 'Export Product'?" In Joseph V. Montville, ed., *Conflict and Peacemaking in Multiethnic Societies,* 107–14. Lexington, Mass.: Lexington Books, 1990.

Susokolov, A. A. "Etnosy pered vyborom." *Sotsiologicheskie issledovaniia* 1988, no. 6: 32–40.

Swettenham, John A. *The Tragedy of the Baltic States.* New York: Praeger, 1954.

Szporluk, Roman. "The Imperial Legacy and the Soviet Nationalities Problem." In Lubomyr Hajda and Mark Beissinger, eds. *The Nationalities Factor in Soviet Politics and Society,* 1–23. Boulder, Colo.: Westview Press, 1990.

Taagepera, Rein. "Estonia's Road to Independence." *Problems of Communism* (November–December 1989): 11–26.

———. "Ethnic Relations in Estonia, 1991." *Journal of Baltic Studies* 23 (Summer 1992): 121–32.

———. "A Note on the March 1989 Elections in Estonia." *Soviet Studies* 42 (April 1990): 329–39.

Tarrow, Sidney. "'Aiming at a Moving Target': Social Science and the Recent Rebellions in Eastern Europe." *PS: Political Science & Politics* 24 (1991): 12–20.

Tiryakian, Edward A., and Ronald Rogowski, eds. *New Nationalisms of the Developed West: Toward Explanation.* Boston: Allen and Unwin, 1985.

Tishkov, V. N. "O novykh podkhodakh v teorii i praktike mezhnatsional'nikh otnoshenii." *Sovetskaia etnografiia.* 1989, no. 5: 3–14.

Tolz, Vera. *The USSR's Emerging Multiparty System.* New York: Praeger, 1990.

Topilin, A. V. "Vliianie migratsii na etnonatsional'nuiu strukturu." *Sotsiologicheskie issledovaniia* 1992, no. 7: 31–42.

Trapans, Andris. "Moscow, Economics and the Baltic Republics." In Jan Arveds Trapans, ed., *Toward Independence: The Baltic Popular Movements*, 85–100. Boulder, Colo.: Westview Press, 1991.

U.S. Commission on Security and Cooperation in Europe. *Referendum on the Soviet Union*. Washington, D.C.: U.S. Government Printing Office, April 1991.

U.S. Commission on Security and Cooperation in Europe. *Report on the Supreme Soviet Elections in Latvia*. Washington, D.C.: U.S. Government Printing Office, 2 April 1990.

U.S. Congress. House. *Baltic States Investigation: Hearings before the Select Committee to Investigate the Incorporation of the Baltic States into the U.S.S.R.*, on H.R. 346, 83d Cong., 1st sess., 1953.

U.S. Congress. House. *Implementation of the Helsinki Accords: Baltic Dissidents: Hearing before the Commission on Security and Cooperation in Europe*, 100th Cong., 1st sess., 1987.

Van Dyke, Vernon. *Human Rights, Ethnicity, and Discrimination*. Westport, Conn.: Greenwood Press.

———. "The Individual, the State, and Ethnic Communities in Political Theory." *World Politics* 29 (April 1977): 343–69.

Vardys, V. Stanley. *The Catholic Church, Dissent and Nationality in Soviet Lithuania*. Boulder, Colo.: East European Quarterly, 1978.

———. "Democracy in the Baltic States, 1918–1934: The Stage and the Actors." *Journal of Baltic Studies* 10, no. 4 (1979): 320–36.

———. "Sajudis: National Revolution in Lithuania." In Jan Arveds Trapans, ed., *Toward Independence: The Baltic Popular Movements*, 11–24. Boulder, Colo.: Westview Press, 1991.

Weigle, Marcia A., and Jim Butterfield. "Civil Society in Reforming Communist Regimes: The Logic of Emergence." *Comparative Politics* 25, no. 1 (October 1992): 1–24.

Weiner, Myron, and Samuel Huntington, eds. *Understanding Political Development*. Boston: Little, Brown, 1987.

Weitzer, Ronald. *Transforming Settler States: Communal Conflict and Internal Security in Northern Ireland and Zimbabwe*. Berkeley: University of California Press, 1990.

White, Stephen. "Soviet Political Culture Reassessed." In Archie Brown, ed., *Political Culture and Communist Studies*, 62–99. Armonk, N.Y.: Sharpe, 1985.

Widmer, Michael Jean. "Nationalism and Communism in Latvia: The Latvian Communist Party under Soviet Rule." Ph.D. diss., Harvard University, 1969.

Young, Crawford. *The Politics of Cultural Pluralism*. Madison: University of Wisconsin Press, 1976.

———. "The Temple of Ethnicity." *World Politics* 35 (July 1983): 652–62.

Young, Iris Marion. *Justice and the Politics of Difference*. Princeton: Princeton University Press, 1990.

Zaslavsky, Victor. "The Evolution of Separatism in Soviet Society under Gorbachev." In Gail W. Lapidus, Victor Zaslavsky, with Philip Goldman, eds., *From Union to Commonwealth: Nationalism and Separatism in the Soviet Republics*, 71–97. Cambridge: Cambridge University Press, 1992.

———"Nationalism and Democratic Transition in Postcommunist Societies." *Daedalus* 121 (Spring 1992): 97–121.

———. *The Neo-Stalinist State: Class, Ethnicity and Consensus in Soviet Society*. Armonk, N.Y.: Sharpe, 1982.

Zile, Zigurds L. "The Legal Framework of Minorities' Policies in Latvia: Background, Constitution, and the League of Nations." *Journal of Baltic Studies* 11 (1980): 3–24.

Zvidriņš, P., and P. Eglīte. "Demogrāfiskā situācija un demogrāfiskā politika Latvijā." *Latvijas PSR Zinātņu Akadēmijas Vēstis* 1990, no. 5: 51–54.

Index